P9-CLA-884

FUTURE INTERVENTIONS WITH BATTERED WOMEN AND THEIR FAMILIES

Sage Series on Violence Against Women

Series Editors

Claire M. Renzetti
St. Joseph's University

Jeffrey L. Edleson
University of Minnesota

In this series. . .

I AM NOT YOUR VICTIM: Anatomy of Domestic Violence
by Beth Sipe and Evelyn J. Hall

WIFE RAPE: Understanding the Response of Survivors and Service Providers
by Raquel Kennedy Bergen

FUTURE INTERVENTIONS WITH BATTERED WOMEN AND THEIR FAMILIES
edited by Jeffrey L. Edleson and Zvi C. Eisikovits

FUTURE INTERVENTIONS WITH BATTERED WOMEN AND THEIR FAMILIES

Jeffrey L. Edleson
Zvi C. Eisikovits
editors

SVAW
Sage Series on Violence Against Women

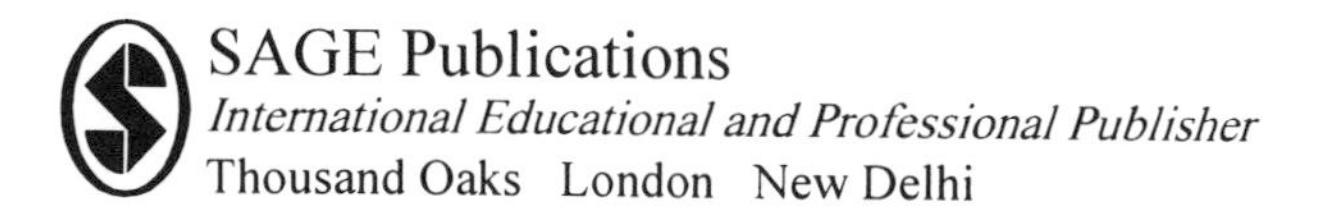

SAGE Publications
International Educational and Professional Publisher
Thousand Oaks London New Delhi

For information address:

SAGE Publications, Inc.
2455 Teller Road
Thousand Oaks, California 91320
E-mail: order@sagepub.com

SAGE Publications Ltd.
6 Bonhill Street
London EC2A 4PU
United Kingdom

SAGE Publications India Pvt. Ltd.
M-32 Market
Greater Kailash I
New Delhi 110 048 India

Printed in the United States of America

Library of Congress Cataloging-in-Publication Data

Main entry under title:

Future interventions with battered women and their families: Visions for policy, practice, and research / editors, Jeffrey L. Edleson, Zvi C. Eisikovits.
p. cm.—(Sage series on violence against women; v. 3)
Based on several meetings of the International Study Group on the Future of Intervention With Battered Women and Their Families, which convened in Haifa, Israel, in March 1995, sponsored by the Women's League for Israel.
Includes bibliographical references and index.
ISBN 0-8039-5944-3 (cloth: acid-free paper).—ISBN 0-8039-5945-1 (pbk.: acid-free paper)
1. Abused women—Services for—Congresses. 2. Wife abuse—Prevention—Congresses. 3. Family violence—Prevention—Congresses. 4. Crisis intervention (Psychiatry)—Congresses. I. Edleson, Jeffrey L. II. Eisikovits, Zvi C. III. Series.
HV1442.5.F87 1996
362.82′928—dc20 96-4515

This book is printed on acid-free paper.

96 97 98 99 00 01 10 9 8 7 6 5 4 3 2 1

Sage Production Editor: Vicki Baker
Sage Typesetter: Andrea D. Swanson

This book is dedicated to our sons,
Nir, Daniel, and Eli,
in the hope that they may grow older in a more peaceful world.

Contents

Acknowledgments

A number of years ago, we envisioned a group of activists, practitioners, and researchers coming together for an intensive discussion of what future interventions may be possible for battered women and their families. Our vision became reality when the International Study Group on the Future of Intervention with Battered Women and Their Families was convened in Haifa, Israel, in March 1995. The Study Group was made possible by the strong support of a number of organizations and individuals.

This book—and the study group from which it grew—was made possible by generous support from the Women's League for Israel (WLI) and its supporters in the United States and Israel. In particular, Rina Lazar, Director of the Haifa Branch of the Women's League for Israel, and both Dr. Nili Porath, the former Director General, and Ahuva Talmon, the present Director General of the WLI, provided much of the support that made the study group meetings possible. The School of Social Work at the University of Haifa also provided a great deal of support to this project, especially Professor Gabriel Warburg, Professor and Head of the School of Social Work. Yael Koresh, a Research Associate in the Center for Youth Policy at the University of Haifa, played a major role in successfully organizing these meetings. Reli Robinzon provided administrative support and coordinated the entire study group.

Finally, Sage Publications—through Terry Hendrix, Sage's Interpersonal Violence Editor—provided us with the opportunity to share our discussions in Haifa through the pages of this book. Support from Sage not only made this book possible but also helped to structure and support the work of the study group, from conference planning to conclusion.

1

Visions of Continued Change

Jeffrey L. Edleson
Zvi C. Eisikovits

It has been more than 20 years since the first formal battered women's shelters were established in both Great Britain and the United States. The intervening years have witnessed a tremendous growth in the number of shelters around the world and in the types of other social interventions and public policies created to address the issue of woman battering. The United Nation's Fourth World Conference on Women, held in Beijing in 1995, revealed the diversity of approaches that governmental and nongovernmental organizations are taking to address a wide range of issues related to violence against women, woman battering being but one form of such violence. The innovative character of the international battered women's movement is evident in countries around the world and is a tribute to the results of 20 years of often difficult and life-threatening work.

This volume addresses the diverse aspects of the battered women's movement. Chapters reflect a progression of activities that include a search for cross-national linkages and collaboration in designing global responses to violence against women, efforts to enlist legal and social control systems on behalf of groups of abused women, and grassroots movements aimed at directly helping individual battered women.

Progress has often appeared slow, but a great deal has actually been accomplished. Shelters have been established in many parts of the world and have dramatically expanded their numbers in many Western countries. Advocacy services, job training, and transitional housing have been added to the basic services of shelters. Governments, such as Israel, have devoted significant resources to support the expansion of grassroots efforts. Programs for violent offenders have been established, have been tested, and have expanded their reach. Services for children who witness violence at home have also been developed, tested, and expanded. Social systems previously uninterested in the plight of battered women have begun to intervene and policymakers appear concerned.

During this period of innovation and growth, we have become aware of how difficult lasting change is to achieve and how much more work is still required, even in those countries that began addressing this issue more than 20 years ago. Battered women's programs in the United States and other countries provide assistance to larger numbers of women and their children each year, yet—as Susan Schechter points out later in this book—these women and children represent only a small portion of those in need of assistance.

As new efforts toward ending violence against women take shape around the globe, it is important to stop and reflect on our progress. It is also an important moment to suspend our current assumptions and reach beyond to envision ways of creating even greater social change in the future. It is a moment to treasure successes but also to revise some of our current approaches, seek new arenas for change, and test new interventions.

At the same time, we must be vigilant about continuing the changes now begun. Violence against women has become *the* issue of the moment in a number of countries. It has become both the focus of media attention and the work of many policymakers. Many professions that had never expressed concern for the topic now define violence against women as an important focus of time and resources. Yet there is a danger that this issue will become a fad and will soon pass and disappear from the public agenda. The history of social problems is filled with examples of such past fads.

Concern for the future of interventions, how to take advantage of current interest in violence against women, and how to extend this interest beyond a particular period of intense social activity is what brought 15 activists, practitioners, and researchers to Haifa, Israel, in March 1995, to the International Study Group on the Future of Intervention with Battered Women and Their Families. The Study Group's 3 days of meetings were supported by several organizations that enabled us to come together and subsequently produce this book. The Women's League for Israel supplied major funding for the study group and helped bring 10 American and British participants to the meeting. The League also acted as our gracious host for two public events, one of which drew more than 150 people from across Israel for a day of consultations and exchanges with study group participants. The University of Haifa's School of Social Work provided meeting space and the substantial logistical support required to organize and conduct the meetings. And finally, Sage Publications provided support for producing this book that also allowed us to structure and support our work for the study group.

Those gathered in Haifa represented a diverse group of Americans, British, and Israelis who have long worked in domestic violence programs and studied their effects. Each participant prepared a written document, in advance of the meeting, which was then circulated among all participants. As we gathered in a conference room at the top of the University of Haifa's main tower, our time was spent in honest and open discussions about the strategies for future global, national, and programmatic changes we described in our papers. Many of the original conference papers were substantially revised after our discussions. The final set of chapters appearing in this book are the result of this collective effort by the authors.

Participants in this study group shared a common vision that multiple forms of change are required to address the social problem of violence against women. The chapters in this book reflect this view and cover a range of perspectives. The ideas expressed here range from the pragmatic to the idealistic. They offer individual and collective prescriptions for change that are dynamic and therefore are constantly changing.

The book begins with Part I, focused on "Changing Societies." In the first chapter of this section, Lori Heise provides a comprehensive vision of global change regarding the broad arena of violence against women. Valli Kanuha follows with a chapter on how race has been removed from much of the U.S. debate on domestic violence and why that needs to change.

Part II of the book focuses on "Changing Community Responses" and begins with a chapter by Susan Schechter on new directions in institutional reform, particularly in health and child welfare. Next, Liz Kelly explores the expanded use of informal community-based networks to end violence against women. And finally, Muhammad Haj-Yahia provides a vision for change within the Israeli Arab community, one that may also be applicable to other countries and communities.

The final section of the book, Part III, focuses on a variety of approaches to "Intervention With Survivors, Perpetrators, and Their Children." Mary Ann Dutton leads this section with a focus on expanding our current thinking about battered women's situations and the fabric of their lives. Einat Peled offers a multifaceted approach to expanding intervention with children who survive violence in their homes. Jeffrey Edleson and Richard Tolman examine a range of issues regarding intervention with perpetrators, from underlying assumptions about treatment to alternative sanctions for perpetrators. Finally, Zvi Eisikovits and Eli Buchbinder suggest a phenomonological approach to intervention with individual cases of wife assault, and Michal Shamai argues that couple counseling can coexist with other approaches as a safe and useful intervention.

Where do all these ideas take us? In the concluding chapter, we are joined by Guy Enosh in examining the commonalities and differences that characterize the great diversity of ideas reflected in this book and draw some conclusions. We leave it to you, the reader, to take these ideas, combine them with your own, and help make the many changes that the next 20 years require.

PART I

CHANGING SOCIETIES

2

Violence Against Women
Global Organizing for Change

Lori L. Heise

In recent years, violence against women has gained a fragile foothold on the global policy agenda, especially as a health and human rights issue. The Organization of American States (OAS) recently negotiated an Inter-American Convention on the Prevention, Punishment and Eradication of Violence Against Women (OAS, 1994); The United Nation's General Assembly passed a Declaration calling on member states to "pursue by all appropriate means and without delay a policy of eliminating violence against women" (U.N. resolution 48/104); and the World Bank issued a major report titled *Violence Against Women: The Hidden Health Burden* (Heise, 1994).

This international recognition comes on the heels of more than two decades of activism by grassroots women to draw attention to gender-based abuse. Around the world, women have joined forces to provide shelter, lobby for law reform, and challenge the attitudes and beliefs that undergird men's violence. In the past 5 years, these individual efforts have coalesced into a truly global movement dedicated to ending gender-based abuse.

But the international movement now stands at a crossroads. Having captured the world's attention, antiviolence activists must begin the difficult task of designing viable and sustainable interventions that go beyond saving individual women one at a time. The movement must begin to ask itself some deeply searching questions: How can we overcome the infighting and competition that divide us? How can we secure a funding base that will sustain ourselves and our work in an environment of reduced social spending? And how do we find the proper balance between dealing with women in crisis today versus working on prevention?

In a spirit of mutual learning and exploration, this chapter will explore these and other issues that face the antiviolence movement as we prepare to enter the next century. Based on my involvement in the battered women's movement in the United States and 9 years of networking and joint action with women's groups overseas, I will also offer some reflections on possible future strategies that deserve our considered attention, especially in resource-poor settings.

A look to the future, however, requires knowledge of the past. Given that few activists have had the luxury to study violence prevention strategies across cultures, I will begin with a brief history of how violence emerged as an issue in various regions of the world. Then I will describe the confluence of forces that helped propel violence onto the international scene, focusing especially on women's strategic organizing to frame violence as an abuse of human rights and as a health and development issue. Finally, I will use this historical backdrop to offer some thoughts on the challenges ahead for national movements as well possible strategies that may hold promise for the future.

The Emergence of Violence Against Women as a Global Issue

A variety of forces have converged to propel gender-based abuse onto the world stage. Undoubtedly, the most important has been the emergence of well-organized women's movements at the grass roots that have identified gender-based abuse as a priority concern. Indeed, violence against women has emerged as a global issue despite the official indifference of world leaders, not through international leadership.

Another crucial factor has been the emergence of regional and international women's nongovernmental organizations (NGOs) and foundations that have facilitated linkages among antiviolence activists. In the past 5 years, there has been a flood of conferences, meetings, and exchange programs that have allowed women to share strategies and build coordinated campaigns for reform. This cross-fertilization of ideas has been critical to the growing sense of global solidarity around issues of gender-based abuse.

Finally, a number of world events have served to validate women's concern by focusing attention on the reality of sexual and physical violence against women. The AIDS epidemic, for example, has highlighted the lack of power many women have to control the terms of sexual encounters. For the first time, researchers have been asking women deeply searching questions about their sexual lives, and violence and coercion have emerged as important themes. Likewise, the recent mass rape of women in Bosnia and Haiti has served to focus popular attention on the prevalence and brutality of gender-based persecution.

Violence Against Women as a National Issue

In industrial countries—Australia, Canada, Europe, and the United States—violence against women emerged as an issue during the 1970s, largely as an outgrowth of renewed interest in women's rights. In the United States, for example, women began organizing separately when it became clear that their needs and concerns were consistently marginalized in the other progressive movements of the day, including the Civil Rights Movement and the Left. Through weekly consciousness raising groups, women began to discover the myriad ways in which society oppressed them and to develop a new analysis of how gender operated as a key variable in defining women's options in life (Dobash & Dobash, 1992; Schechter, 1982).

Early feminist analysis often focused on sexual exploitation and male control of female sexuality. It is little wonder, then, that rape emerged as the primary focus of early Western feminist debate and action. Women's groups organized rape crisis centers, lobbied for law reform, and developed their unique approach to lay advocacy that still forms the backbone of many antiviolence movements. The battered women's movement emerged several years later as rape crisis hot lines became overwhelmed with calls from abused women seeking escape from violent relationships. Building upon the skills honed during the earlier rape crisis years, feminists took up this new cause with equal energy and commitment: starting shelters, training police, and lobbying for new laws on domestic violence (Heise & Chapman, 1992).

In developing countries, the issue of violence also emerged in the context of increased organizing by women, as part of either national democratic movements, international development projects, urban community struggles, or emerging feminist movements (Schuler, 1992). In Brazil, Argentina, Chile, and the Philippines, for example, the movement had its roots in women organizing against military/authoritarian regimes. As women came together to protest state repression, they began to analyze the gender oppression in their own lives. In India, several notorious rape cases in 1979 focused public attention on women's plight and galvanized the nascent women's movement to press for new legislation to address sexual violence and dowry harassment (Basu, 1987).

Elsewhere, organizing around violence evolved within the context of the U.N. Decade for Women, which focused attention on the role of women in international development. For the first time, international money became available to support women-focused NGOs. Preexisting women's organizations, as well as new ones, were able to use the legitimacy conferred by the Decade for Women to deepen their analysis of the social context of their lives.

In both the industrial and the developing worlds, organized action against violence generally began with isolated groups of concerned middle-class women and professionals—psychologists, activists, lawyers—coming together to provide training, information, legal services, and other support for women. Some of the groups specifically focused on providing services for women who had been beaten or raped, whereas others were more generic organizations aimed at women's empowerment. The mere presence of legal services, support groups, and women-only discussions, however, encouraged women to come forward in droves, quickly overwhelming the capacity of existing groups to respond. Daily contact with raped and abused women also served to highlight how social service agencies, the police, and the courts revictimized women and failed to respond to their needs. Frustrated with the existing system, women's organizations began to form coalitions to push for systemic reform.

Such coalitions have used diverse strategies to achieve their goals. In Malaysia, the Joint Action Group Against Violence Against Women sponsored a 5-year, multifaceted campaign consisting of workshops, media campaigns, demonstrations, lobbying, petitions, and community organizing (Fernandez, 1992). In 1988, Mexico's *Red Nacional contra la Violencia hacia la Mujer* held a National Forum on Sex Crimes, which presented 88 papers and testimonials about rape and domestic violence to the Mexican House of Deputies (Shrader-Cox, 1992). And in Bolivia, *La Platforma de la Mujer* organized a major campaign to reform the country's rape laws, including widespread media coverage, dialogues with parliamentarians, and popular mobilization. In 1 month, the campaign collected more than 40,000 signatures denouncing violence (Montano, 1992).

Strategic Organizing at the International Level

In the late 1980s, activists began to work strategically to raise international awareness of violence against women. Despite its prominence at the grass roots, violence was virtually absent from policy and funding agendas at the international level. Because women's groups—especially those from developing countries—are almost entirely dependent on international donor support, this blind spot in the international agenda had severe consequences for groups seeking to survive in an era of shrinking resources.

The strategy adopted by activists was to gain credibility and funding for violence-related projects by demonstrating how gender-based abuse relates to issues already high on the international agenda: human rights, health, and socioeconomic development. Indeed, much of the progress made within mainstream institutions has been the result of directed efforts on the part of advocates to construct arguments about violence compelling to different constituencies.

Among the initiatives whose primary aim has been to articulate the links between violence and other mainstream issues have been the Women's Rights Project of Human Rights Watch; the Institute for Women, Law and Development; the Campaign for Women's Human Rights (based out of the Center for Women's Global Leadership); the Gender Violence and Health Initiative of the Health and Development Policy Project; and the work on violence as an international development issues, undertaken by the United Nations Development Fund for Women (UNIFEM) and the Canadian NGO, Match International. The most successful of these efforts has been the campaign to frame gender violence as an abuse of human rights. Slightly less well-developed, but

Table 2.1 Advantages of Health and Human Rights Frameworks

Human Rights	*Public Health*
Concepts:	*Concepts:*
Persuasive power of "rights language"	Focus on prevention
Appeals to "bodily integrity" and "security of person"	Social analysis of health
	Interdisciplinary approach
Tools:	*Tools:*
International law and conventions	Epidemiology
Human rights machinery	Opportunity for early intervention
Fact finding and documentation	Social science research
Access to sanctions	Access to health services
Experience with international campaigns	Experience with behavior change

still promising, has been work to link abuse to health and development concerns such as unwanted pregnancy, AIDS and sexually transmitted disease (STD) transmission, and women's participation in development projects.

The decision to frame violence as a *health* and *human rights* issue was a conscious strategy designed to marshal the resources and technical know-how of two large and influential communities. Both the health and the human rights communities represented a "pot of resources" that could be tapped to garner increased investment in the problem of abuse. Each field also provided certain key concepts and methodological tools that offered useful ammunition for marshaling increased attention toward violence against women (see Table 2.1). The field of human rights, for example, offered the persuasive power of rights language and access to the fact-finding and accountability mechanisms of the United Nations and its human rights machinery. By contrast, framing violence as a public health issue helped emphasize the role of prevention and helped enlist the constructive engagement of health workers in the battle against woman abuse. It was these strategic considerations that helped crystallize health and human rights as the central metaphors of the international movement against violence in the early 1990s.

The Campaign for Women's Human Rights. Despite the existence of many international instruments that guarantee all individuals the right to life, bodily integrity, and security of person, mainstream human rights discourse has failed—until recently—to recognize rape or domestic violence by private individuals as an abuse of women's human rights. This incongruence stems in part from a general reluctance of the human rights community to take women's issues seriously. It is reinforced by the mainstream's insistence on maintaining a distinction between abuses in the public and the private sphere. Indeed, traditional human rights theory focuses primarily on violations perpetrated by the state against individuals, such as torture, wrongful imprisonment, and arbitrary execution. Under this framework, theorists do not recognize wife assault and other forms of violence against women as human rights violations, because such acts are perpetrated by private individuals, not the state (Culliton, 1993).

The tendency of traditional human rights approaches to ignore abuses in the private sphere evolves from a variety of interrelated factors. As Sullivan (1995) observes, international law originally evolved as a set of rules intended to regulate relations among states; hence, *the State* has tended to dominate human rights discourse and practice. Moreover, despite formal recognition by the international community of the indivisibility of human rights, the human rights institutions in the West have tended to privilege civil and political rights over economic, social, and cultural rights. In the United States, for example, rights are perceived as the obligation of governments not to interfere in the civil and political liberties of their citizens. By contrast, many Third World theorists consider economic and social rights equally important, arguing that human rights create positive obligations upon governments to meet the basic needs of their citizens. In this formulation, the duty of government extends beyond refraining from perpetrating abuses itself to helping ensure the full enjoyment of rights. The hegemony of the civil and political rights discourse, however, has meant that mainstream human rights institutions have concentrated largely on abuses perpetrated by the State.

The public/private distinction is especially prejudicial when it comes to violations of women's human rights. From a woman's standpoint, it makes little difference whether her assailant is an agent of the State, a stranger, or a friend. Rape and assault are brutal violations of a woman's bodily integrity and her security of person regardless of who the perpetrator may be. In fact, feminist theorists have argued that the public/private distinction is largely an illusion, a legal fiction that shifts periodically to accommodate the concerns of men. As Susan Ross observes, whenever you see the word *public,* substitute the word *important,* and whenever you see the word *private,* substitute the word *unimportant* (Goldstein, 1995; p. 1316). "Disappearances," for example, have been considered a violation of international law for more than 20 years, even though they are often perpetrated by private individuals. And the United Nations has entire conventions against slavery, racial discrimination, and other private abuses. "The public/private distinction," notes Goldstein (1995), "is no more—and no less—than a male judgment of what is important enough to try to fix" (p. 1316).

In the late 1980s, however, women came together to protest the failure of the human rights community to address gender-based forms of persecution. Eventually, more than 1,000 women's groups joined the Campaign for Women's Human Rights, an international effort to get the United Nations to integrate gender into all facets of its human rights machinery. The campaign included major initiatives to redefine the contours of human rights law to include rape and domestic violence as violations of human rights, regardless of who is the perpetrator (Friedman, 1995). At the 1993 Second World Conference on Human Rights, in Vienna, Austria, women presented delegates with almost a half million signatures from 128 countries demanding that they recognize violence as an abuse of women's rights. They also held an international tribunal, moderated by an esteemed panel of judges, where women presented well-documented and moving cases of gender-based abuse (Bunch & Reilly, 1994). Widely recognized as the best organized lobby at the conference, women eventually achieved virtually all of their demands. The final declaration out of Vienna recognized violence against women in the private sphere as an abuse of human rights and affirmed that women's rights are an "inalienable, integral and indivisible part of universal human rights" (World Conference on Human Rights, 1993).

More than just a symbolic gesture, the reframing of violence as a human rights issue has yielded some concrete benefits. In response to the campaign, the United Nations has appointed a *Special Rapporteur on Violence Against Women,* charged with investigating and reporting on gender-violence worldwide (U.N. Commission on Human Rights, 1994). This means that a U.N. emissary with high-level clearance and investigatory powers can now help ensure that ignorance of abuse can no longer be an excuse for inaction. In March 1994, the Commission on Human Rights appointed Radhika Coomaraswamy, a Sri Lankan lawyer and activist, to this 3-year post. The Rapporteur's terms of reference are broadly defined, giving Ms. Coomaraswamy authority to investigate the underlying "causes and consequences of abuse," in addition to flagrant violations.

Major human rights NGOs have also implemented women's programs to undertake field missions designed to document violence against women in the same way that they have traditionally documented abuses of civil and political rights, such as wrongful imprisonment. The Women's Rights Project of Human Rights Watch, for example, has published detailed reports of domestic violence in Brazil, rape in Pakistan, abuse of Asian maids in Kuwait, trafficking in women from Burma to Thailand, and the imposition of forced "virginity tests" in Turkey. These reports—which would not have been published without the reframing of violence in rights terms—have been instrumental in lending credibility and substance to women's claims of gender-based abuse.

And finally, with the signing of the Inter-American Convention of the Prevention, Punishment and Eradication of Violence Against Women, abused women will now have recourse to the Inter-American Court and the Inter-American Commission on Human Rights. These new fora provide women an opportunity to pursue justice at a regional level, an option especially critical for victims facing uncooperative enforcement agencies or judiciaries in their home countries. Already, a case is being prepared on behalf of 20 women who were allegedly raped by military officers in Haiti (Grossman, 1995).

Framing Violence as a Health and Development Issue. Despite the rhetorical power of rights language and the usefulness of testimony as a form of documentation, the human rights field has little to offer in terms of services for victims or insights for prevention. Thus, in the late 1980s, a small group of activists began working to frame gender violence as a public health and international development issue. Increasingly, evidence was emerging that documented the links between abuse and women's physical and mental well-being as well as their ability to participate fully in social and economic development (Carrillo, 1992). Thus, the health and development community appeared as an obvious constituency to target for increased involvement in the issue of abuse.

As a strategy, framing violence as a health issue poses both certain opportunities and certain risks. The field of public health offers extensive experience in research and in the design and implementation of interventions to change behavior and social norms—skills badly needed in the antiviolence movement. A public health perspective also adds an important emphasis on the *prevention* of violence rather than focusing solely on its victims. Finally, health and family planning services are one of the few institutions that regularly have ongoing contact with women, making health centers an ideal site for identifying and referring women to other available support services.

A major danger in framing violence as a health issue is in the risk of "medicalizing" what is essentially a social and political issue. Medicalization is the process whereby a social phenomenon, such as alcoholism, hyperactivity, or pregnancy, becomes framed in medical rather than moral, social, or political terms (Conrad, 1992). The main critique of medicalization is that it decontextualizes social issues, brings them under medical control, and individualizes what might otherwise be seen as a collective social issue (Conrad, 1992).

Advocates have resisted medicalization of battering by drawing guidance and support more from the field of public health than from medicine per se. A public health perspective helps keep the focus on prevention and sociocultural change rather than on treatment and cure. Further advocates have been quick to criticize any drift toward models of battering that frame abuse as pathology or abused women as "patients" in need of treatment (e.g. Tavris, 1992). Given the historical reluctance of the medical profession to take up the issue of wife abuse (Kurz, 1987), advocates have generally felt that the potential advantages of claims making in the health arena have outweighed the dangers of medicalization.

Already, women have achieved some major successes in their efforts to engage the international health and development community. As a result of women's lobbying, the World Health Organization sponsored a major panel discussion on violence against women as part of its Geneva-based activities on World Health Day 1993. Likewise, the World Bank's *World Development Report 1993, Investing in Health* included a box highlighting the health impacts of gender-based abuse (World Bank, 1993). A recent World Bank document on women's health includes screening and referral for abuse as part of its package of "essential minimum services" (Tinker et al., 1994).

Perhaps most impressive, however, have been collaborations between advocates and the Pan American Health Organization (PAHO). The Women Health and Development Program at PAHO made violence against women its priority theme in 1994. With input from advocates, PAHO has raised more than $4 million to be invested over the next 4 years on violence and health projects in Central America and the Andean countries (P. Hartigan, personal communication, August 10, 1995).

Challenges for the Next Decade

As the global movement enters the final years of this millennium, many local and national movements face similar questions. Needless to say, I cannot offer answers to these dilemmas, but I would like to explore some of the challenges that appear most pressing for local and national movements worldwide.

Issues of Sustainability

Perhaps more than any other matter, issues of sustainability loom large in all countries. How can women's groups raise the funds necessary to sustain their services? What are the benefits and dangers of demanding service or resources from the State? How can women's groups hold the State accountable without losing their autonomy?

These are age-old questions that have no simple answer. Most antiviolence groups, regardless of country, begin as loosely organized collectives that rely almost exclusively on volunteer labor. (In developing countries, it is common for groups to be entirely staffed by individuals who hold down other full-time jobs.) As work expands beyond available resources, groups are generally forced to institutionalize to meet the terms and expectations of outside funders. Eventually, many collectives evolve into legally recognized NGOs—but generally only after substantial upheavals due to ideological and personal conflicts.

In general, this growth path represents a positive evolution toward a more realistic and sustainable organization. Formalizing mechanisms of accountability, divisions of labor, and areas of work can help organizations function better and more effectively. There has been a self-destructive tendency in the women's movement to equate any structure with hierarchy and domination, leading to organizations that are driven by personalities, with no clear lines of accountability. This often leads to what has been termed the *tyranny of structurelessness,* where power—rather than being exorcised—is wielded in covert and destructive ways (Freeman, 1974).

But this evolution can also be fraught with danger if groups allow the demands and priorities of funders to undermine the organization's integrity, personal style, and vision. Many battered women's organizations in the United States lost their political edge as they became reliant on government money (Pharr, 1987; Schechter, 1982). Even seemingly benign "strings" attached to grants, such as credential requirements for staff, can have subtle but profound effects on an organization's mission and style. With the recruitment of more credentialed staff, for example, can come a shift away from *social action* and toward *social work* (Schechter, 1982).

At the same time, operating with little or no external funding means that groups can, at most, touch only a handful of the women in need. History suggests that autonomy often comes at the expense of achieving adequate scale. Moreover, developing a parallel set of feminist social services means that vital movement energy is being diverted from activism and prevention toward providing services that are arguably the responsibility of the State to provide. This is especially problematic in developing countries where structural adjustment programs and privatization schemes are increasingly being used to justify huge cuts in social services, under the false assumption that civil society will be able to make up the difference (Chossudovsky, 1992).

In effect, movements are caught in a dilemma: Do they provide the services for victims themselves, thereby ensuring quality and the group's political autonomy (but reaching only a handful of women and letting the State off the hook)? Or do they demand that the state either provide the service or allocate funding to nongovernmental groups for its provision, thereby running the risk of co-optation or poor quality services?

These questions obviously take on different hues depending on the historical relationship of civil society to the State. Movements vary by time and place in their orientation to the State: some see it as hostile, others benevolent, and still others neutral (for a more in-depth discussion, see Dobash & Dobash, 1992). Also relevant to the calculus of decision making is the presence or absence of other sources of funding. In most Latin American countries, for example, there is almost no tradition of private philanthropy, severely limiting the availability of nonstate funding for local endeavors (C. Krueger, private communication, July 6, 1995). In such settings, NGOs must either survive on volunteer labor, reconcile with the State, or seek funding from international donors (primarily from the United States and Europe).

Feminist groups, especially those emerging from the Left, have traditionally been reluctant to engage with the State, preferring to provide parallel services and criticize from afar, rather than make demands for government accountability. This strategy has come with costs, in both terms of coverage and energy available for prevention. In my opinion, women's groups in the next decade will have to concentrate more on working with State actors to enact gender-sensitive programs if lasting change is going to occur. Feminist NGOs can and should strive to develop model services and interventions, but eventually they must shift from being sole provider to helping adapt model services for mainstream systems. To the extent that women's groups continue to provide services in lieu of the State, such as shelter, employment counseling, and legal services, the groups should be reimbursed for these activities. The trick becomes how to negotiate the terms of this reimbursement/grant making in order to minimize red tape and guarantee the group's autonomy.

There is a variety of things groups can do to help resist co-optation by outside funders (Capps 1982; Pharr 1987). First, groups must establish and maintain a clear vision of their priorities and the political analysis that they bring to their work. This provides the perspective from which the movement makes its demands on the State and evaluates offers of outside resources. With any offer or opportunity for funding, groups should ask themselves, "What do we gain, what do we lose, and what are the contradictions inherent in each choice?" Likewise, groups should challenge up front any requirements or restrictions that they fear may threaten their organizational style or autonomy. Funding conditions are sometimes negotiable given sufficient pressure. Finally, organizations should strive to diversify their funding so that survival is never dependent on any one grant. This ensures a measure of freedom from influence and buys maneuvering room to adhere to certain bottom-line positions.

Ultimately, however, sustainability implies much more than mere financial solvency. Groups must begin to take more seriously the task of recruiting and maintaining quality staff. Burn-out and staff turnover are critical problems that deserve our considered attention and resources. Dealing with issues of violence day in and day out is grueling work, and groups must attend to the emotional needs of staff by offering support groups, access to counseling, or other stress reduction techniques. We must also make a concerted effort to seek out and encourage new leadership. Our movements are only as strong as the women who follow in our footsteps.

Issues of Focus

Another issue that virtually all movements share is the question of focus: What is the proper balance between dealing with women in crisis today versus working toward fundamental social change? What are the advantages and disadvantages of a predominantly justice system approach to violence?

To date, most movements have invested the bulk of their energy in assisting victims and reforming how the justice system responds to gender-based abuse. Although understandable, this strategy has had certain costs. Clearly, any struggle that claims to work on behalf of abused women must respond to their immediate needs; but too often, the political goals of the movement have become lost in the daily grind of keeping shelter doors open.

I have become increasingly convinced that we must simplify our service models and invest more time and energy into changing the underlying beliefs and attitudes that undergird men's violence (see section below for elaboration). This is especially true in countries where it is still widely held that men have a right to physically "chastise" their wives. Until there is a cultural consensus that intimate violence is wrong, it will be difficult to make progress.

I have also begun to question the wisdom of relying so heavily on a criminal justice system approach to violence. We must begin to explore other mechanisms to raise the social costs of violence besides the formal justice system, especially given that so many judicial and police systems worldwide are corrupt and misogynist (see section below). Relying on typical criminal justice solutions (such as incarceration) raises even more vexing issues in developing country settings, where women generally do not want or cannot afford to have their husband go to jail.

As in the United States and Europe, many developing country movements have largely focused their institutional reform efforts to date on the police and legal system. Many groups have invested substantial resources in police training and law reform or in developing all-female police stations. Although these initiatives are important and necessary, I worry that Third World movements may go the way of those in the United States, where virtually all the movement's systems advocacy has focused on the justice system, rather than engaging and reforming the response and attitudes of family and community members or of institutional structures like health and social service agencies or religious institutions.

In large measure the U.S. emphasis on the justice system evolved not by design but by default. Women's groups turned to the police during the early days of the movement when they realized that advocates alone could not protect women if the police did not do their job. Not only did changing police behavior prove more difficult than groups expected, but women also soon learned that it didn't help to change police behavior if the prosecutors did not prosecute. And it wasn't enough to change the prosecutors if the judges were still racist and misogynist. Slowly, without realizing it, the U.S. movement was sucked into the black hole of justice system reform. Given how conservative, bureaucratic, and male-dominated most justice systems are, it is not surprising that trying to eliminate victim blaming and gender bias from the U.S. justice system was enough to exhaust the movement's energy (Heise & Chapman, 1992).

This is not to say that movements should ignore law reform or abandon work with police and judges. Efforts to criminalize domestic violence, for example, are an important way to redefine the frontiers of acceptable behavior. The question, however, is one of emphasis. Each movement should think strategically about the relative amount of energy to devote to sensitizing groups such as the police as compared to working with other professional groups (e.g., clergy, nurses, social workers), who may be more receptive to training (and may have more to offer developing country women). The point is not to shift wholesale away from justice system reform but to be attentive to other opportunities for influence.

Issues of Group Solidarity

A third issue becoming increasingly salient in many movements is within-group solidarity. I fear that in many feminist movements worldwide, our effectiveness is being compromised by ideological infighting, turf battles, and political correctness. Although internal debate is healthy and necessary, debate can turn destructive if it is informed by personal rivalries, backstabbing, and identity politics. Regrettably, the other side of the feminist credo, "the personal is political," has been the tendency to personalize the political—attacking the credibility and worth of the woman instead of the value of her ideas.

Such problems are not unique to feminist movements, nor are they surprising in movements where organizations must compete for the same small pie of resources. Nonetheless, it is behavior that I think we can no longer afford. I encourage all of us to begin dialogues in our own settings about holding ourselves and each other to certain basic standards of respect. Women with sufficient standing in their movements must begin to challenge critics when a woman is the focus of censure instead of her ideas, when personal animosities begin to define organizational politics and direction, or when women are judged by the color of their skin and not by the quality of their work or ideas.

Female activists working on violence issues from within minority communities must face their own set of solidarity issues. It is always difficult to criticize elements of one's own culture when the group as a whole is marginalized and judged by a dominant culture. The fear is that by airing one's dirty laundry in public, activists will in effect feed into stereotypes and negative attitudes about their community held by the society at large. The issue of group loyalty in the face of an oppressive dominant culture is becoming ever more salient as groups of people increasingly migrate around the globe.

As an international movement, we must become more aware of these dynamics and find ways to support women from minority communities who are willing to take up the issue of violence against women. We must also be aware of how insensitive attacks on cultural practices from outsiders can lead to cultural retrenchment and defensiveness, even among individuals who otherwise would not defend a practice. This is all the more reason that we must seek out and support progressive women leaders from within all cultural groups.

The Question of Men

A fourth challenge facing our movements is the issue of men: What role can and should men have in the fight against abuse? How can we recruit and train more men to work with adolescent boys and batterers? To what extent should women's groups take up issues of men and masculinity?

There has always been an uneasy relationship between men and the antiviolence movement. Many women have felt that it is inappropriate to invest resources in men when women are still dying for lack of protection (Schechter, 1982). Even when pro-feminist men have taken on the task of working with their abusive peers, activists have feared that treatment programs would siphon resources away from women's organizations.

Although not without merit, the feminist impulse to invest exclusively in women ignores both the desires of many battered women to have interventions for their partners and the larger political need to engage men as partners in the battle against abuse. Clearly, the task of mounting programs for batterers is best left to sympathetic male allies. But working to end abuse of necessity requires working directly with men and boys around issues of masculinity, power, and gender roles. The more I work on violence, the more convinced I become that the answer partly lies in redefining what it means to be male—in decoupling masculinity and dominance, aggression and violence, and in creating more flexible gender roles. This is a task for all of society, and especially women, who are the mothers of our next generation of men.

Nonetheless, it is also a task that can only be achieved in cooperation with men. The challenge of how to begin and sustain a dialogue around issues of sexuality, gender, and abuse among the wider community of men is one of the major outstanding questions of the movement. Long-term social change requires that we seek out and cultivate ways to recruit more men and boys to work with their peers on issues of gender and power.

Issues of Style and Strategy

A final set of issues concern strategy: How much should we fashion our messages so that they can be heard rather than seek ideological purity? Is it acceptable to couch feminist agendas in the language of "crime control," "community safety," or "family," if this will win converts and assure funding?

These issues of style and strategy are particularly important as the movement gains strength in developing countries, where feminist values are often perceived as a threat to culture and family. Rightly or wrongly, feminist antiviolence groups are widely perceived in many cultures as antimale and antifamily.

Recently, when I traveled to Zimbabwe to work with the battered women's group, the Musasa Project, I noted on my immigration card that the purpose of my trip was "research collaboration." When the immigration officer asked me who I would be collaborating with, he exclaimed: "The Musasa Project! Well, I hope you have not come here to attack Zimbabwean men. They hate us men at the Musasa Project."

Some of the uproar is clearly an attempt to discredit local groups by claiming that their ideas are imported from the West and will destroy families. But there is also a sincere discomfort among many with any idea that seemingly pits women against men and portrays all men as evil. Especially in Africa, where community and family are valued and recognized far above individual rights, any effort that appears divisive will face fierce opposition.

This raises the question of the extent to which movements should bow to initial discomfort with ideas of gender equality in order to initiate a dialogue about abuse. When it is cast as an issue of men versus women, many individuals, especially in developing countries, immediately reject antiviolence activism. There may be a way to talk about violence in general or violence in the family as being unacceptable before focusing on the gender dimensions of the issue.

In Zimbabwe, for example, discussions of violence were heard more clearly when the facilitator began by talking about families: What makes a good family? What do people need from a family? Should a family be a safe place? Then she proceeded to discuss the reality of certain families. Are there families where people don't always get what they need? Do you know a family where one member is often hurt or abused? Through this line of questioning, the group begins to formulate intimate violence as a threat to the family, an important social institution. When the facilitator began by talking about violence against women, the conversation seldom got beyond the group's felt need to defend the community's men.

To be honest, I am unsure how I feel about the wisdom of this approach. I find it unsettling to underplay what is in fact a critical dimension of the problem, but feminist ideas are seen as so threatening in some contexts that it is impossible to open dialogue. I tend to think that it is acceptable—indeed, important—to craft messages so that they can be heard, as long as groups recognize that this is a conscious strategy to overcome resistance and not a permanent capitulation to antifeminist forces. Eventually, these more benign messages must be supplemented with new ones that directly challenge issues of gender and power.

A similar issue arises in terms of seeking funds for services. I recently visited a very well-equipped crisis center for victims of violence in Monterrey, Mexico. The center has a staff of 40, including lawyers, counselors, prevention workers, and medical staff, and receives substantial funding from the State. Rather than being promoted as a women's crisis center, it is framed as a center for victims of crime in general, even though 80% of its clients are female victims of domestic violence or rape. As the center's dynamic director explained, if she had tried to sell her idea as a women's center, she would never have gained the political support and funding she needed. As it is, the governor can tout the center as part of his efforts to deal with issue of crime while women get well-funded, efficient services.

Again, the issue is one of strategy: Are such reframings of feminist agendas a benign way to garner much needed resources in the short run, or do they jeopardize the movement in the long run by compromising our core values?

Some Thoughts for the Future

The most important shift that antiviolence groups could make to improve their effectiveness is to place greater emphasis on primary prevention. The emphasis on primary prevention is purposeful. In public health terminology, *primary prevention* refers to broad based efforts designed to change social norms and behaviors that promote violence toward women. This is in contrast to *secondary prevention,* which focuses on assisting individuals who have already been identified as being at risk. Programs that focus on at-risk populations can have the negative side effect of further oppressing certain groups by labeling them as a "social problem." Consider, for example, the heightened stigmatization of prostitutes and Haitians that accompanied the early days of the AIDS epidemic (see Sabatier, 1991).

In this regard, the movement would do well to study the community-based strategies of grassroots AIDS organizations, especially those operating in developing nations. Despite an overwhelming need for victim services, the international AIDS community recognized early that it had to focus the bulk of its energy on prevention programs aimed at changing sexual behavior and it has developed increasingly sophisticated strategies for doing this. At the same time, AIDS advocates have not ignored victims. Instead, they have developed low-cost programs of home-based care that draw upon the indigenous resources of family and community.

Similarly, antiviolence activism must shift its emphasis from assisting victims to organizing entire communities against gender-based abuse. In this final section, I would like to share some of my recent thoughts on approaches to violence prevention that deserve our considered attention.

Community Organizing and Consciousness Raising

To date, the model for feminist organizing around violence has been one of service provision, community outreach, and systems advocacy. At the core of this approach is a network of woman's NGOs that provide services for victims and engage in community outreach and system level advocacy (e.g., police training) as funding allows.

An alternate model that deserves consideration—especially in resource poor settings—is a *community organizing* approach to gender-based abuse. Here, women's groups would hire organizers who would work with communities over the long term to analyze issues of violence and mobilize local resources to respond. This approach would be especially appropriate for small towns and rural communities.

The goal of the organizer is fourfold: (a) to help build a local cadre of women committed to ending violence and assisting victims; (b) to help them establish a low-cost method of meeting victims' needs; (c) to initiate a multifaceted community-based prevention campaign that combines media, street theater, religious groups, and other local resources; and (d) to convene a coordinating council of local representatives from the police, courts, health facilities, schools, and the like to begin a process of group reflection and action on how to improve existing responses to victims of abuse.

An organizer might begin, for example, by working with a local women's group—a mother's club, a women's cooperative, or a group convened of representatives from local church groups—to help it undertake a participatory community diagnostic on violence. Is it a problem? How are victims treated? How does it affect our families? Generally, from such exercises, potential leaders emerge who are interested in working further on the issue.

Building on the work of Paulo Freire, the organizer could help these women gain a *critical consciousness* about gender, power, and how violence operates in women's lives (Freire, 1974). Freire's approach is built on a group process of critical reflection and transformative action and has been widely used in developing countries around issues such as land reform and community development. The development of critical consciousness starts with the recognition of the problem and then moves on to analysis, action, and then to organization. In the Frierian model of group learning, the facilitator/leader does not impart "knowledge" to passive subjects, but engages as a partner in a common search for insight about relevant problems.

The organizer could also work with the group to develop a low-cost method of meeting the immediate needs of victims. A group of community women, for example, could be trained as peer counselors/educators to assist women in crisis and accompany them to the hospital, police station, or other location. Where phones are available—and they increasingly are in developing countries—the group might consider investing in a cellular phone or pager system to serve as a hot line, staffing it with group members on a rotating basis. Otherwise, members of the group could run a drop-in center or self-help support group out of a borrowed space in a local church.

Once a support network for victims is established, the organizer and the peer counselors/educators could begin enlisting the help and support of other sectors by convening a coordinating council of representatives from the police, legal services, local churches, women's groups, and the like to begin improving the treatment of local victims. A coordinating council in Gweru, Zimbabwe, has worked with a local legal services project and the magistrate's court to improve the process for abused women applying for child support payments.

Eventually, the peer counselors, organizer, and coordinating council could work collaboratively to develop a broader campaign against violence by enlisting the help of local churches, community leaders, and the like. In many parts of the world, there is still much work to be done to dispel beliefs regarding a man's right to beat a woman, victim-blaming attitudes, and mythology around rape. As with AIDS awareness and legal literacy programs, there is much potential to use indigenous communication media such as drama, street theater, and song.

Campaigns to Create More Social and Family Support

Many women remain trapped in abusive relationships because they are repeatedly told by family, clergy, and others important to them that it is their duty to stay. In many developing countries, they also remain because their cultures fail to recognize any legitimate role for nonmarried women. Frequently, single women are considered prostitutes and "free game" for any passing man. Violence prevention campaigns that specifically target these attitudes could help create a more supportive environment for women wishing to leave abusive relationships.

In India, for example, the women's organization, Jagori, runs a Single Women's Project, specifically named to counter the negative stereotypes of single women and to challenge marriage as women's only option. Group members work against early marriage, desertion, dowry demands, and family violence. Likewise, programs aimed at the opinions and behaviors of those surrounding the victim may also prove important. Slogans such as "Parents, help keep your daughters safe" and "It is better to be single and safe than be sorry" could be used to encourage new attitudes when women disclose abuse.

Indeed, social science research emerging from the AIDS epidemic suggests that the attitudes and norms of individuals in one's social network greatly affects the ability and willingness of individuals to take protective action, such as using condoms (Fisher, Misovich, & Fisher, 1992; Romer et al., 1994). The influence of peer norms and beliefs is so powerful in fact that AIDS prevention programs are increasingly focusing on creating positive attitudes about condoms among peer groups and family members in an effort to support condom use among individuals at high risk of HIV. Similarly, campaigns designed to change the norms and biases of individuals close to battered women may help women to take protective action in their own best interest.

Raising the Social Costs of Violence

In industrial countries, society relies heavily on the justice system to impose social costs on certain unacceptable behaviors. But the justice system—especially the criminal law—offers only a limited number of remedies for women. Putting a man in jail, for example, may harm the woman and her children as much as the offender if she is entirely dependent on her husband for income.

But there are a variety of other ways to raise the social cost of violence. In some developing countries, for example, women have taken to publicly shaming men who batter or rape. Women in India, for example, have humiliated male abusers by picketing their site of employment, socially ostracized families that harass daughters-in-law over dowry, and publicly paraded men naked who have abused their wives (Kelkar, 1992). The Indian police also deploy female officers on crowded buses to stem the tide of "Eve teasing"—the sexual groping and harassment of women in public. When an officer catches an offender, she loudly denounces him, humiliating him in public, before charging him a fine (Moore, 1995). Likewise, during the Sandinista regime, women in the urban poor neighborhoods of Managua instituted their own "women's court," where abusers were summoned and chastised by women's advocates (Dolan, 1995).

Standard courts could implement alternative sentencing schemes that build on the same principle. Batterers could be sentenced to weekend detention or to community service (cleaning parks, public toilets, etc.) and be forced to wear colored overalls that would publicly brand them as abusers. Likewise, there are other such costs that in some settings may serve as more of a deterrent to abuse than a night in jail—things like revoking an abuser's driver's license. Some advocates fear that alternative sentencing schemes would trivialize violence against women by treating it differently from other criminal offenses. But in situations where women do not want or need their partner jailed, such schemes deserve consideration.

Greater Attention to the Role of the Media

To date, there has been little feminist attention to issues of violence in the media, with the exception of pornography. This has been an important oversight. More than 1,000 separate studies and reviews now attest to the fact that media violence facilitates aggressive and antisocial behavior and desensitizes viewers to future violence (Comstock & Strasburger, 1993). Moreover, there are cross-cultural studies that show that violence against women is high in cultures where other forms of interpersonal violence are common and where violence is perceived as an acceptable means to resolve conflicts

(Levinson, 1989; Sanday, 1981). Given this evidence, the movement would do well to join forces with other groups interested in stemming media depictions of all forms of gratuitous violence. Because much of the violent programming worldwide is exported from the United States, the U.S. women's movement has a special responsibility to take on this issue.

There is some evidence that the globalization of the world media is in fact driving the rate of violence in American television and movies. Even though surveys show that American audiences would like less violence on American TV, producers must now shoot to attract global audiences. To be considered profitable, shows must have potential for being sold overseas, and the one thing that sells well without translation is violence (M. Kelly, private communication, July, 1995).

Developing New Models of Child Rearing

Ultimately, prevention means going beyond saving individual women to creating a generation of men and women who believe that violence is unacceptable and who have the skills necessary to build egalitarian relationships. To reach this point, child rearing will have to become a feminist issue, as indeed it should be. Cross-cultural research shows that violence against women is lowest in cultures that do not link masculinity to notions of dominance, aggression, or male honor and that have flexible gender roles (Counts, Brown, & Campbell, 1992; Levinson, 1989; Sanday, 1981). Prevention programs will have to go beyond "conflict resolution" programs in schools to challenging the very definitions of appropriate male and female behavior and roles. Programs on parenting, gender socialization, sexuality, and relationships must be integrated into school curricula and community-based programs for out-of-school youths.

To mainstream such programs, activists will have to confront some deeply rooted fears on the part of parents, especially with respect to homosexuality. One of the strongest enforcers of traditional gender roles is parent's fear that their child will turn out gay if their son indulges in "feminine" pastimes or their daughter is allowed to act "like a boy" (Miedzian, 1991). Although gender and sexual orientation are separate constructs, many parents strongly believe that they are linked and fear that permitting nonstereotypical behavior will lead to "homosexual tendencies." If there is to be any hope of dismantling the destructive gender roles that currently hold sway, the movement will have to take up the issue of homophobia and seek ways to help parents and society past its fears.

The movement will also have to find ways to help support those parents and children who are at the forefront of social change. Even parents who intellectually believe in transforming gender roles are understandably reluctant to have social change happen on the backs of their children. All parents want their children to be liked, to be popular (which generally requires conformity to prevailing stereotypes about male and female behavior). Parents and children need positive reinforcement and skills to help them resist playground jeers and social censure toward children who dare to be different.

Conclusion

These are but a few of the many ideas worthy of consideration as the global movement against violence enters its third decade. By no means should these reflections be considered definitive; they are merely points of departure for further discussion and action. Although many challenges remain, one important battle has been won: The world community now recognizes violence as a legitimate social issue. It remains for activists to translate this rhetorical recognition into concrete change in the lives of women and men.

References

Basu, A. (1987). Alternative forms of organizing women in India: The challenge of difference in the Indian Women's Movement. *The Barnard Occasional Papers on Women's Issues, 2,* 39-61.

Bunch, C., & Reilly, N. (1994). *Demanding accountability: The global campaign and tribunal for women's human rights.* New Brunswick, NJ: Center for Women's Global Leadership.

Capps, M. (1982). *The co-optive and repressive state versus the battered women's movement.* Paper presented at the annual meeting of the Southern Sociological Society, Nicholls State University, Thibodaux, LA.

Carrillo, R. (1992). *Battered dreams: Violence against women as an obstacle to development.* New York: United Nations Development Fund for Women.

Chossudovsky, M. (1992). *Structural adjustment, health and the social dimensions: A review.* Ottawa, Canada: Canadian International Development Agency.

Comstock, G., & Strasburger, G. (1993). Media violence: Q & A. *Adolescent Medicine: State of the Art Reviews, 4*(3), 495-509.

Conrad, P. (1992). Medicalization and social control. *Annual Review of Sociology, 18,* 209-232.

Counts, D. A., Brown, J., & Campbell, J. (Eds.). (1992). *Sanctions and sanctuary: Cultural perspectives on the beating of wives.* Boulder, CO: Westview.

Culliton, K. (1993). Finding a mechanism to enforce women's right to state protection from domestic violence in the Americas. *Harvard International Law Journal, 34*(2), 507-561.

Dobash, R. E., & Dobash, R. P. (1992). *Women, violence and social change.* New York: Routledge.

Dolan, M. (1995). Estrategias Juridicas Contra La Violencia en Los Hogares Urbanos de Nicaragua. *Revista Mexicana de Sociologia. 57*(1), 151-166.

Fernandez, I. (1992). Mobilizing on all fronts: A comprehensive strategy to end violence against women. In M. Schuler (Ed.), *Freedom from violence* (pp. 101-120). New York: UNIFEM.

Fisher, J. D., Misovich, S. J., & Fisher, W. A. (1992). Impact of perceived social norms on adolescent's AIDS-risk behavior and prevention. In R. DiClemente, (Ed.), *Adolescents and AIDS: A generation at risk* (pp.117-136). Newbury Park, CA: Sage.

Freeman, J. (1974). The tyranny of structurelessness. In J. Jaquette (Ed.), *Women in politics.* New York: John Wiley.

Freire, P. (1974). *Education for critical consciousness.* New York: Seabury.

Friedman, E. (1995). Women's human rights: The emergence of a movement. In J. Peters & A. Wolper (Eds.), *Women's rights, human rights: International feminist perspectives* (pp. 18-335). New York: Routledge.

Goldstein, A. T. (1995). Remarks of Anne Tierney Goldstein. *The American University Law Review, 44*(4), 1315-1318.

Grossman, C. (1995). The inter-American system: Opportunities for women's rights. *The American University Law Review, 44*(4), 1305-1309.

Heise, L., & Chapman, J. R. (1992). Reflections on a movement: The U.S. battle against women abuse. In M. Schuler (Ed.), *Freedom from violence* (pp. 257-294). New York: UNIFEM.

Heise, L. (with Pitanguy, J., & Germaine, A.). (1994). Violence against women: The hidden health burden. Discussion paper 255. Washington, DC: The World Book.

Kelkar, G. (1992). Stopping the violence against women: Fifteen years of activism in India. In M. Schuler (Ed.), *Freedom from violence* (pp.75-99). New York: UNIFEM.

Kurz, D. (1987). Emergency department responses to battered women: Resistance to medicalization. *Social Problems, 34*(1), 69-80.

Levinson, D. (1989). *Family violence in cross-cultural perspective.* Newbury Park, CA: Sage.

Miedzian, M. (1991). *Boys will be boys: Breaking the link between masculinity and violence.* New York: Doubleday.

Montano, S. (1992). Long live the differences, with equal rights: A campaign to end violence against women in Bolivia. In M. Schuler (Ed.), *Freedom from violence* (pp. 213-226). New York: UNIFEM.

Moore, M. (1995, February 14). Indian police take on "Eve-teasers." *Washington Post,* p. A20.

Organization of American States (OAS). (1994). *Inter-American Convention on the Prevention, Punishment and Eradication of Violence Against Women* (OAS/ser.L/II.2.27, CIM/doc.33/94).

Pharr, S. (1987). *Do we want to play Faust with the government—(or how do we get our social change work funded and not sell our souls?).* Mimeograph. Little Rock, AK: The Women's Project (on file with author).

Romer, D., Black, M., Isabel, R., Feigelman, S., Kalijee, L., Galbraith, J., Besbit, R., Hornik, R., & Staton, B. (1994). Social influences on the sexual behavior of youth at risk for HIV exposure. *American Journal of Public Health, 84*(6), 977-985.

Sabatier, R. (1991). *Blaming others: Prejudice, race and worldwide AIDS.* London: Panos Institute.

Sanday, P. R. (1981). The socio-cultural context of rape: A cross-cultural study. *Journal of Social Issues 37*(4), 5-27.

Schechter, S. (1982). *Women and male violence: The visions and struggles of the battered women's movement.* Boston: South End.

Schuler, M. (Ed.). (1992). *Freedom from violence.* New York: UNIFEM.

Shrader-Cox, E. (1992). Developing strategies: Efforts to end violence against women in Mexico. In M. Schuler (Ed.), *Freedom from violence* (pp. 175-198). New York: UNIFEM.

Sullivan, D. (1995). The public/private distinction in international human rights law. In J. Peters & A. Wolper (Eds.), *Women's rights, human rights: International feminist perspectives* (pp. 126-134). New York: Routledge.

Tavris, C. (1992). *The mismeasure of women.* New York: Simon & Schuster.

Tinker, A., Daly, P., Green, C., Saxenian, H., Lakshminarayanan, R., & Gill, K. (1994). *Women's health and nutrition: Making a difference.* Washington, DC: World Bank.

U. N. Commission on Human Rights. (1994). *Resolution 1994/45, E/1994/24.*

World Bank. (1993). *World development report 1993: Investing in health.* New York: Oxford University Press.

World Conference on Human Rights. (1993). *Vienna Declaration and Programme of Action* (U.N. Doc. A/CONF.157/24).

3

Domestic Violence, Racism, and the Battered Women's Movement in the United States

Valli Kanuha

There are few places in the United States where domestic abuse is an unknown problem. Beginning more than 25 years ago, our collective knowledge and understanding of violence against women has evolved from a grassroots social change movement among feminist activists into an international social problem of note among academicians, legal scholars, and social policy analysts. Although some activists have bemoaned the fact that the early vibrancy of the battered women's movement has at best become lackluster, and at worst lost to State co-optation, it is a measure of the movement's success that the issue of domestic violence has gained enough prominence in 25 years to become mainstream, as evidenced by the hundreds of programs and services now available to women, children, and men across the United States (National Coalition Against Domestic Violence [NCADV], 1992; Pirog-Good & Stets-Kealey, 1985; Sullivan, 1982).

Often discussed but never well-elucidated, analyses of domestic violence in the relationships of women and men of color have been disappointingly meager. Equally important, the impact of race and ethnicity upon one's experience in both the private and the public domain of spouse abuse has also been poorly documented or studied. As one who counts herself among the ranks of the battered women's movement, how this movement and its collateral institutions have had such an influential and sustaining effect on American political and social life while at the same time virtually ignoring the relationship between spouse abuse and the most salient and controversial issues of our time—racism and race relations—is something of an enigma to me.

The purpose of this chapter is to present an analysis of the elements that have contributed to the failure of the American battered women's movement to address race as a significant factor in our understanding of spouse abuse. My primary framework for analyzing the connection between race and domestic abuse is a social construction perspective of social problem formulation, in specific the ways spouse abuse and battered women have been defined and conceptualized in the United States. This analysis is not intended to be a definitive explanation for the underrepresentation of race issues in domestic abuse theory building and intervention. Rather, it is proposed as a heuristic model for understanding the contextual underpinnings that may have affected theory building and interventions with battered women of color in the United States over the past two decades, and as such is intended as a work in progress.

Social Construction and the Etiology of Domestic Violence

Spouse abuse as a social problem of interest garnered attention as defined within and as an extension of the feminist movement beginning in the 1960s. The etiology of spouse abuse has been extensively studied across disciplines with varying degrees of interest and focus on the victim, the offender, the marital relationship, the family, the children, and respective families of origin (Dutton, 1992; Edleson & Tolman, 1992; Hampton, 1987; Peled, Jaffe, & Edleson, 1995; Sonklin, 1987; Yllo & Bograd, 1988).

Although most contemporary explanations of partner abuse probably combine a number of epistemological and practice areas, feminist thought has predominated the analysis of wife abuse initiated first by battered women's movement activists and reinforced in the academy (Dobash & Dobash, 1979, 1992; Martin, 1976; Pagelow, 1981; Roy, 1977; Schechter, 1982; Walker, 1979).

Social constructionism, as originally conceived by Berger and Luckmann (1966), has been most frequently applied to a feminist analysis of spouse battering by emphasizing a number of factors. First and foremost, wife abuse is attributed to both ascribed and endowed expectations for males and females. These roles are manifested along gendered lines wherein the existence of historically constructed social contexts (marriage, dating, family life) have reinforced that males are not only expected to but also have the means to maintain control over all aspects of social life, and the lives of women in particular. Second, many males employ a particular engendered repertoire of individual and institutional control over women, which may include both physical and psychological dimensions. And finally, the overt sanction of many influential social institutions such as schools, the media, police, courts, and legislatures have historically reinforced all of the preceding factors to create an environment of male dominance in which violence against women may be one result. Although there are other perspectives that explain the causes and nature of domestic abuse, there are very few analysts who would disagree that the preceding factors are significant if not minimal conditions under which spousal battery may occur.

The examination of partner abuse from a social construction perspective has, however, been primarily rooted in defining the *causes* of woman abuse, and not the processes by which the so-called problem of woman abuse emerged and has now become more commonplace across all communities and nations. I believe that there has been not only an implicit assumption about the moral right of our (speaking of the collective battered women's movement, in which I include myself) theoretical analyses of spouse abuse but also the presumption of spouse abuse as *a social problem.* Because we begin with the given that spouse abuse has been occurring privately, "behind closed doors" for centuries, the role of social activists has been merely to open those doors and expose the problem to the public so that it can be addressed and eventually alleviated. In the operationalizing of the problem of spouse abuse, however, very little attention has been paid to the private and public processes by which we defined the parameters of the battered woman problem and therefore who the battered woman is or was.

Let me emphasize a caution here: I am not criticizing the application of the social construction model to explicating the causes and dynamics of spouse abuse, because I adhere to this perspective along with most feminists. We know that every day women and girls are violated in their homes; this fact is not to be disputed. However, as we approach the third decade of our work to end this devastation in women's lives, I believe that our analysis and understanding of who those women and girls are, and subsequently what we as a society do to stop the violence against them is our *only,* but largely underdeveloped, concern. Inattention to how battering has been defined as a social problem is in part responsible for the absence of race perspectives in our analysis of spouse abuse.

Construction of Domestic Violence as a Social Problem

The relegation of certain social phenomena to the status of social problem is a complex process that has been a longstanding subject of study for social scientists. The most common sociological explanations of social problems include social pathology, social disorganization, labeling theory, deviance, and others, all of which have generated a variety of models and applications from which social problems are understood and analyzed (Rubington & Weinberg, 1989). Although the more traditional view of social problems suggests that problems are objective social conditions that are "found to be harmful to individual and/or societal well-being" (Bassis, Gelles, & Levine, 1982, p. 2), in the past 20 years the social constructivist perspective has gained prominence among many activists and social scientists. This viewpoint forms the basis of my critique of the absence of race perspectives in domestic violence theory building and intervention.

In general, the constructivist analysis of social problems posits that they are phenomena that are not necessarily objectively problematic; that is, they may not be innately troublesome occurrences nor are they necessarily situations endowed with negative characteristics (Spector & Kitsuse, 1977). Instead, problems become defined to a public audience through a complex series of activities, called *typification,* in which interested individuals and groups, known as *claims makers,* engage.

Applying the perspective to battered women, constructivists would state that spouse abuse only exists as a social problem because battered women's activists made public claims about the conditions in some women's lives in which they are violated by their intimate partners. The most important claims-making activities regarding the problem of domestic abuse include both defining what spousal battering or abuse is and delineating the behavioral, psychological, and other characteristics that describe the battered woman. For example, a single slap in a 40-year marriage may be an abusive act but may not necessarily constitute a pattern of domestic violence.

Although some feminist theorists and activists have challenged the contributions and limitations of social constructivism in our understanding of spouse abuse, the particular analysis of battering as a socially constructed problem has not been fully developed (Fine, 1985; Tierney, 1982). In her study of a battered women's shelter, Loseke (1992) offers a particularly cogent example of wife abuse as a social construction of a social problem. I suggest that the movement, as exemplified by its leadership, theory builders, and activist/service providers—claims makers all—has constructed what Loseke defined as a collective representation of both the battered woman problem and the battered woman, which not only included but also excluded many women who have been and are currently being abused in their intimate relationships.

For example, Loseke and others (Walker, 1990) suggest that our construction of the battered woman includes such typifications as her lack of culpability for her violent situation. Therefore, if a woman is perceived as being responsible in any way for her predicament, such as her fighting back, initiating abuse, being mutually violent, or any myriad of ways in which she might be *perceived* as accountable for her abuse, the benefits usually accorded her are abrogated. We know of too many incidents when we were unsure whether a battered woman was "deserving" of protection or other kinds of intervention because of particular behaviors she manifested that didn't fit our image of the battered woman.

Mahoney (1994) theorizes that the dual concepts of agency (acting for oneself) and victimization create contradictions in our analyses and expectations of the battered woman because "in our society, agency and victimization are each known by the absence of the other: you are an agent if you are not a victim, and you are not a victim if you are in any way an agent. . . . This all-agent or all-victim conceptual dichotomy will not be easy to escape or transform" (p. 64). Therefore, if we construct the battered woman as having agency, we expect her to be able to leave; however, if she is a victim, it undermines the inherent survival skills and strengths that many battered women typify each day they live with violence.

What is the purpose of analyzing the battered women's movement from this perspective? The reason to study social problems using this framework is to develop social theory about multilevel interactions and, most important, to elucidate those structural features of social problems that help us understand why problems are manifested in particular ways. The reason to examine domestic abuse from a social problems perspective is that the American battered women's movement has arrived at a critical juncture in its development as a social movement, wherein the theoretical underpinnings, intervention models, research and policy priorities, and perhaps all aspects of our work need a critical review. If a crucial role of social change work is the promotion of an epistemology and requisite ideology that informs the public about the condition of spouse abuse, what terms best represent for whom we work and toward what goals? As Loseke (1992) states in her introduction,

> I will be emphasizing how this social problems industry reflects characteristics of modern day America. In many ways, wife abuse and the battered woman are merely case examples demonstrating general cultural characteristics—what types of situations Americans define as troublesome and what types of people we define as worthy of help. In the final analysis, wife abuse and the battered woman exemplify the social problems work of producing and reproducing collective images and thereby producing and reproducing social structure. (p. 9)

The next section presents an analysis of how race and racism, as manifested in the battered women's movement, have indeed reproduced the prevailing social structure of race relations in the United States.

Spouse Abuse as a Problem "Regardless of Race"

Women of color have—from the inception of the modern-day American women's movement—challenged feminism's underrepresentation of race/ethnicity as a cofactor with gender discrimination.

These concerns about feminism have included the shortage of race/ethnic perspectives in theory building (Allen, 1986; Anzaldua, 1990; Chow, 1989; Mohanty, Russo, & Torres, 1991; Moraga & Anzaldúa, 1983) and the exclusion of women of color in feminist leadership and scholarship (Hill-Collins, 1990; Hull, Scott, & Smith, 1982). Although this criticism of feminism has unfortunately been a consistent theme for more than three decades of the modern women's movement, women of color rather than white women continue to be the primary voices raising the issue of not only the absence of race but also other forms of oppression in our understanding of the status of women.

As an extension of a broad based women's movement, it is not surprising that the battered women's movement suffered from many of the same limitations in its analyses and intervention strategies with regard to women of color. Early in the domestic violence movement, women of color began to challenge movement leaders and service providers about the absence of women of color's experiences in our analysis of battered women (American Indian Women Against Domestic Violence, 1984; Burns, 1986; Davis, 1985; NCADV, 1990; Rimonte, 1989; Rios, 1985; Rogers, Taylor, & McGee, n.d.; White, 1985; Zambrano, 1985). Yet, little empirical literature exists to guide intervention within communities of color.

In particular, many have criticized those claims makers who have used—and continue to use—what I refer to as "the Other" tag line. This is the common caveat too often tagged on to the end of a statement of analysis or theory, such as describing sexism as the oppression of "all women, regardless of race, class, or sexual orientation" or domestic abuse as a problem affecting "every person, across race, class, nationality, and religious lines." The use of this tag line is not only a token attempt at inclusion of diverse perspectives but also evidence of sloppy research and theory building.

Defining a concept, theory, or social problem as "regardless of race" implies that people of color are comprised in a collective identity based on racial minority status as the dichotomous opposite from the racial majority group. This bipolar analysis of racial stratification is problematic for both whites and people of color, especially in its connotation that either group is unidimensional. In a racial hierarchy, lumping together the dominant group only maintains its hierarchical status and accompanying power and privilege. For people of color, such grouping not only conflates their unique differences but by so doing also structurally mitigates any claims for a redistribution of resources and power in the hierarchy. That is, for battered spouses who also happen to be women, poor, lesbians, and nonwhite, the fact of their racial minority status alone does not tell the whole picture of their lives as victims of abuse; the tag line that domestic violence affects everyone equally trivializes both the dimensions that underlie the experiences of these particular abuse victims and, more important, the ways we analyze the prevalence and impact of the violence against them.

Crenshaw (1994) outlines an important concept called *intersectionality,* which refers not only to the inclusion of perspectives of women of color in all of our analyses but also to consideration of the *shared effects of race and gender* (and other relevant factors such as class, nationality, language, and other cultural elements) upon the construction of social problems and upon the requisite solutions to them. Similar to previous and ongoing challenges to the broader women's movement, women of color have articulated the multiple oppressions that battered women of color face, which therefore require perhaps a different but surely more expansive vision of who *all battered women* are.

There are ongoing concerns about the historical and the current failure of the battered women's movement to address the issues of women and men of color and, more important, Crenshaw's (1994) intersectionality of race and gender with domestic violence.

Race/Ethnicity as an Important Factor

A number of things have occurred relative to race/ethnicity in defining spouse abuse as the problem and subsequently the battered woman as the primary victim of that problem. As stated earlier, feminist theorists often did not mention possible differential effects for women of color (or other women with multiple oppressive life conditions or identities). More frequently still, they stated that spouse abuse was a problem common to all women, regardless of race, class, or other factors (Martin, 1976; Pagelow, 1981; Walker, 1979). When constructing an ideology of battering as a social problem, including the race tag line is usually intended to communicate two things: that the social problem *may apply* to all women or that it *should apply* to all women. In most cases, the analysis is rarely more extensive or substantive than a tag line, because it is apparent that there is little empirical evidence to either support or refute that race is or is not a salient cofactor. More troubling, however, is the implication not only that battering applies to all women equivalently but also that the conditions and experiences under which spouse abuse is manifested are also equivalent.

Why is the tag line still a common strategy among domestic violence theorists and workers? There are two primary reasons: First, because of our initial reliance on the traditional, objectivist definition of spouse abuse as a social problem, the concepts of race and racism were poorly defined as part of the early ideology of battering. Until the mid-1970s, spouse abuse was not defined as a social problem. Only when feminist activists began to describe the experiences of battered women within the context of heterosexual relationship violence did spouse abuse gain some credibility as a problem in the United States. Therefore, for white feminists who primarily constructed the ideology of the early battered women's movement, their racism—reflecting societal racism—necessarily limited their notions of who the battered woman could be.

A tautological barrier naturally ensued for the white, feminist claims makers in the movement. Lacking a concept for *the battered woman of color,* they were not able to construct race as a factor in the analysis of spousal violence; and without defining race as a construct, we could not know battered women of color. Therefore, we also could not know about the experiences and lives of their children or abusive male partners.

There is another reason we have not done very well in addressing race as part of our analysis, intervention, or research strategies about battered women. Movement claims makers perceived and engaged in claims-making activities to reinforce the movement's dual role of protecting people of color and itself from backlash by attenuating the importance of the race issue. The ideology of all women as potentially battered women has always been more palatable not only to the movement but also to our external constituents. The battered woman as "the bad woman" who is poor, or drug addicted, or a racial/ethnic minority, or all of these seemed less palatable. To reinforce in the hearts and minds of the public that not just so-called bad women are battered, the movement appealed to the highest common denominator in its construction of the battered woman by portraying her as the victim without agency (Mahoney, 1994), as morally deserving of public protection and attention (Loseke, 1992), as one who does not fight back (Richie, 1992), and as therefore fitting some collective interpretation of Everywoman, which, for mainstream America, is often equivalent to white, middle-class, moral, "good" women.

Crenshaw (1994) suggests that, to minimize the challenges to both the battered woman problem and the race problem, the violence against women movement abandoned women of color in its collective representation and construction of battering and the "acceptable" battered woman. She states,

> By pointing out that violence is a universal problem, elites are deprived of their false security, while nonelite families are given reason not to be unduly defensive. Moreover all battered women may well benefit from knowing that they are far from alone. But there is, nonetheless, a thin line between debunking the stereotypical beliefs that only poor or minority women are battered, and pushing them aside to focus on victims for whom mainstream politicians and media are more likely to express concern. (p. 105)

Although not suggesting that white women are solely culpable for this situation, the inherent racism of the movement left very few areas of support for activist women of color to address these deeply conflicting struggles.

A related dynamic that has affected the absence of race perspectives involves revealing negative aspects of an already oppressed identity group. The basic nature of prejudice and oppression requires that marginalized individuals and groups lessen the conditions for their oppression by minimizing any part of their identity, behavior, history, values—essentially, their culture—that may be construed as deviant by the dominant social and political environment in which they live. At particular moments in history, the distinction of a marginalized group's private cultural identity is more or less consistent with its public identity. These distinctions are directly proportional to the threat of loss of an already minimal status relative to the place of either the dominant group or other competing marginal groups. With regard to the battered women's movement, as women of color struggled for a place at both the feminist and the racial identity tables, neither hosts had set a welcome place for them. The predominantly white battered women's movement was not able to easily confront racism in its work, and communities of color could not prioritize the needs of women, much less battered women, over their longstanding fight to promote an agenda of racial equality.

In terms of protecting women in communities of color, there is an obvious—though not simplistic—element of hypocrisy in claims makers' wanting to protect communities of color when the foundation of the movement was to protect battered women, among which there would be non-Caucasian women.

Another related analysis, which requires much more discussion than this chapter permits, is the representation of batterers, and particularly men of color as batterers. If the empirical literature is sparse about battered women of color, it is practically nil with regard to men of color who are abusers. As Davis (1985) has suggested, the characterization of the African American man and by extension all men of color as the quintessential rapist, abductor of white women, and demon has a long tradition in historical and contemporary depictions. Although mindful of these degrading stereotypes, the activity of protecting men of color who are batterers from further racial stigmatization has in fact resulted in our collusion with their gendered violence. Somehow, both the antiviolence movement and communities of color have claimed through default that it is more important for men of color to be protected in all aspects of their lives than it is for women of color to be protected in the most intimate and private aspect of their lives. The result of this ill-formed strategy is to do just the opposite of what claims makers and tag line users have professed: All women *can* be battered, but only some will be protected. And all men *can* batter, but only some will be held accountable.

In summary, the claims-making activities of the battered women's movement have lacked a very simple theoretical formulation in their ideology of the battered woman problem. The conceptualization of gender as the primary—if not sole—foundation of battering as a social problem mitigated consideration of race (or other factors) as significant in our analysis and theory building about domestic violence. As Loseke (1992) stated, we have produced images of battered women that have not included women of color as abused or men of color as abusers, and by doing so, we have also reproduced the existing social structure of American life in which race is a defining element of social stratification. We must produce additional images of domestic abuse that include those many men, women, and children who are experiencing this devastating condition of family life. Until we do so, the battered women's movement not only will reinforce the existing social institutions and norms, of which racism is a historical and ingrained dimension, but also will lack the moral vision that has made it one of the most important social change movements of this century.

The Future of Theory Building in the Movement

In a succinct definition of feminism and antiracism, Sohng (1995) states that her understanding of an oppressed class is informed primarily by those at the margins of that class; for example, feminism is constructed only through representations of women of color, lesbians, poor women, immigrant women, women with disabilities, and other women for whom gender is but a part of their marginalized status. As this analysis comes to a close, I conclude that the battered women's movement, in its collective ideology and construction of the battered woman problem, has indeed failed to represent those women—battered women—most at the margins. This situation is not easily rectified but must be. However, it will require a certain commitment and will to change for us to reconceptualize not just the very nature of our work but, more important, those for whom we work.

Although the primary aim of this chapter was to offer a theoretical analysis upon which to frame our reflections of domestic violence and race, I offer the following recommendations with a view toward the future.

Culturally Competent Research. Where are all the men and women of color who are living with domestic violence? Collaborative research efforts with communities of color to document the incidence, service usage, treatment outcomes, and intra- and inter-group differences of spouse abuse by race/ethnicity and other factors *must* begin. We know too much, have too many talented scholars with intersectionality perspectives, and have counted too many women dying and men in jail to allow this travesty of invisibility to continue.

The methods of research must be participatory, empowering, and based in a community action model, as is appropriate for most if not all ethical studies of marginalized populations. If we are to mitigate not only the negative ramifications upon communities of color but also movement fears of racial stigmatization regarding the social deviancy of battering, our research efforts must be responsive and reflexive to the various participants.

This activity is the single most important item on the American domestic violence agenda for the years to come. Issues for people of color with regard to domestic violence may be neither unique nor equivalent to majority groups. This, however, is the problem; we just don't know. As most feminists of color have stated, hiding the extent or nature of spouse abuse within communities of color is not a protective act for battered women in those communities (Crenshaw, 1994; Richie, 1985; Richie & Kanuha, 1993). Victim safety and offender accountability should also apply to women and men of color, as we have espoused that it should for everyone else. How and when and where it should occur are our more relevant concerns.

Including Diverse Voices. There are many women and men of color, and our allies who are not only living with abuse but who are engaged in work to end domestic violence in communities of color. These voices and experiences must be heard across different perspectives, from different theoretical disciplines, and in different forms. As many of us know, living with and doing domestic violence work are not necessarily compatible with claims-making activities in the public arena. Therefore, many women of color are excluded from sharing their experiences of domestic violence through writing, speaking, theater, or other media. Mentorship and collaborative efforts to support claims-making activities of women and men of color are the only ways these absent voices in the battered women's movement will be heard. Mentorship is not an invitation to participate; it involves active engagement in the experiences and subsequent development of those with whom you are collaborating. This is a necessary precursor to correcting the paucity of feminist and other perspectives on the race-domestic violence issue.

Internationalizing Theory. Domestic violence theorists and practitioners from other countries bring different and important perspectives to the sometimes ethnocentric analyses developed in the United States. Sharing theory, interventions, and policy development strategies across nations and cultures may inform our limited American view of this cross-cultural phenomenon. Although I have focused my critique on the American battered women's movement, most international domestic violence workers have done no better in addressing race issues in their countries and programs (Borkowski, Murch, & Walker, 1983; Hopkins & McGregor, 1991; Pahl, 1985; Walker,

1990). However, I believe there are particular structural aspects of race and racism that transcend national boundaries, and these are the international dialogues we should be engaged in.

Increasing the Scope of Theory. This chapter has highlighted the necessity of considering the intersectionality of race and gender in our conceptualization of spouse abuse. There are, however, many other marginalized women who are battered and to whom we must also give voice. Renzetti (1992) and I (Kanuha, 1990) have both written about lesbian violence, Nishioka (1992) and Takagi (1991) have discussed the complex issues facing immigrant battered women, and Haj-Yahia (this volume) has examined the historical, religious, and cultural conflicts for Arab communities dealing with spouse abuse. There are many other women whose experiences have not been illuminated to demonstrate both the complexity and the commonplace nature of domestic abuse. The intersectionality perspective offers a much richer level of analysis of violence in the home, and I suggest this perspective is one that should inform our work across the many and varied examinations of this problem.

Refocusing on Social Action. Given the current political climate in the United States, is there a role for the battered women's movement to remobilize as a social action endeavor? In 1995, is there still a battered women's movement, or, as longtime battered women's advocate Ellen Pence suggests, is there just a "stagnant women's movement"? Critical analysis and reflection about the role, if any, of movement politics in the current plethora of domestic violence initiatives is overdue.

Making Assumptions Explicit. Finally, I challenge activists, scholars, educators, policymakers, and anyone concerned with domestic violence at the public level to consider the ethical imperative inherent in addressing this issue without explicitly stating upon what their analyses are based. Most analyses of battering are offered toward a social goal of ending violence against women, children, and some men. However, the limitations of any conclusions or recommendations, including upon whom those findings are based, must become a professional and moral requisite of claims makers and claims-making activities. More of us need to admit to the shortcomings of our constructs, study samples, and theories as they contribute to our understanding of domestic violence. I would even suggest that we cease using the tag line, substituting instead an analysis about what conditions of social and political life have contributed to the absence of certain perspectives in our work. We would start from the viewpoint of *who* is excluded and *why,* rather than the assumption that everyone is included and how.

After almost three decades, the need to include diverse perspectives in our definition of violence and battered women is not merely to correct a longstanding gap in our theory building and interventions. Integrating an analysis of multiple oppressions into our gendered perspective of violence against women will only deepen our understanding of this problem and our subsequent efforts to end it—surely and finally for *all* women, children, and their partners.

References

Allen, P. G. (1986). *The sacred hoop: Recovering the feminine in American Indian tradition.* Boston: Beacon.

American Indian Women Against Domestic Violence. (1984). *Position paper.* St. Paul: Minnesota Coalition for Battered Women.

Anzaldúa, G. (Ed.). (1990). *Making face, making soul = Haciendo caras: Creative and critical perspectives by women of color.* San Francisco: Aunt Lute Foundation Books.

Bassis, M. S., Gelles, R. J., & Levine, A. (1982). *Social problems.* New York: Harcourt Brace Jovanovich.

Berger, P. L., & Luckmann, T. (1966). *The social construction of reality.* Garden City, NY: Anchor.

Borkowski, M., Murch, M., & Walker, V. (1983). *Marital violence: The community response.* London: Tavistock.

Burns, M. C. (Ed.). (1986). *The speaking profits us: Violence in the lives of women of color.* Seattle: Center for the Prevention of Sexual and Domestic Violence.

Chow, E. N. (1989). The feminist movement: Where are all the Asian American women? In Asian Women United of California (Ed.), *Making waves: An anthology of writings by and about Asian American women* (pp. 362-376). Boston: Beacon.

Crenshaw, K. W. (1994). Mapping the margins: Intersectionality, identity politics and violence against women of color. In M. A. Fineman & B. Mykitiuk (Eds.), *The public nature of private violence* (pp. 93-120). New York: Routledge.

Davis, A. Y. (1985). *Violence against women and the ongoing challenge to racism.* Latham, NY: Kitchen Table: Women of Color Press.

Dobash, R. E., & Dobash, R. (1979). *Violence against wives: A case against the patriarchy.* New York: Free Press.

Dobash, R. E., & Dobash, R. (1992). *Women, violence and social change.* London: Routledge.

Dutton, M. A. (1992). *Empowering and healing the battered woman.* New York: Springer.

Edleson, J. L., & Tolman, R. M. (1992). *Intervention for men who batter: An ecological approach.* Newbury Park, CA: Sage.
Fine, M. (1985). Unearthing contradictions: An essay inspired by *Women and male violence. Feminist Studies, 11*(2), 391-407.
Hampton, R. J. (Ed.). (1987). *Violence in the black family: Correlates and consequences.* Lexington, MA: Lexington Books.
Hill-Collins, P. (1990). *Black feminist thought: Knowledge, consciousness and the politics of empowerment.* Boston: Unwin Hyman.
Hopkins, A., & McGregor, H. (1991). *Working for change: The movement against domestic violence.* North Sydney, Australia: Allen & Unwin.
Hull, D., Scott, P., & Smith B. (1982). *All the women are white, all the blacks are men, but some of us are brave: Black women's studies.* New York: Feminist Press.
Kanuha, V. (1990). Compounding the triple jeopardy: Battering in lesbian of color relationships. In L. S. Brown & M. P. P. Root (Eds.), *Diversity and complexity in feminist therapy* (pp. 169-184). New York: Haworth.
Loseke, D. R. (1992). *The battered woman and shelters: The social construction of wife abuse.* Albany: State University of New York Press.
Mahoney, M. R. (1994). Victimization or oppression? Women's lives, violence and agency. In M. A. Fineman & B. Mykitiuk (Eds.), *The public nature of private violence* (pp. 59-92). New York: Routledge.
Martin, D. (1976). *Battered wives.* New York: Simon & Schuster.
Mohanty, C. T., Russo, A., & Torres, L. (Eds.). (1991). *Third world women and the politics of feminism.* Bloomington: Indiana University Press.
Moraga, C., & Anzaldúa, G. (Eds.). (1983). *This bridge called my back: Writings by radical women of color.* Latham, NY: Kitchen Table: Women of Color Press.
National Coalition Against Domestic Violence (NCADV). (1990, July). Women of color and domestic violence. In *Women of Color Institute Manual* from the proceedings of the National Coalition Against Domestic Violence Conference, Amherst, MA.
National Coalition Against Domestic Violence. (1992). *A current analysis of the battered women's movement.* Denver: Battered/Formerly Battered Women's Task Force of the National Coalition Against Domestic Violence.
Nishioka, J. (1992, November). Asian women and the cycle of abuse. *New Moon,* 3. Boston: Asian Task Force Against Domestic Violence.
Pagelow, M. A. (1981). *Woman-battering.* Newbury Park, CA: Sage.
Pahl, J. (Ed.) (1985). *Private violence and public policy: The needs of battered women and the response of the public services.* London: Routledge & Kegan Paul.
Peled, E., Jaffe, P. G., & Edleson, J. L. (Eds.). (1995). *Ending the cycle of violence: Community response to children of battered women.* Thousand Oaks, CA: Sage.
Pirog-Good, M., & Stets-Kealey, J. (1985). Male batterers and battering prevention programs: A national survey. *Response to the Victimization of Women and Children, 8*(3), 8-12.
Renzetti, C. M. (1992). *Violent betrayal: Partner abuse in lesbian relationships.* Newbury Park, CA· Sage.
Richie, B. E. (1985). Battered black women: A challenge for the black community. *The Black Scholar, 16,* 40-44.
Richie, B. E. (1992). *Gender entrapment: An exploratory study of the link between gender-identity development, violence against women, race/ethnicity and crime among African American battered women.* Unpublished doctoral dissertation, City University of New York.
Richie, B. E., & Kanuha, V. (1993). Battered women of color in public health care systems: Racism, sexism and violence. In B. Blair & S. E. Cayleff (Eds.), *Wings of gauze: Women of color and the experience of health and illness.* Detroit: Wayne State Press.

Rimonte, N. (1989). Domestic violence among Pacific Asians. In Asian Women United of California (Eds.), *Making waves: An anthology of writings by and about Asian American women* (pp. 327-336). Boston: Beacon.

Rios, E. (1985). *Double jeopardy: Cultural and systemic barriers faced by the Latina battered woman.* Unpublished manuscript.

Rogers, B., Taylor, M., & McGee, G. (n.d.). *Black women and family violence: A guide for service providers.* St. Paul: Minnesota Coalition for Battered Women.

Roy, M. (1977). *Battered women: A psychosociological study of domestic violence.* New York: Van Nostrand Reinhold.

Rubington, E., & Weinberg, M. S. (1989). *The study of social problems.* New York: Oxford University Press.

Schechter, S. (1982). *Women and male violence: The visions and struggles of the battered women's movement.* Boston: South End Press.

Sohng, S. (1995, February). *Pedagogy: The medium is the message.* Paper presented at the Women of Color in Academia Panel Discussion Series, Northwest Center on Research on Women, Seattle.

Sonklin, D. J. (Ed.). (1987). *Domestic violence on trial: Psychological and legal dimensions of family violence.* New York: Springer.

Spector, M., & Kitsuse, J. (1977). Social problems: A reformulation. *Social Problems, 21,* 145-159.

Sullivan, G. (1982). Cooptation of alternative services: The battered women's movement as a case study. *Catalyst, 14,* 39-56.

Takagi, T. (1991, Spring). Women of color and violence against women. In National Network of Women's Funds and Foundations/Corporate Philanthropy (C. Mollner, Ed.), *Violence against women supplement* (pp. S1, S6). St. Paul, MN: National Network of Women's Fund and Foundations/Corporate Philanthropy.

Tierney, K. J. (1982). The battered women movement and the creation of the wife beating problem. *Social Problems, 29*(3), 207-220.

Walker, G. A. (1990). *Family violence and the women's movement: The conceptual politics of struggle.* Toronto: University of Toronto Press.

Walker, L. E. (1979). *The battered woman.* New York: Harper Colophon.

White, E. C. (1985). *Chain, chain, change: For black women dealing with physical and emotional abuse and exploring responses to it.* Seattle: Seal.

Yllo, K., & Bograd, M. (Eds.). (1988). *Feminist perspectives on wife abuse.* Newbury Park, CA: Sage.

Zambrano, M. A. (1985). *Mejor sola que mal accompanada: Para la mejor golpeada* [For the Latina in an abusive relationship]. Seattle: Seal.

PART II

CHANGING COMMUNITY RESPONSES

4

The Battered Women's Movement in the United States

New Directions for Institutional Reform

Susan Schechter

Between 1975 and 1995, the battered women's movement in the United States focused on the following three major initiatives: (a) establishing and maintaining shelters and other crisis support services for women and their children, (b) expanding women's options for legal protection, and (c) educating the public about domestic violence. Over the past 20 years, grassroots activists have set up more than 1,200 shelters and safe homes projects, reformed protection order legislation in every state, expanded safeguards for women seeking custody of their children, and offered education about domestic violence to hundreds of thousands of professionals and lay people.

Over the past several years, feminist activists have come to see that these extremely important initiatives have limitations; for example, current strategies (a) leave out key sectors of the community involved in responding to domestic violence (e.g., the health care and child welfare systems, the schools, and the religious community); (b) rely heavily on criminalizing the problem of domestic violence and punishing perpetrators (The battered women's movement has argued for coordinated community responses to domestic violence, but until very recently this has meant only that *criminal justice* system interventions are coordinated.); and (c) offer little in the way of prevention.

This chapter examines the first problem, the failure of key sectors in the community to respond to domestic violence, and argues that the domestic violence movement should target the child welfare and health care systems as the next major arenas for institutional reform. Describing the handful of new and innovative initiatives to help battered women developed in health care and child welfare settings, the chapter explores the dilemmas, concerns, and hopes that this new institutional reform agenda suggests for the domestic violence movement.

Why Reform the Health Care and Child Welfare Systems?

A 1992 study of domestic violence in Massachusetts paints a compelling picture of the need to expand the number of systems that should intervene in domestic violence. Extrapolating from national survey data, the authors (Schechter with Mihaly, 1992) estimated that approximately 43,000 married and cohabiting women in Massachusetts experienced severe violence in 1991. Another 149,000 women endured some form of abuse (defined, for example, as pushing and slapping).

Although this estimate of 192,000 women victimized by their male partners is problematic for a number of methodological reasons, it stands in stark contrast to the service statistics provided by the member programs (28 shelters) of the Massachusetts Coalition for Battered Women Service Groups in the same year. In 1991, Massachusetts shelters reported that their advocates accompanied 9,400 women to court. Nineteen hundred abused women were offered shelter, and 8,700 participated in a support group (Schechter with Mihaly, 1992). Assuming that this is an overlapping population of women—many women who attended support groups also lived in shelters and asked an advocate to accompany them to court—it is clear that domestic violence services reach only a small number of the women who actually need help.

Between 1990 and 1991, the Massachusetts state legislature expanded legal protection for battered women who were living with or dating their partners. As a result, the number of restraining order petitions to courts skyrocketed, from 33,000 orders granted in 1990, most of them to battered women, to 44,000 in 1991 (Schechter with Mihaly, 1992). At best, only approximately 9,000 of these women were accompanied to court by an advocate from a domestic violence program.

These statistics suggest that the vast majority of battered women in Massachusetts are not currently served by a program for battered women. Even the most severely victimized women, numbering approximately 43,000, are not reached through the network of services currently in place. The statistics regarding children are even more disheartening. Responding to a 1991 survey, 23 Massachusetts shelters reported that they employed a total of 12 paid child advocates although they provided housing to more than 2,500 children in the study year. On average, each paid child advocate was responsible for at least 125 sheltered children annually. Only 6 of 23 programs could provide support groups for resident children; and in the entire state, approximately 80 children of battered women living outside shelters received support group services in 1991 (Schechter with Mihaly, 1992).

From these data, it might be argued that the government needs to provide more funding for services to domestic violence programs and more financial support for court-based advocacy efforts for battered women. Both are undoubtedly true. Urban shelters in Massachusetts are still turning away more women than they serve. If shelters and court projects were adequately funded, far more women and children would be helped.

Yet many women and children are reluctant to reach out to a shelter, call the police, or petition the court for an order of protection. Others call these agencies only after experiencing years of abuse. These are the women who could be served if other systems, like health care and child welfare, change.

One example from a health care site illustrates the profound potential for helping abused women who are using neither shelter nor the courts. Statistics compiled by AWAKE (Advocacy for Women and Kids in Emergencies), a project for battered women with abused children at Children's Hospital, Boston, indicate that in the first 9 months of 1994, 166 women with 279 children were identified by hospital staff as abused and asked for the help of an AWAKE advocate. Only 3 of those 166 women reported that they had ever been a resident of a shelter and only 6 reported that they had ever obtained a restraining order (J. Robertson, personal communication, December 1994). AWAKE advocates were often the first people within any formal institutional setting who had inquired about the domestic violence and offered the women help. Many of these women were young mothers with young children.

The data suggest that health care settings provide services to many women and children affected by domestic violence. Unfortunately, many of these settings are unaware of the incidence and prevalence data that make them ideal sites to develop a response. Hospitals and clinics, for example, treat hundreds of thousands of battered women annually. In several studies of emergency room visits in the United States, 22% to 35% of women presenting with any complaint were there because of symptoms related to domestic violence (Council on Scientific Affairs, 1992). Stark, Flitcraft, and Frazier (1979) found that almost one battered women in five in their study presented to emergency rooms at least 11 times with trauma. Several studies report as many as 37% of obstetrics patients are physically abused during pregnancy (Council on Scientific Affairs, 1992). Many battered women also seek medical care for problems like depression, anxiety, suicide attempts, and substance abuse although medical providers are often unaware of the connection of the presenting problem to recurrent domestic abuse.

Many battered women are also using services (or are forced to use services) in child welfare settings, especially child protection agencies. In a review of 200 substantiated child abuse and neglect reports, the Massachusetts Department of Social Services (the state agency mandated to investigate child abuse and neglect) found that more than 30% of its case records mentioned adult domestic violence (Herskowitz & Seck, 1990). A recent replication of the study found domestic violence in 48% of the substantiated cases (J. Whitney, personal communication, 1994). A Massachusetts Department of Social Services study also found that 29 of its 67 child fatalities (43%) were in families where the mother identified herself as abused. Interestingly, in 20 of the fatality case records, domestic violence was noted by the worker although there was no indication that any interventions to respond to the mother's abuse were offered (Massachusetts Department of Social Services, 1994). The Oregon Department of Human Resources also reported a link between severe and fatal child abuse and domestic violence. In a 1993 study, 41% of the families with a critical injury or death of a child also experienced domestic violence (Oregon Department of Human Resources, 1993).

National survey data seem to corroborate the finding that there is a link between domestic violence and child abuse. In their national survey of more than 6,000 American families, Straus and Gelles (1990) reported that 50% of the men who frequently assaulted their wives also frequently abused a child, a substantiation of what the state child protection agencies are finding.

Other parts of the child welfare system also intervene in domestic violence without adequately or meaningfully responding to it. Families First, Michigan's statewide family preservation program, reports domestic violence in 30% of its families (S. Kelly, interview with author, October 1993). Healthy Start, Hawaii's model child abuse and neglect prevention program, estimates that 35% of the women screened immediately after delivery of a baby or in the course of receiving in-home services report domestic violence (B. Pratt, interview with author, March 1994).

Because child welfare and domestic violence agencies serve a huge overlapping population of clients, it simply makes good sense that child welfare become a significant part of the coordinated community response to domestic violence. But there are other reasons to push for reform in this direction. It is my estimate that child welfare agencies in the United States (including Child Protection Services [CPS], family preservation and support initiatives, Healthy Start Programs, Head Start, school-based health and mental health clinics) annually respond to hundreds of thousands of battered women although the agencies are unaware of this fact. This is far more women than domestic violence services will ever reach.

Domestic violence and child welfare agencies could build significant alliances to improve public policies for women and children in the United States. Right now, unfortunately, the fields often stand at odds with each other, especially over the supportive stance that feminists take toward the women who they help. Often in the child welfare community, women's needs and children's needs fail to be seen as complementary and are pitted against each other. However, from the work recently developed at several model program sites, we are seeing the possibility of a new synthesis of domestic violence and child welfare issues.

AWAKE: Integrating a Health Care and Child Welfare Response

AWAKE, a project set up at Boston Children's Hospital in 1986, offers an exciting synthesis of a response to domestic violence and child abuse within a health care setting. It opens up the possibility of new intervention sites to help battered women and their children.

In 1985, several disturbing incidents spurred the staff of the Family Development Clinic at Boston Children's Hospital to question its response to family violence. The first occurred during an evaluation ordered by the court to explore allegations of child abuse. During the initial interview with the child's parents, the father started to pace around the room and then unexpectedly lunged for his wife's throat. Pulling him away, the stunned staff had little idea of what to do next. What, they later wondered, should be done to protect the mother?

In several other cases, violent fathers assaulted or threatened their wives on hospital grounds. In still others, hospital staff had to recommend the placement of children in foster care because of domestic violence and in spite of the children's close attachment to their mothers.

These cases led to the development of an innovative project, Advocacy for Women and Kids in Emergencies (AWAKE). Borrowing from the ideas of the battered women's shelter movement, hospital staff created a program that offered advocacy and support to abused mothers at the same time that the hospital provided services for their children.

AWAKE was the first program in the United States located in a pediatric setting that provided dual advocacy for both battered women and their abused children. AWAKE staff believe that by providing help to battered women in conjunction with clinical services to children, both populations are more effectively served. The basic premise of the AWAKE project is to broaden the view of child abuse to include intervention on behalf of battered women and to unite the services that are often offered separately to women and their children. Battered women with abused children are paired with an advocate at AWAKE who has had personal experience with family violence. This advocate collaborates with hospital staff and outside agencies to devise a safety plan and to offer help to keep mothers and children free from violence and, whenever possible, together. This help includes ongoing counseling support, housing help, court advocacy, referrals for legal and medical care, and support groups for women and children (Schechter with Gary, 1992).

Currently, AWAKE employs three advocates and a project director. In the years 1986 to 1991, AWAKE staff provided advocacy and consultation to more than 600 women and their children. In 1993 alone, 346 women and 179 children received advocacy or consultation services from AWAKE staff (J. Robertson, personal communication, December 1994).

In a small evaluation study of 46 adult women followed by the AWAKE project on average for 16 months, approximately 80% of the mothers reported that they and their children were no longer living with their assailants and were no longer being abused. Of significance is the low rate of foster care placement for children of AWAKE women. Only two children were in foster care at the time of the study (Schechter with Gary, 1992).

The intervention model developed at AWAKE—linking advocates for battered women to a system of children's services—has also been adopted by the Massachusetts Department of Social Services, the state agency mandated to investigate child abuse reports. Massachusetts is the first—and, to date, only—state child protection agency in the United States to try to integrate domestic violence services into its response to child abuse. The department has established an internal Domestic Violence Unit with its own director and 11 domestic violence advocates who work with regional child protection offices, offering help to CPS workers and their battered women clients around the state.

The department has also established external and internal advisory boards to review policies and procedures for their impact on mothers and children who are experiencing domestic violence. It has also set up pilot projects in two area CPS offices that allow workers to specialize in domestic violence/child abuse cases and offer advocacy and support for battered women in their caseloads. In each of these two pilot projects, multidisciplinary working groups have been formed, and service planning for cases includes trying to find ways to protect the woman and children and hold the abusers accountable. Through its Domestic Violence Unit, the department has also funded two visitation centers where children who have witnessed domestic violence can be safely exchanged between parents (Schechter, 1994).

Strengths of System Responses

Each of these innovative interventions, AWAKE at Children's Hospital and the Domestic Violence Unit of the Massachusetts Department of Social Services, offers promising directions for the future of domestic violence interventions. Staff from each agency report that many women reveal abuse for the first time in interviews with hospital workers or CPS staff. Although some women are clearly, and wisely, reluctant to tell a CPS worker about the domestic violence, others are using the CPS system to find safety for themselves and their children.

Both of these interventions suggest the possibility that many abused women can be reached at sites that are traditionally concerned with children. At AWAKE, staff find that many abusers permit their female partners to seek health care for the children while denying the women any access to help for themselves. Once the staff at Children's Hospital understood this dynamic, they were willing to set up extra appointments for children in order to provide their mothers with help.

Because AWAKE and the Domestic Violence Unit await careful program evaluations, caution must be exercised in describing their results. Reports from the two sites indicate that young mothers with young children are asking to work with an advocate. Staff from both programs also report that because they provide extensive training to hospital and child welfare personnel and concrete help for victims, many professionals within both settings have significantly changed attitudes toward battered women, dropping their more hostile and judgmental attitudes toward mothers and abandoning the accusations against the women of failing to protect their children. This lessening of victim blaming could lead to a significant improvement in institutional response to battered women and their children. The two projects also report that in some cases health care providers and CPS workers have shifted their paradigm: They understand the feminist argument that one of the most effective ways to protect children is to protect mothers, and they want to incorporate this philosophical change into their daily practice and agency policies.

Finally, the significance of these two interventions seems to lie in their creation of more community-based safe sites for battered women and their children. Traditionally, the domestic violence movement has waited for abused women to come to its programs; the women must call a shelter or support group and request help. If, however, a nurse or social worker in a hospital or a CPS worker routinely inquires about threats, harm, and safety, the possibility of help is made immediately apparent to the abused woman. Given the isolation and terrorizing tactics that many battered women experience, it seems that the more possibilities for help and information that are available, the more likely it is that one of them will work for her.

The Future of Collaboration: Dangers and Promises

Many health care organizations in the United States have called for a new response to domestic violence. The American Medical Association has held several national meetings about the problem and has issued Diagnostic and Treatment Guidelines for Physicians. The Nursing Network Against Violence Against Women has also coordinated several national conferences and training seminars about domestic violence, and many of its most active members are now publishing research and practice articles in nursing and medical professional journal. Two former Surgeons General of the United States have called domestic violence an epidemic. Many medical specialty groups, like the American College of Obstetrics and Gynecology, have issued guidelines for victim care to their members or have increased training efforts.

In spite of these initiatives, it is very difficult to determine if health care *interventions* are changing. Are physicians, nurses, social workers, and chaplains in hospitals and clinics actually inquiring more frequently about domestic violence and doing anything to help its victims? Only a handful of sites around the country have initiated advocacy efforts like those at AWAKE in Boston.

The United States has been through a difficult debate about health care reform, and the failure to pass federal legislation now means that health care reform may be fought over in each state. In this climate of managed care, caution, and cost cutting, it has been difficult to see how to interject domestic violence into the debate, although lack of concern for women's health has drawn increasingly sharp criticism from many quarters. It is also difficult to envision a pared-down medical system that will be able to respond to battered women in humane ways.

Many advocates have argued that primary care physicians should screen all female patients for domestic violence. But because physicians in the United States are only reimbursed by insurance companies for their services if a diagnosis is attached to the patient, the domestic violence community has proceeded cautiously. The battered women's movement has been reluctant to advocate for an intervention that forces a potentially stigmatizing diagnosis on battered women. These dilemmas are still unresolved.

Similar concerns hamper reform efforts within the child welfare system. The United States Advisory Board on Child Abuse and Neglect has declared the child protection system in a national emergency. The system is overwhelmed by increasing numbers of reports—close to 2 million in 1994—and is reluctant to take on a "new" issue like domestic violence.

Additionally, a history of mistrust and suspicion categorizes the relationship between domestic violence advocates and child protection workers. Many domestic violence programs define child protection as the enemy of battered women, removing their children precipitously and blaming mothers for the violence that their male partners perpetrate. For their part, CPS workers often see domestic violence advocates as blindly loyal to women and as willing to ignore female-perpetrated child abuse and neglect.

The same criticisms leveled between CPS and domestic violence are also made between domestic violence and the recently emerging field of family preservation. These new services, designed to prevent the unnecessary placement of children in foster care, have sprung up throughout the United States. Battered women's advocates have been frightened that these interventions will push women to stay with abusive partners as a way of preserving the family. Although progressive family preservation programs deny this intention and, in fact, define the protection of mothers as part of their mission, the fear remains.

Several positive initiatives between child welfare and domestic violence have recently occurred in the United States. A June 1994 national meeting between leaders in the two fields was extremely productive, and, as a result, many national child welfare organizations have published articles about domestic violence and are including workshops about it at their annual conferences. Over the past 18 months, the Family Violence Prevention Fund's collaboration with two key family preservation programs, HOMEBUILDERS and Families First, has produced the first national domestic violence curriculum for the family preservation field. In the next year, at least five states will write domestic violence curriculum modules for their child protection workers. In January 1995, the U.S. Department of Health and Human Services held a 1-day workshop for its senior staff to explore the connections between domestic violence and child welfare. And the newly created Resource Center on Domestic Violence: Child Protection and Custody has convened a public policy working group from both fields to develop a research, service, and policy agenda.

The argument that health care and child welfare systems must respond to domestic violence causes many victim advocates to worry that their vision of women's safety and empowerment will disappear. Advocates also fear others will not adopt the analysis that has guided their social change efforts for the past 20 years. Domestic violence organizations have clearly articulated that violence against women is a social problem, embedded in the larger problems of gender inequality. This framework has led to demands for institutional reform in criminal justice practice and housing policies and for new resource allocations at local, state, and federal levels. As more mainstream organizations start to respond to battered women, advocacy organizations fear that the demand for institutional reform and resources for grassroots organizing will disappear, along with the analysis that names gender domination as the core of the problem to be solved. If this analysis disappears, the social change strategy of empowering women, holding perpetrators responsible for their behavior, and insisting that institutions stop condoning violence against women is also likely to mostly disappear.

These concerns need to be balanced against the fact that many battered women turn to agencies in their communities for help and receive little of what they need. To maintain the vision that has historically guided domestic violence interventions and, at the same time, improve the community response system, the guidelines below are proposed. Although these guidelines do not begin to resolve the many contradictions and complexities of practice with battered women and their families, they set parameters for conversations between domestic violence, child welfare, and health care practitioners and offer possibilities for working together.

Assumptions for Guiding Future Interventions and Policy

What assumptions should guide future interventions in domestic violence within these systems? Within the child welfare system, they should include the following:

1. Women have the right to be safe from harm. Children have the same right. Most battered women want to protect their children. The goal of interventions is to foster simultaneously the safety of the adult and child victims. Safety planning for battered women and their children should be an essential part of child welfare interventions.
2. In many cases, the best way to protect the child is to protect the mother from an assaultive partner.
3. Traditionally, society has unfairly placed sole responsibility on mothers to make the family a safe place. Communities need to revise their frameworks for intervention and hold assailants—not their victims—accountable for abuse.
4. Battered women with abused children constitute a significant subset of child abuse cases, numbering in the hundreds of thousands, that require different interventions from those traditionally used. For example, although respite care, day care, or parent education may be useful to some battered women, these interventions fail to respond to the core of the mother's major problem: the assaults, threats, rapes, terrorizing tactics, isolation, and harassment directed at her by her partner. In this subset of child abuse cases, effective intervention must include advocacy for the woman and upholding her right to be safe and independent. No battered woman should ever be encouraged to stay in a situation that is abusive or dangerous.
5. When domestic violence occurs, the family unit to be preserved should be the children and the nonabusing parent.
6. In these cases, the goal of keeping the family together—if defined as mother, father, and children—is a dangerous one. Couple and family treatment are contraindicated for cases in which terror and coercion form the core of the abuser's behavior (Schechter with Gary, 1992).

The Family Violence Prevention Fund (Warshaw, 1995) recently published the manual, *Improving the Health Care System's Response to Domestic Violence.* In it, a set of guiding principles for health care clinical intervention is described that parallels those proposed for the child welfare system:

1. Respecting safety of victims and their children as a priority.
2. Respecting the integrity and authority of each battered woman over her own life choices.
3. Holding perpetrators responsible for the abuse and for stopping it.
4. Advocating on behalf of victims of domestic violence and their children.
5. Acknowledging the need to make changes in the health care system to improve the health care response to domestic violence (Warshaw, 1995).

Conclusion

To date, there are no national, state, or local plans that lay out a broad agenda for reforming the health care and child welfare systems. Although there are pockets of progressive work within each system, there is no broader vision and plan for reform. As a next step, the domestic violence movement needs to use its many new allies within child welfare and health care to help answer the difficult public policy, political, and resource questions raised by entering these arenas. With allies, the domestic violence movement needs to create public policy working groups, model program sites, and a new research agenda. It is unclear where the resources will emerge to tackle the problems that health care and child welfare systems create for battered women. That these systems need to change is obvious: They offer the possibility of help for hundreds of thousands of battered women who are untouched by the current networks of services in their communities.

References

Council on Scientific Affairs, American Medical Association. (1992, June 17). Violence against women: Relevance for medical practitioners. *Journal of the American Medical Association,* 267(23).

Herskowitz, J., & Seck, M. (1990, January). *Substance abuse and family violence: Part 2. Identification of drug and alcohol usage in child abuse cases in Massachusetts.* Boston: Massachusetts Department of Social Services.

Massachusetts Department of Social Services. (1994). *An analysis of child fatalities, 1992.* Boston: Author.

Oregon Department of Human Resources. (1993, June). *Task force report on child fatalities and critical injuries due to abuse and neglect.* Salem: Oregon Department of Human Resources, Children's Services Division.

Schechter, S. (1994, June 8-10). *Model initiatives linking domestic violence and child welfare.* Paper prepared for the conference, Domestic Violence and Child Welfare: Integrating Policy and Practice for Families, Wingspread, Racine, WI.

Schechter, S., with Gary, L. T. (1992). *Healthcare services for battered women and their abused children: A manual about AWAKE.* Boston: Children's Hospital.

Schechter, S., with Mihaly, L. K. (1992). *Ending violence against women and children in Massachusetts families: Critical steps for the next five years.* Boston: Massachusetts Coalition of Battered Women Service Groups.

Stark, E., Flitcraft, A., & Frazier, W. (1979). Medicine and patriarchal violence: The social construction of a "private" event. *International Journal of Health Services, 9,* 461-493.

Straus, M. A., & Gelles, R. J. (Eds.). (1990). *Physical violence in American families.* New Brunswick, NJ: Transaction.

Warshaw, C. (1995). Identification, assessment and intervention with victims of domestic violence. In C. Warshaw, A. L. Ganley, et al. *Improving the health care system's response to domestic violence: A resource manual for health care providers.* San Francisco: Family Violence Prevention Fund.

5

Tensions and Possibilities

Enhancing Informal Responses to Domestic Violence

Liz Kelly

> Community attitudes towards rape, rapists and rape victims are measured not by the sympathetic and outraged pronouncements of public officials but by the services that are and are not available. . . . The quality, speed and sensitivity of services provided by law enforcement, medical, mental health and social services agencies measures the true regard, dignity and safety that a community extends as a matter of course to members who become victims.
>
> Koss & Harvey, 1991, p. 104

Although this quotation refers to rape, it can be applied to any form of victimization of women and children. Nor is it solely the responses of agencies within communities that express regard and affect women's dignity and safety but also those of individuals—within women's kinship and friendship networks, their neighborhoods and workplaces. This aspect of community is seldom addressed in domestic violence initiatives, yet in the long run it may prove to be a key resource not only in establishing safety for women and children, but also in beginning to decrease the prevalence of domestic violence.

In this chapter, the term *domestic violence* is used in reference to the violence men direct at current and former female partners. Violence within lesbian and gay relationships is not included in this discussion. This decision was made out of an unhappiness with approaches that "add in" lesbian and gay relationships to models and approaches developed in relation to heterosexuality (see Kelly, 1996).

My interest in exploring community responses emerges out of these simple facts: (a) domestic violence occurs within communities where members of neighborhoods, kinship networks, and friendship networks know about domestic violence long before any outside agency is approached—they see and hear it happening, they see the physical consequences on women's bodies or they are the ones women speak to about it; (b) women and children who are escaping violence either relocate to new neighborhoods or are attempting to secure safety in their current ones; and (c) the prevalence of domestic violence means we will never create enough specialist services to cope with the actual, let alone potential demand. Developing these ideas has involved remembering where our work began in community organizing and thinking beyond where many individuals and organizations in Britain, and other Western countries, are now, more than 20 years later.

Each community of which women and men are members can condone or challenge domestic violence, can recognize it as an issue or ignore it, can support women who are abused or exclude them. Judy Carne, a British actress who starred in Rowan and Martin's *Laugh-In* in the 1960s, has spoken movingly of how the Hollywood community shunned her when she named Burt Reynolds as a wife batterer (Carne, 1982). The responses women encounter will generally be a contradictory and confusing mixture of solace, support, and advocacy alongside skepticism, indifference, and exclusion. The balance contributes to or subtracts from her sense of personal and social power to resist and refuse abuse. Abusive men may encounter anger, sanction, and exclusion or forms of explicit or implicit support for their actions—the balance contributes to or subtracts from his sense of personal and social power over his partner.

In most Western industrialized countries, the focus for change in relation to all forms of sexualized violence has been institutions and agencies, particularly those that belong to the national or local state: the law, justice system, welfare, health, and social services. The implication of these bodies in the toleration of violence against women has been well documented, and attempts to change them have met with more or less success in various jurisdictions. This concentration has unintentionally reinforced divisions between the public and private; an ironic consequence, given the original intentions and thinking within "the battered women's movement." One result has been a neglect of other important locations of toleration and potentials for change. Attempts to create meaningful change for individuals and broader social change efforts need to embrace all the locations in which toleration persists and the potential for resistance exists.

Most women and girls who have experienced sexual violence first tell someone they trust in their social network, and most who have been victimized marshal as much, possibly more, support over the long term from informal networks than from formal services. It is these two realities that form the rationale for this chapter. They are, in turn, connected to recent perspectives on prevention, developed in both Canada and Scotland, which attempt to create zero tolerance of men's violence within community settings.

Although some models for developing informal community responses exist within Western countries (Kelly, 1993), they are localized and small scale. More extensive examples exist in developing countries, where the significance of community in the absence of developed national and local state formations makes informal sources of support essential elements in assistance. Some of the work undertaken in India, the Philippines, Thailand, and Latin America also illustrates the ways in which community or political education can combine individual support with collective action. The perspective outlined in this chapter, however, draws primarily on Western societies, and particularly that of Britain. This context makes clear that any attempt to enhance the role of informal networks must distinguish itself from right-wing governments and administrations placing responsibility for social care on individuals and families; itself a euphemism for the traditional role of women. What is proposed is not an individualized or familial model of responsibility but a collective potential for change within which the family itself is the subject of critical analysis.

Rethinking Community

Although the word *community* is frequently used, its meanings are multiple and range from a deeply conservative traditionalism to a radical vision of the future. One of the most frequent contexts in which the concept of community is evoked involves a nostalgic recalling of the past, a reference to idealized forms of social connection and interaction. During the past two decades, the use of the concept within social theory has declined, but its invocation within social policy has increased. Two of the reasons accounting for the decline in academic usage are the lack of consensus about what *community* denotes and the emergence of new social movements that questioned presumptions of unified neighborhoods and social groups. Rather than abandon it to either the conceptual scrap heap or conservative social policy, a rethinking of the concept is needed (Kelly & Thorpe, 1994). It is only possible here to sketch out some of the conceptual work this involves.

Implicit in many discussions of community is a division between public and private life. The *loss of community* refers to an increase in impersonal forms of human connection, which is contrasted to face-to-face personalized interactions. Moreover, personal and enduring connections are presumed to be positive and enhancing and are often exemplified in references to the family and village or rural life. Research on the family, especially that done by feminists, questions this simplistic interpretation of the past and present.

The formation of families, historically and cross-culturally, has often been linked to contractual (or exchange) relationships, with women being the property that is exchanged (Rubin, 1974). It is relatively recently, and in urban Western contexts, that a familial/heterosexual ideology emerges that stresses intimacy and personal connection as the basis of familial relationships (Davidoff & Hull, 1987; 1976 Gittins, 1993). Anthropological work has documented the multiple and ongoing tensions between kin and within small social groups, tensions that can be intense and have many consequences, including violent conflict (Dobash & Dobash, 1992; Kelly, 1988; Saraga & MacLeod, 1988).

Most definitions of community contain implicit and explicit exclusions and confusions, for example, that communities exist within a bounded geographical area, which is frequently presumed to coincide with social space; divisions and conflicts within social groups are thus ignored or minimized, permitting definitions of community to use concepts such as homogeneity, shared history, connection to place/others, and the presence of similar interests. Common identity and history are frequently presumed to be coterminous with geographical areas in which planning, service delivery, and decision making occur. In the process, administrative and bureaucratic needs construct a definition of community that has little, if any, reference to actual social relations between people.

The stress on similarity in definitions of community means that variable experiences of social life that accrue by virtue of gender, class, race, age, and sexuality cannot be acknowledged, let alone studied. The common life that communities are presumed to share disguises the fact that every community, from the family outward, contains within it a variety of unequal relationships that inform, if not always determine, individual and social experience.

In a previous paper (Kelly & Thorpe, 1994), the potential diversity of communities was explored by suggesting a number of forms of community and possible variations within and between them. The forms explored were *place* (localities, neighborhoods, history, diaspora); *interest* (churches, leisure, professions, political parties, organizations); *identity and experience* (race, gender, sexuality, disability, class, age); and *circumstance* (workplaces, residential institutions, schools, colleges). Across and within communities, variations were also possible.

How issues are raised in each of these forms may be similar or different, and many forms overlay each other in both individual and collective experience. Community was conceptualized as a possibility, something that is struggled for and created, rather than a pregiven state. The tradition that draws most on this model is the theory and practice of radical community development, which has origins in the work of Alinsky (1971) and Freire (1976). Both saw education as the key to the creation of communities that were directed toward social change. In its application, it has been limited to localities and has inheritors in action research, participatory research, and education. All communities, however, have to be created and sustained, even ones that are directed toward maintaining the status quo.

Rather than the late 20th century representing a loss of connection and values, it is equally possible to argue that we have witnessed the emergence of new forms of social identity and connection. These changes, adaptations, and possibilities in forms of social life have been the subject of much interest in sociological theory, but few have explored the implications for how community is understood, experienced, and constructed. Little attention has been given to those social relations that are not locality based but nonetheless are powerfully linked to social identities or histories, mutual support, and ongoing social networks—for example, diasporic communities, friendship networks, and kin relations that may span considerable distances.

The emergence of a range of identity-based social movements in the mid- to late 20th century presents a fundamental challenge to traditional conceptions of communities. Part of the intent of such movements has been to foster a strong sense of belonging between members, and for those who form around shared oppression to create a different and positive sense of self. The goal of most social movements is social change, through developing a sense of and possibilities for collective resistance.

In attempting to recognize and make sense of the complexity of oppression and disadvantage, the possibility that identities can be multiple and fragmented and communities divided and fractured has emerged. Fundamental to this framework are power relations and the fact that they structure social relationships and social groups. Any new conceptualization of community necessitates a framework that begins from an analysis of power relations, rather than an ideal type that stresses consensus, shared history and values, attention shifts to tensions, contradictions, conflicts, and alliances. Relationships of dominance and subordination are present in families and kinship networks, in localities and institutions, making the achievement of community much more complex than previously envisaged.

Communities are complex amalgams of both potential and actual alliances and divisions. One can become more important than others in particular circumstances. For some oppressed groups, one aspect of identity may be most salient in the public sphere and another in private; unsurprisingly, it is often gender that is privatized. This creates contradictions for many women in accessing support, because to do so involves prioritizing gender in the public sphere.

Part of what needs to be explored here is how far the tension between subjective identities is internal to women themselves, and how far it is constructed, recreated, or reinforced by others. For example, it has become something of a truism in discussions of violence against women to say that black women are less likely to report to the police. But both research data and official records show that black women do report, and sometimes in proportionately higher numbers than white women. Here, commentators have both prioritized race and presumed a unitary influence of racism on black women's decision making. In the process, what black women *actually* do is not noticed.

To put this another way, do institutions respond first to identities other than gender? Are women able to hold, and public agencies able recognize, more than one identity at the same time? One response to these tensions has been the establishment of specialized services where it is possible to hold multiple identities simultaneously, for example, a black woman, a disabled woman. Although important elements in developing appropriate responses, these services form a fraction of those available, and the overall aim must continue to be making all forms of support as accessible and relevant as possible to all women who might need them.

Recognizing the complexity of power relations has implications for social policy. This ranges from how need and service provision is addressed to who is seen and asked to speak for and represent communities. Those who suggest that there are only unitary interests and needs within particular communities—be they neighborhoods or social groups within neighborhoods—are either unaware of or concealing the differences and tensions within. The possibility that individuals are, and feel themselves part of, multiple communities complicates simplistic notions of consultation, choice, and need that now underpin the majority of social policy planning and resource allocation in Britain. One example of this in action is the way male religious leaders are frequently invited to speak "for" ethnic minority communities, thus excluding secular women's organizations who have a critical perspective on aspects of religion and tradition that oppress women. Simplistic multiculturalism silences these radical voices (Southall Black Sisters, 1990, 1994).

Exploring Community and Crime

Domestic violence is a crime that occurs in localities but seldom in the street. Public sphere community policing or "visible policing" has limited relevance to this form of crime. Its location in the home and its context within families have provided a historic justification for nonintervention. Policing of the private has had minimal support from political traditions of either Left or Right. It has been women's organizations, during the past century and this one, who have pointed to the ideological function of privacy. "Respecting privacy" results in women and children being left at the mercy of men in their households. Moreover, in this context, the fact that there is no singular unified community interest is starkly obvious in both the household and the locality. Rather, there are conflicting interests of the victimized (predominantly women), the victimizers (predominantly men), and the witnesses (usually children and neighbors). Placing domestic violence within a discussion of community policing forces the difficult question of which community is being served and whose interests are to be prioritized. Domestic violence also illustrates the fact that the issue is not simply what form of law enforcement is acceptable, but that some crimes are deemed less criminal, less deserving of law enforcement, than others.

Part of the explanation for this is the construction of the criminal as Other, an outsider who threatens and harms "us," the insiders. Young people—black youths in particular—drug users, prostitutes, the poor have all been defined in this way. One outcome has been the locks-and-bolts approach to crime prevention, whereby forms of protection involve surveillance and protection from and detection of outside intrusion. Domestic violence challenges this version of crime prevention because it requires recognition that crime is committed by us—the insiders.

Changes, albeit limited and variable, over the past decade in police policy and practice have produced some recognition that interpersonal violence experienced by women and children is a matter of concern. It is within this changed context that some of the most innovative and substantive connections between police officers and other agencies or organizations are occurring. Sampson, Stubbs, and Smith (1988) remark on this in their study of interagency work. They note that what distinguishes these areas from others, where the cooperation seldom extends beyond a "talking shop" format in which police maintain control of the agenda, is that the connections turn on gender; women inside and outside the police are able to form alliances that have content as well as form. Thus, the recognition of women and children as communities or constituencies with particular interests, and the building of women's networks across professional boundaries, have been critical factors in creating change. These changes, however, will be of limited impact where overall police priorities continue to focus on the public sphere and fail to address the divisions within communities.

This issue is explored from a different starting point by Campbell (1993), in her analysis of the 1991 riots in Britain. These were outbreaks of conflict between the police and groups of young people in various locations in Britain. Unlike previous riots, the participants were predominantly white. Campbell argues that these were confrontations between young men in the community and young men in uniform, and that communities were basically abandoned by the police except for occasional crackdowns.

Campbell makes an interesting comparison: The riots were located "in communities that were like battered women left alone to manage their marauding men" (Campbell, 1993, p. 93). The few examples of successful intervention involved proactive police action, where they "became part of a larger coalition wrapped around endangered people and places" (p. 87). In these contexts, insightful senior officers were aware of the need to support women's challenge to men's dangerousness.

A recent small-scale study on the possibilities of enhancing community responses to domestic violence (Bindel, Kelly, Regan, & Burton, 1994) examined the consequences of simplistic constructions of communities and crime. An attempt was made, in the inner-city area studied, to recreate localized community. It involved prime movers—many of whom did not live in the area—constructing a consensus about what the area's problems are. The problem identified was crime, defined narrowly in terms of prostitution and drugs, with those responsible for crime defined as outsiders. Defining drug users and women who work in the sex industry as the problem meant that links between these activities and domestic violence were unlikely to be made. This in fact proved to be the case. None of the local agencies addressing drugs or prostitution had considered that domestic violence might be a potential issue for their clients, let alone that it may have been directly connected to their illegal activity. Localized crime prevention and urban regeneration activities were not simply reflecting the crime problem in the area, they were constructing it. Both domestic violence and possibilities for women to develop community support networks were casualties of the exclusions.

A contrasting example is Southall Black Sisters (SBS). It is one of the oldest black women's groups in Britain and has an impressive record of combining services for local women with local and national campaigning (see Farnham, 1992; Southall Black Sisters, 1990). One of the key components of SBS's philosophy is that although racism is a primary concern for black people, their communities are not unified and women and men's interests are not necessarily the same. SBS has highlighted the silencing of women's voices and experiences in areas where religious leaders are accepted as speaking for the community.

SBS has both been part of local coalitions challenging racist policing and, at the same time, insisted that the police respond to domestic violence as a crime in their community. It has provided a support service for women and girls in Southall, and a high proportion of this work involves domestic violence. SBS has also been at the center of a number of effective campaigns focused on homicides in families. The group's most recent work focuses on how British immigration law traps migrant women in violent relationships.

Both the longevity of SBS and the national respect for its work clearly demonstrate that women can be both members and critics of communities. SBS also exemplifies the possibility and effectiveness of linking support for women with political activism; many of the women who come seeking help become involved in the campaigning side of SBS's work. Their victimization is both the reason and the motivation for wanting to be part of creating change.

Domestic Violence and Informal Networks

Most studies exploring women's help seeking find that relatives and friends, especially female ones, are the most likely sources of immediate and often long-term support. This pattern is also found in relation to rape and sexual abuse in childhood. Female friends and relatives are the most likely to be told initially, and frequently become primary supporters over time.

Cavanagh (1978) has proposed a model of help seeking that begins in informal networks and moves through to formal agencies when the informal sources fail to enable the woman to end or escape violence. We currently know very little about women for whom informal sources are effective, for whom enough resources and protection can be marshaled to end violence without any formal record of it.

Data from several recent local research projects in Britain confirm this pattern. In one study (McGibbon, Cooper, & Kelly, 1989) women who both had and had not experienced domestic violence were asked who they would never approach and who they actually did approach for help. More than one third said they would never approach the police, but 24% had done so. Less than one third said they would not approach family and friends, whereas 38% had and a further 31% contacted their mothers. The combination of informal supporters is almost three times larger than approaches to the police, who were the most likely formal agency to be contacted.

Contrary to popular myth, most relatives and friends were helpful, offering emotional support and sanctuary. Although a temporary respite, this seldom resolved the problems and could compound them if the violent man chose to threaten the woman's supporters. What was less evident in informal responses, though, were either explicit challenges to the violent man by supporters or their acting as informed advocates for women in discovering what her options were through more formal responses.

Alongside this more common pattern were unsupportive responses, which either blamed the woman or suggested that there was nothing that could be done. This traps women even further in the violence. Hanmer's (1995) study of women's coping strategies has revealed the lengths to which some women will go to support each other. One of the subsamples is a group of Asian women, a number of whom told of women relatives enabling their escape, on condition that they never reveal that they had done so. Loyalty to these courageous supporters was such that women would not reveal who they were in research, which guaranteed anonymity.

Mooney's (1994) study confirms that friends and relatives are the most commonly used support. She asked who women had told about violence against them. She found that friends (46%) and relatives (31%) were most frequently told about domestic violence. This was followed by doctors (22%), police (22%), solicitors or lawyers (21%), social services (9%), and women's refuges or shelters (5%).

Enhancing community responses means taking seriously the support that women already access, and attempting to build this into something more effective and enduring. Some of the tensions for women turn on how much and how many times they can ask for support; and some of the dilemmas for supporters turn on how many times they are willing or can afford to provide it. Education and information, which outlines how ending violence is a complex process, beginning with recognizing abuse and its consequences, and shows that women use many strategies to prevent it, might shift some of the unease felt on both sides. A more detailed understanding is also needed of the fact that even when women reach the point of saying "enough is enough," they still face the monumental task of finding the means to leave and ensure both their survival and that of their children. A book aimed at supporters of women—both workers and friends—has recently been published in Britain (Glass, 1995), but such recognition is still the exception rather than the rule.

Women who find a place in refuges (or shelters) are a minority for two reasons. First, in Britain and many other countries, the number of refuge places falls far short of the need. Second, leaving is a response of last resort, and other sources of support will be used until that point is reached. Currently, the costs and losses of leaving for women are huge, and many realistically assess the negative impacts on them and their children and either never leave or leave and return home. We also know that leaving a violent man is no guarantee of safety and in fact can be the most dangerous thing for a woman to do.

Leaving an abusive man in some communities may result in additional losses: of the community that is her only defense against racism; of her "right to stay"; of the home and friends she has had for a generation or more; or of custody of her children. Many women in these situations are so terrorized by both their abuser and the implications of leaving that they never reach out for help; some seek help and encounter hostility and prejudice from those they contact; and some—despite all the odds against them—manage to get free.

If we take seriously the extensiveness of informal support that women seek out and create for themselves, we also need to ask which women may have least access to this. Women who have moved to a new area, a new country, who are isolated geographically (either through separation from their networks or in rural settings), linguistically, or in terms of physical mobility and ill health, are some obvious examples. These women need greater access to formal support, yet they are often the least able to access it.

Developing alternatives to and a variety of routes of access into formal agencies is therefore essential. The following example offered by a crisis intervention support worker in a London project demonstrates this point:

> One woman told me that had it not been for her picking up a leaflet on the "Zero Tolerance" campaign, she would not have been aware of the various nonstatutory services and resources available to her. She explained that after discussing the issue with the worker at her mother-and-toddler group, she then found the courage to contact us. It was obvious to me that until she had this kind of support, she had always been anxious and indeed afraid to approach the police. (Research interview by author for evaluation of domestic violence matters, April 1994)

This woman did subsequently approach police during a violent assault by her partner, and he was arrested and charged. Thus, a combination of public education, informal networks, and a voluntary organization created a context that enabled this woman to seek support from agencies she would not otherwise have approached. She was supported and the man's behavior was sanctioned.

Importance of Community Support for Individuals

In this section, I draw heavily on Judith Lewis Herman's (1994) book, in which she provides a framework for understanding the importance of support from community members for women and children who have experienced *chronic abuse*—physical, sexual, and psychological violence over a period of time. The traumatic impacts on them are not comparable to those of single events, because they are both cumulative and also interfere with attempts to cope with and survive abuse. She regards one of the most important impacts of prolonged abuse to be damage to relational life. Doubts emerge about self and others, self in relation to others. The violation that occurs is both of the self and of human connection. This damage to social relations means that those close to women and children have the power to influence not just their ability to escape but also the long-term effects of abuse: Supportive responses may mitigate impacts; hostile and negative ones compound the damage. A positive sense of self (as opposed to more therapeutic notions of self-esteem) develops in connections with others. One of the major qualities of refuges is that they combine provision, which addresses physical safety and survival, with collective living, which seeks to reestablish positive and affirming social connection.

Herman (1994) notes how, within communities, the perpetrator often enjoys higher status than his victim. This may prompt even greater withdrawal by women, and the potential loss of work, friendships, and neighborhoods. The creation of isolation is a deliberate strategy, intended to separate the woman or child being abused from information, advice, and emotional support. Misinformation is also often given: that they will be blamed; that negative consequences such as deportation or loss of child custody will result. A "jealous surveillance" develops, whereby the destruction of attachments is achieved and women and children come to see the world through the opinions of their abusers. One survival response to this unbearable reality is a fragmentation of life and identity.

Alongside these coping responses are the social expectations of women to care for others, and their anticipation of others' responses. Although some supporters might be sympathetic, they seldom hold accurate information about either domestic violence or its effects on individuals:

> Survivors are thus placed in the situation where they must choose between expressing their own point of view and remaining in connection with others. . . . Restoration of the breach between the traumatized person and the community depends, first, upon some form of community action. Once it is publicly recognized that a person has been harmed, the community must take action to assign responsibility for the harm and to repair the injury. These two responses—recognition and restitution—are necessary to rebuild the survivor's sense of order and justice. (Herman, 1994, pp. 67, 70)

The role of individuals in contributing to justice for women and children who have been victimized by naming and opposing violence has been recognized implicitly in much feminist analysis, but limited attention has been paid to developing it as a political strategy. The loss of community as a consequence of seeking to end violence has been recognized as a significant factor in many women's decision-making processes. In emphasizing the right to professional or specialist support, however, we have at best taken for granted and at worst neglected the importance of support from social networks, and minimal attention has been paid to finding ways to transform losses into gains and possibilities at both an individual and a social level. Herman (1994)—despite being a therapist—argues that one of the most effective ways of creating new connection and meaning for those who have been abused is through social action.

Moving On

There are compelling practical gains and possibilities in exploring how informal networks might be enhanced and developed; not the least being that they can be built and adapted within all societies and sections of societies. They also offer a strategic way to extend and make more effective responses to hard-to-reach groups of women. Even within the most embattled communities, there are women who publicly question male dominance, and many more undoubtedly do so in private. Thinking about community approaches involves imagining and creating ways in which isolated individuals and actions can be linked into a more collective context.

The proposal to make community organizing and political education a key element in coordinated approaches to domestic violence is seen not as an alternative to formal intervention but as a critical element within a coherent approach. The outline presented of ways this might be effected are initial thoughts, sparks to the imaginations and creative talents of those who wish to do more than "first aid" work. They open up the possibility for new alliances between those already working in the field and community workers and activists who have not yet integrated violence against women into their working practices.

The central requirement is a range of forms of public education, encompassing high-profile awareness and prevention campaigns through local women's group meetings, and an additional focus on these activities already occurring in some areas. Alongside the messages that domestic violence is both common and unacceptable, the fact that most people come into contact with it would be stressed, as would our collective responsibility to do something about it. Literature that currently focuses only on what you can do if this is happening in your life would be supplemented with advice on how to support someone and how to challenge both known abusers and attitudes that tolerate abuse. Individuals and local groupings would be encouraged to take the issues into their community networks—be they relatives, friends, churches, or clubs of various kinds.

The basic principles of crisis intervention could be conveyed very simply as the basis for individual support and supplemented with advice about issues involved in supporting someone over the longer term. Localized activity makes possible the development of networks of temporary safe houses and spaces and strategies for challenging and changing men.

The basis for developing community approaches must be coordinated outreach and education. The precise forms these take will vary according the kinds of communities involved. There are, however, several core components, below, that will be common.

Understanding and Belief

Here, basic myths and stereotypes are addressed, in relation to how common domestic violence is, what it is, and who experiences and perpetuates it; the content in much of our basic awareness training for professionals. These myths represent the first-line barriers to being able to support women and challenge men. For example, although there is some acceptance that domestic violence is relatively common, certain groups are often excluded—elderly people, people with disabilities, and professionals being the most common. Holding limited definitions of what counts as violence can also act as a barrier: where the abuse is primarily forms of coercive control; where it can be defined as a "lovers' tiff" between young people; when it is infrequent, or not connected to alcohol abuse, or both. Holding stereotyped images of battered wives (weak, submissive, and traditional) or batterers (domineering, aggressive, drunks) acts as a barrier to both belief and understanding.

Finding ways to question these commonsense ideas through simple, visual means as well in printed word formats will increase the effectiveness of the strategies. The basic aim is to communicate that domestic violence takes a number of forms and occurs in all social groups—that men who use violence and women who suffer it are our relatives, our neighbors, our friends, our colleagues, our customers and service users.

Broaden and Enrich Knowledge

Communicating in accessible ways what we have learned over 20 years of activism and research is the aim in this domain. Some of the most important elements to include are the strength and creativity in women's attempts to manage and survive abuse; the long-term impacts of living with abuse in terms of faith in oneself and others, as well as in physical and mental health; the ways men deny, minimize, and displace responsibility; that leaving can be both dangerous and costly in other ways; the losses to women and children in ending relationships, including the additional issues faced by many groups of women; what living with violence is like for children; the failure of governments and agencies to provide protection and support; and the importance of offering women options rather than telling them what to do. Practical advice on options and strategies is useful only when people have a framework of understanding in which to use and apply it. All such advice should be prefaced, in verbal or written form, by knowledge about the reality and complexity of living with abuse.

Creating New Linkages

Several examples of this have already been offered earlier in this chapter. As an organizing strategy, creating new linkages means building awareness of domestic violence, and what can be done in groups and organizations that are neither focused on domestic violence nor offering generalist services that ought to encompass it (e.g., the police, legal advice centers). In terms of reaching women in ethnic minority communities, women with disabilities, and elderly women, it may be far more effective to build awareness within already existing services and networks than to wait until it is possible to establish specialist services. There are extremely effective and extensive women's organizations in rural areas, and some of these—in Britain, at least—have passed resolutions on the issue of domestic violence.

There are many potentials for building networks of support and resistance. One example involves thinking of institutions as communities in which levels of tolerance can be changed. Achieving this requires more than one-time education and awareness programs. Taking a school as an example, the creation of a whole-school policy that aims to create zero tolerance would integrate domestic violence with other forms of violence and abuse. The kind of prevention programs that have already been developed would be only one element in a coordinated approach, which would address curriculum issues, the ways in which forms of coercive control are used by adults in relation to children and young people, and that gender as a form of power is reproduced daily (for a more detailed discussion of whole-school policies in relation to sexual abuse and sexuality, see Kelly, 1992).

Another example is the difference taking this approach would make to the talks many of us involved in work on domestic violence give to a variety of audiences. These are often done either as an abstract issue or through describing the particular service to which we are connected. In the proposed model, we would begin from explicit recognition that domestic violence is an issue in all communities—from neighborhoods to workplaces—and that most people have experience of it, whether their own or that of friends, neighbors, or colleagues. Our aim would be to provide knowledge and insight that refers directly to the problems and possibilities that coping with domestic violence creates for the woman herself and for those from whom she seeks support. We would offer ideas and strategies that anyone could use to support women and challenge men, alongside the more usual information about specialist services and legal rights. Where there is willingness and interest in taking work further, we would keep in touch, encouraging local activity, networking with similar groups locally (and, where relevant, nationally and internationally), and critically reflecting on attempts to create change.

Anticipating Tensions and Possibilities

Part of the knowledge that can be shared in these endeavors is the complexity of the issue in relation to individuals and communities. Serious reflection on what the unanticipated consequences might be of supporting women and challenging men would provide a less romanticized view of this work and offer the possibility of anticipating common difficulties. Within this process, care must be taken to ensure that issues of difference and diversity are understood and that the principle of zero tolerance is not taken up in ways that either endanger women or merely displace the problem. For example, at the study group meeting in Haifa, examples were offered in which whole families had been hounded out of Canadian neighborhoods, and young people excluded from school. In such situations, intolerance is not focused on the violence but on the individuals who are using it, and on those experiencing it. Integrated community approaches involve planting and tending seeds of resistance, wherever possible, to create ripples of change. This in turn will contribute to local climates in which domestic violence is increasingly unacceptable.

Concluding Thoughts

In outlining this model, I am all too aware of the extent of change it requires and I am not suggesting that this can be achieved quickly or easily. I offer it as an alternative framework for thinking about local strategies, which can be developed in many different ways; these will be discovered and adapted in action. In offering such a limited outline, I am attempting to suggest a necessary core while avoiding a prescriptive model. Developing community responses requires recognizing that moving too fast, or without anticipating the consequences of certain actions, can overwhelm local resources, ride roughshod over local traditions and tensions, and fail to notice and use the potentials that already exist. For example, in many established neighborhoods, strong women act as local "fixers" who are turned to in emergencies. They, and women in all communities who have survived domestic violence, are critical resources in building networks of support and resistance.

What community approaches involve are sensitive, focused, successive, incremental, and linked strategies that are connected to both short- and long-term goals and a knowledge of what exists already at the formal and informal levels. They are *not* substitutes for formal services and indeed, if effective, would both generate more demand for some of those services and be powerful voices in demanding that existing services respond to and meet the needs of women and children.

One of the barriers to the development of this model in Western countries in which strong movements against domestic violence already exist is raised in Heise's earlier chapter in this book: ownership and control of the issue. To encourage local informal networks is to take risks, to dare to share the issue many of us have struggled for years to put on political agendas. It is time to recognize that we have succeeded, for the moment, in doing that. Moving on means finding ways to make it part of everyone's agenda and to support those who have and continue to struggle to find ways to support and challenge, but outside the networks that have sustained many of us over the years.

If we were successful in finding ways to link our hard-won but now fairly extensive knowledge with the willingness of many others to "do something," we might have a realistic chance of creating not only "the true regard, dignity, and safety that a community extends as a matter of course to members who become victims" (Koss & Harvey, 1991, p. 104) but also zero tolerance of victimization itself.

References

Alinsky, S. (1971). *Rules for radicals: A practical primer for realistic radicals.* New York: Random House.

Bindel, J., Kelly, L., Regan, L., & Burton, S. (1994). *Whose agenda, whose community? Exploring community response and resources for women in the King's Cross area.* Final report to Islington Council Women's Committee.

Campbell, B. (1993). *Goliath: Britain's dangerous places.* London: Methuen.

Carne, J. (1982). Keynote address at National Coalition Against Domestic Violence conference, St. Louis, MO.

Cavanagh, C. (1978). *Battered women and social control.* Unpublished master's thesis, University of Stirling, Scotland.

Davidoff, L., & Hull, C. (1987). *Family fortunes: Man and woman of the English middle class, 1780-1850.* London: Hutchinson.

Dobash, R. E., & Dobash, R. P. (1992). *Women, violence and social change.* London: Routledge.

Farnham, M. (1992). Writing our own history: Interview with Southall Black Sisters. *Trouble and Strife, 23,* 41-52.

Freire, P. (1976). *Education—The practice of freedom.* London: Writers and Readers.

Gittins, D. (1993). *The family in question* 2nd ed. London: Macmillan.

Glass, D. (1995). *"All my fault": Why women don't leave abusive men.* London: Virago.

Hanmer, J. (1995, January). *Women's coping strategies.* Keynote address, ROKS conference, Stockholm.

Herman, J. L. (1994). *Trauma and recovery: From domestic abuse to political terror.* London: Pandora.

Kelly, L. (1988). *Surviving sexual violence.* Cambridge, UK: Polity.

Kelly, L. (1992). Not in front of the children: Responding to right wing agendas on sexuality and education. In M. Arnot & L. Barton (Eds.), *Voicing concerns: Sociological perspectives on contemporary education reforms* (pp. 20-40). London: Triangle.

Kelly, L. (1993). Towards an integrated community responsibility to domestic violence. In Child Abuse Studies Unit, *Abuse of women and children: A feminist response* (pp. 14-32). London: Essential Issues: University of North London Press.

Kelly, L. (1996). When does the speaking profit us? Reflections on the difficulties of developing a feminist approaches to abuse and violence by women. In M. Hester, J. Radford, & L. Kelly (Eds.), *Women, violence and male power* (pp. 34-49). Buckingham, UK: Open University Press.

Kelly, L., & Thorpe, M. (1994). *Setting the context: A brief overview of sociological uses of the concept of community.* Unpublished paper for Catchment and Community project, University of North London.

Koss, M., & Harvey, M. (1991). *The rape victim: Clinical and community interventions.* Newbury Park, CA: Sage.

McGibbon, A., Cooper L., & Kelly, L. (1989). *"What support?": An exploratory study of council policy and practice, and local support services in the area of domestic violence within Hammersmith and Fulham.* London: Hammersmith and Fulham Council, Community and Police Committee.

Mooney, J. (1994). *The hidden figure: Domestic violence in North London.* London: Islington Police and Crime Prevention Unit.

Rubin, G. (1974). The traffic in women: Notes on the "political economy of sex." In M. Reiter (Ed.), *Toward an anthropology of women.* New York: Monthly Review Press.

Sampson A., Stubbs, P. & Smith, D. (1988). Crime, localities, and the multi-agency approach. *British Journal of Criminology, 28,* 478-493.

Saraga, E., & MacLeod, M. (1988). Challenging the orthodoxy: Towards a feminist theory and practice. *Feminist Review: Family Secrets: Child Sexual Abuse, 28,* 16-55.

Southall Black Sisters. (1990). *Against the grain: A celebration of survival and struggle—SBS 1979-1989.* Southall, UK: Author.

Southall Black Sisters. (1994). *Asian women and domestic violence.* Southall, UK: Author.

6

Wife Abuse in the Arab Society in Israel

Challenges for Future Change

Muhammad M. Haj-Yahia

> Men are the managers of the affairs of women, for God has preferred in bounty one of them over another. . . . And those you fear may be rebellious admonish; banish them to their couches, and beat them.
>
> *Quran*, Sura 4 (The Women), Verse 38

> A woman is like a snake. If you raise your leg above her head she will bite you; and she is like a rug . . . the more you beat her the cleaner she will be.
>
> Two Arabic proverbs

For the past two decades, the problem of wife abuse and battering has been widely acknowledged, particularly in Western postindustrial societies. This acknowledgment is manifested in several areas, including public awareness, development of empirical knowledge, legal and social policy, development of services, and allocation of resources. Nevertheless, the Arab society in Israel is far from having attained full acknowledgment of this serious problem. Although professional and public interest in wife abuse and battering in the Arab society has increased in recent years, the issue has hardly been given the attention it deserves, particularly in view of its dangerous and destructive implications. The prevailing attitude toward abusive and violent husbands in this society has been lenient, and women—who are the victims of violence—have been blamed and held accountable for their misery (Haj-Yahia, 1991).

The family is considered the most sacred system in Arab society, and wife battering is not considered grounds for breaking up the family. It is not even viewed as grounds for the wife to leave home, nor is it a basis for legally evicting or removing the abusive and violent husband from the home. Moreover, family members are expected to maintain the privacy of the family (Haj-Yahia, 1995). In this connection, wife abuse and battering is not considered a sufficient reason to disclose the private affairs of the family to public authorities.

All of this explains the lack of outside (formal and informal) intervention in cases of wife abuse in the Arab society in Israel, and the paucity of research on the topic. However, there are also structural constraints that preclude more effective intervention in cases of wife abuse and battering.

The most salient structural constraints are the lack of resources for protection and support of battered women in the Arab society (e.g., shelters, protected community housing for women who choose to leave their homes) as well as lack of skilled human resources who are aware of the unique problems faced by battered women in this society. This chapter will address the problem of wife battering and abuse in the Arab society from a combined cultural and structural perspective. An attempt will be made to illuminate the main challenges faced by social service practitioners, policymakers, women's activists, and the general community in two main fields: direct intervention with battered women and the development of appropriate and accessible public programs and services for victims of wife abuse and battering in the Arab society in Israel. Before discussing these challenges, there is a need to provide basic background on the status and roles of women in the Arab society.

On Women in Arab Society

The status of women in the Arab family has always been lower than that of males (particularly older brothers or brothers who are close in age) and lower than that of the husbands and their parents. Notwithstanding the changes taking place in the Arab society in Israel, Arab women are still expected to be dependent on their husbands, to satisfy their husband's needs, and to maintain the household (Avitzur, 1987; Haj-Yahia, 1994, 1995; Ibrahim, 1993; Shokeid, 1993). The husband usually fulfills the dominant instrumental roles as main provider and protector, whereas the wife fulfills the expressive role as housewife (Barakat, 1985).

The changes in the status of women in the Arab family over the past two or three decades can be viewed as quantitative; that is, more women are educated and working outside the home. However, these changes can hardly be considered basic qualitative changes that completely alter the woman's status in the family vis-à-vis her husband. Similarly, these changes have not affected her status in the community and the extent of her social and political influence (Ibrahim, 1993). The woman's role as mother and wife continues to be traditional and nonegalitarian (Al-Haj, 1987, 1989; Shokeid, 1993). She is expected to maintain the household and it is her responsibility to see that the family functions as a cohesive unit. In contrast, the male partner is not expected to do housework or take care of the children. Thus, in many sectors of the Arab society, it is still believed the woman's place is in the kitchen, and the man's place is out of the home, at work (Barakat, 1985; Haj-Yahia, 1994, 1995). No doubt this distribution of roles enhances the power of women behind the scenes, notwithstanding apparent support for the authority of the husband.

The Arab woman often considers her role as a mother more important than her role as a marital partner. Moreover, assuming that children establish the marriage and cement the marital relationship, motherly love is considered more powerful than a wife's love for her husband (Barakat, 1985).

On the whole, equality between marital partners (even among young couples) is not a priority in the Arab society or in the Arab family. In this context, social, economic, and political institutions relegate marginal status to women. Similarly, personal status codes discriminate against women, particularly in areas such as marriage, divorce, and inheritance. The prevailing religious ideology perceives wives as the source of evil, anarchy (*fitna*), and deception or trickery (*kaid*) (Barakat, 1985; Moghadam, 1992). Among certain groups, particularly Bedouins and inhabitants of small villages, women are still victims of forced marriage, murder for the sake of "restoring and retaining" family honor, and confinement to the home after marriage.

Control over women is encouraged, because they are considered a potential source of social *fitna*; that is, they cause disorder and anarchy. In this connection, Al-Rifaee (1994) argues that in the marital relationship the husband has certain basic rights and the wife is obligated to fulfill certain basic demands, which include the following: to acknowledge her husband's superiority and obey him; to serve him and take care of the children; to thank him for supporting her; to refrain from burdening him with excessive expenses. Based on these traditional norms and the above definition of the woman's status, any wife who questions the authority and power of her husband is making a serious error.

In sum, the fact that some Arab women in Israel have begun to receive a university education and work outside the home has led to relative democratization in their relationship with their husbands. Nevertheless, this process has not brought about a significant change in the hierarchical structure of the Arab family or in basic attitudes toward women. Consequently, the woman continues to be dependent on the male family members (e.g., their father, husband, or brother). Moreover, although wives are expected to be faithful to their partners, husbands are only obligated to provide material support and have no moral obligation toward their wives (Barakat, 1985). Any attempt to deal with wife abuse and battering in the Arab society in Israel should take these aspects of the role and status of Arab women into account.

Some Challenges for Future Direct Intervention With Battered Women in Arab Society

Family members usually solve their problems among themselves, and even issues such as violence are not considered sufficient reason to enlist outside intervention. Consequently, in most cases, battered women in the Arab society do not cope with their victimization by seeking help outside the home. In particular, the battered woman's family and relatives do not expect her to take active measures, such as calling the police or turning to social service agencies. Thus, she often refrains from seeking help even though she desperately needs a protected environment, financial and legal aid, and emotional support.

A battered woman who seeks services often requires them on an emergency basis. Turning to battered women's shelters or to the police is viewed as an attempt to challenge the community's values, and a manifestation of shame. It is also likely to arouse considerable anger and antagonism toward the woman from her family, which may even lead to ostracism. Consequently, the Arab battered woman usually keeps her suffering to herself; and if she decides to leave the "closed castle," she usually asks her parents, siblings, or other relatives to provide her with shelter and support. However, this shelter and support is only provided for a limited period of time and, in most cases, the family will blame the woman for her situation and ask her *where and how she went wrong with her husband.* Moreover, they will make it clear to her that violence is not a sufficient reason to leave home, nor is it a reason for breaking up the family. She will be encouraged to return to her husband as soon as possible, because *he is her man, her husband, and the father of her children.* They may also try to rationalize his behavior while still holding her accountable for the situation.

Relatives from both sides will often mediate between the partners in an attempt to reach a reconciliation. This process is usually humiliating for the wife, who is blamed for the situation and warned *not to repeat her mistake in the future* if her husband batters her again. Without a doubt, this process can even be rewarding for the husband (Gelles, 1983). He is not considered accountable for his violent behavior, nor is he required to participate in therapy. At the same time, he witnesses the accusations directed against his wife. Consequently, she soon learns that she paid a high price for her actions, that is, for daring to challenge family values by actively coping with the violence and leaving the home.

This bleak situation may be alleviated if social service practitioners establish contact with the battered woman and her family as soon as possible after such cases are identified. Even if their physical and social safety are temporarily jeopardized, it is important for the woman and her family to learn that she is not accountable for violence against her and that her husband is solely responsible for his own behavior.

In addition to emotional and physical support, the battered woman may require financial aid, because a considerable percentage of Arab women are unemployed and financially dependent on their husbands (Ibrahim, 1993). Financial support can play a crucial role in helping these women cope effectively with abuse and battering and may also provide them with an important incentive to leave a violent relationship (e.g., Aguirre, 1985; Strube & Barbour, 1983). Moreover, such support can relieve the woman's family of the economic burden, which is often one of their main reasons for rejecting her appeals for help and protection. Existing procedures for receiving financial support can be particularly traumatic for the Arab woman. Oftentimes, for example, the claim for child support is interpreted by the husband, his family, and the wife's family as a bitter complaint against the sacred family system and as a "declaration of war."

Involvement of the police and the justice system is viewed by the wife's family as an opening for outside intervention in the private affairs of the family. Similarly, such intervention is looked upon as a challenge to the husband's authority and to the unity of the family, and as a "declaration of war" against the husband and his family. Clearly, such perceptions and interpretations often provide the basis for the wife's family-of-origin and relatives to reject her, ostracize her, and refuse to support her.

Direct intervention with the battered wife's family-of-origin and her relatives plays a key role in helping her cope. In the process of such intervention, it is important to help the family and relatives realize the need to create a supportive atmosphere for the wife. It should be taken into consideration that Arab society is usually patrilocal (Haj-Yahia, 1995), and that Arab women usually marry men from the city or village where they grew up. Hence it can be assumed that the victim of abuse probably lives near her parents and relatives, and that they are available and accessible when she needs them. However, in view of the limitations of such social networks (Schilling, 1987), women's activists and social service practitioners may help the wife's family and relatives realize the positive and productive role they can play in supporting, protecting and helping the battered woman.

Oftentimes, the abusive husband isolates his wife from her parents, relatives, and friends, because he wants her to remain dependent on him and he seeks to keep the violence within the family. Hence, the battered woman's family can be encouraged to visit her frequently. Such visits may enable the woman's family to witness her suffering and to understand her need for support. This, in turn, would provide an incentive for the wife to break the vicious cycle and release herself from the atmosphere of violence created by her husband.

Finally, the importance of providing counseling and self-help groups for battered women should be emphasized. These groups may be established and initiated by women who have succeeded in coping with violence and also by women's activists and social service practitioners in the Arab society in Israel. Such groups may promote activities aimed toward creating a supportive atmosphere for victims of violence and for women who have left the violent conjugal relationship. In addition, such groups are expected to empower battered women, enhance their sense of self-worth and self-mastery, educate them to be assertive and to defend themselves. At the same time, women in such groups may need to learn how to advocate for and with other battered women. These groups can reinforce the feeling of sisterhood among women who suffer from a common problem.

There is an urgent need to establish nonprofit self-help groups for battered women in the Arab society. Such groups may eventually become bona fide activist organizations. Such organizations can play a major role in initiating and implementing some of the programs proposed below. Moreover, they can be instrumental in preventive programs and community education on violence against women as well as in provision of support services and protection for battered women.

Establishing Public Programs for Improving Interventions With Battered Women

This section discusses several public programs for improved methods of intervention with battered women in the Arab society in Israel. At present, it is assumed that service providers often inadvertently contribute toward the continuation of violence against women and the perpetuation of the atmosphere of terror in which these women live.

Criminal Justice System

Police officers who receive complaints about wife abuse in the Arab society are in most cases Jewish men. These officers are usually not aware of the difficulties faced by the battered Arab woman nor are they aware of and sensitive to her specific needs and problems. Even the Arab officers (who are almost all men) cannot always understand the needs of these battered women and are usually incapable of giving them the support they desperately need.

There is a lack of empirical research examining how Arab and Jewish police officers respond when Arab women request their assistance and intervention against violent husbands and even when complaints are registered about wife abuse and battering in the Arab society. However, the experience of social service practitioners and women's activists working in the Arab society suggests that the police usually prefer not to intervene in cases of domestic violence. Moreover, it has been observed that the police usually contact the family of the battered woman, one of her relatives, or one of the senior members of the community in an attempt to arrange for mediation and reconciliation between the woman and her husband. They rarely take measures to remove or evict the violent husband from the home or arrest him. Clearly, this process can only harm the woman. When she is blamed or held accountable for her husband's violent behavior, an atmosphere of humiliation and intimidation is created (see, e.g., Bograd, 1984). Moreover, this process usually does not provide the battered woman with the security, support, and shelter she requires.

This situation may be alleviated if police officers dealing with battered women in the Arab society receive special training and supervision. Such training and supervision can be provided in conjunction with the existing social service agencies in the Arab society. In this process, efforts should be made to debunk myths about violence in general and wife abuse in particular, with specific emphasis on the problems of battered women in general and Arab battered women in particular. With regard to Arab society, it is important to enhance the awareness of the police officers and help them realize that battered women need protection, shelter, and support, which are not provided by their family and relatives. Without a doubt, it is also important for them to understand the patriarchal structure of the Arab family and how this structure often perpetuates wife abuse and prevents battered women from receiving the shelter and support they need. Similarly, it is important to clarify to the police that the current policy of noninterference can harm the woman who is a victim of terror in the family. In a similar vein, prosecutors and judges can also be encouraged to avoid withholding support and shelter from victims of wife battering and abuse in Arab society on the grounds of traditional values such as *family pride, family privacy,* and *family reputation.*

Religious Courts

The religious judges in Arab society can also become more aware of the needs and problems of battered women. Arab women usually appeal to a religious court for a bill of divorce. The judge—who is usually a clergyman and lacks sufficient legal training—then attempts to achieve a "family peace" arrangement (see, e.g., Layish, 1975). This arrangement usually aims to persuade the partners to keep living together, even if wife abuse and battering is likely to continue. Both the families and relatives of the partners and some senior members of the community are usually involved in the process of negotiating family peace upon the recommendation of the religious judge. Clearly, these individuals do not always realize that battered women need support and protection, nor do they tend to assist her in her attempt to deal with the situation of violence and its implications. Rather, they often advocate traditional solutions along the lines of *family honor, family reputation,* and *family stability and unity.*

Social Services

Social services in the Arab society can cooperate with the judges and help them become aware of the destructive consequences of imposing traditional family peace arrangements on the wife as long as domestic violence persists. Furthermore, it may be helpful if the judges understand the potential risks of involving relatives and community members in the process of family peace. In this connection, the judges might consider the extent to which the family is sensitive to the women's needs and prepared to provide her with support, shelter, and protection. If the woman spontaneously agrees to family peace, implementation of the arrangement may have to be accompanied by professional intervention and advocacy. Social service practitioners and women's activists may have to become involved in the process in order to see that her needs are provided for, and give top priority to her security, welfare, and well-being during this arrangement.

Efforts are also needed to expand existing services and establish new ones in the Arab society. For example, there is a need to establish more hot lines for battered women. At present, there are only a few lines serving Arab communities—and they do not function 24 hours a day. Ideally, there should be at least one line serving every Arab village or town, and volunteers should be recruited and trained to staff the lines around the clock. Although hot lines are not an alternative to direct intervention with battered women, they provide the woman with a supportive and empathetic listener, particularly when she does not want to appeal directly to welfare and health services.

The hot line staff can also provide her with information regarding services she may not have known about and encourage and enable her to seek their assistance (see, e.g., Roberts & Roberts, 1990). Hot lines can also play an important role in identifying battered women and reaching out to those women who do not have access to welfare services. The combination of hot lines and cooperation on the part of the women's families and community welfare services can provide a highly significant network of support, protection, and sustenance for battered women.

The importance of direct intervention with the families and relatives of battered women must also be emphasized. In particular, families may need to be encouraged to provide more support and protection for their daughters rather than pressing them to return to their violent husbands. It is important to clarify to them that such pressure constitutes a net reward for the violent husband that is likely to encourage him to continue abusing his wife.

The battered woman's family often refuses to give her support and shelter. An alternative solution, which may be culturally acceptable, is to enlist *guardian families,* or foster families for battered woman. These families, who may not necessarily be direct relatives of the woman, can be recruited, trained, and supervised by the social service departments and can remain under their supervision as long as the woman is in their custody. The guardian families are expected to provide the necessary support and shelter for the battered woman until she decides what she is going to do, that is, whether she is going to divorce her husband or move back with him. In the latter case, it is important for the social service practitioner or women's activist who referred the battered woman to the guardian family to ascertain that the husband has successfully completed treatment and is likely to refrain from violence against his wife. The guardian family can also serve as a supportive transition (halfway) point before the battered woman goes to a shelter.

Social service practitioners who are involved in this process need to make sure that guardian families meet the necessary criteria for accommodating battered women before they participate in the program. These criteria might at least emphasize the following qualities: willingness to support and protect battered women; awareness of the problems faced by these women and their children, and sensitivity to their needs; basic opposition to violence as a means of solving conflicts; willingness and ability to maintain confidentiality; willingness to accompany the woman in her contacts with different institutions and services; and accessibility to the woman when she needs their help and protection.

Clearly, when a battered wife moves to the home of the guardian family, her family of origin and relatives are likely to express severe opposition. However, it is assumed that these temporary accommodations will be more acceptable to the woman's family than referral to a battered women's shelter, even though the very idea of battered women leaving home is against the values of the Arab society, as mentioned above. On the whole, the strategy of mobilizing and training guardian families can be a first step toward encouraging Arab communities to take responsibility for providing protection and combating violence against wives.

Shelters for Battered Women

It is also important to emphasize the importance of establishing more shelters for battered women in the Arab society in Israel. Clearly, shelters cannot provide a long-term solution to the problem of wife abuse and battering but they can provide immediate support and protection that the woman cannot find in her family of origin or in the community, at least for a certain period of time or until a guardian family becomes available. At present, there is only one shelter for battered Arab women in one of the villages in the northernmost region of Israel. Thus, victims of abuse living in the southern region (the Negev) have to travel for at least 4 hours, and those living in the central region (Triangle) have to travel 2 hours, to get to the shelter. Before the shelter was established, in 1993, battered Arab wives had to go to shelters in Jewish communities. Today, six shelters for battered Jewish and Arab women are located in Jewish neighborhoods. Unfortunately, Arab women usually fail to adjust in these shelters, particularly due to the language barrier and cultural differences.

The Arab shelter in the northern region is run by the Association for the Prevention of Violence Against Women and largely financed by the Israel Ministry of Labor and Social Welfare. The ministry is currently attempting to approve funds for the establishment of another shelter in the Triangle, which will be sponsored by the Association for the Prevention of Family Violence in the Arab Society. The proposal to establish this shelter has met with stiff opposition from the Islamic Movement on the grounds that the shelter "will destroy the Muslim family," and that it will "strengthen the woman vis-à-vis her husband," among other arguments. Clearly, the political coalition is seriously delaying the development of these essential services. Finally, it will be important to establish additional centers for the prevention of domestic violence in the Arab society in Israel. These centers can be involved in the proposed programs dealing with domestic violence in Arab society both on the level of prevention and community education and on the level of direct intervention, research and documentation, and planning and implementation. The programs and projects may be carried out in an atmosphere of coordination and cooperation with the existing welfare, health, and education services as well as with the justice system, the community, and formal and informal women's groups.

Structural Change as Intervention

Programs for intervention with and on behalf of battered women in Arab society will be subject to many obstacles and constraints unless they are accompanied by efforts to generate basic social changes. Such changes should inherently lead to the development of a violence-free environment that is conducive to long-term prevention of wife abuse and battering. In this connection, several dimensions of change may be emphasized.

Special emphasis can be placed on changing norms, values, and beliefs that perpetuate sexism and sex-role stereotyping in the Arab society in an attempt to eliminate values that emphasize the inferiority of women and the superiority of men. Moreover, it is important to oppose behavior codes and actual behavior that reflect these beliefs and values and also to eliminate the practice of differential education and socialization for men and women.

Similarly, there is a need for educational programs aimed at eliminating both the norms justifying violence against women and the erroneous myths about battered women and violent men. In Arab society, as in other traditional patriarchal societies, the battered woman is often perceived as *provocative, one who asks for violence, one who deserves to be beaten,* or *a failure as a wife and mother.* All of these perceptions justify violence against women and reflect an understanding, tolerant attitude toward the violent husband. Hence, these changes need to be accompanied by serious efforts to improve the social, economic, and political status of Arab women in Israel. In particular, government ministries and women's activists can play an active role in these efforts.

Another dimension that should be considered in any plan for social change is the nature of family life and perceptions of the family. Arab society attributes importance to situations such as family consensus, harmony, stability, equilibrium, and homeostasis; therefore, conflict in the family is considered an unacceptable situation that contradicts these norms and can undermine the stability of the family (Barakat, 1985; Haj-Yahia, 1994, 1995). However, it has been shown that such harmony and stability are utopian, ideal, and difficult to achieve and that conflict should be dealt with as an integral part of family life (Farrington & Chertok, 1993; Sprey, 1979). Therefore, it is essential to encourage social change that legitimizes family conflict and delegitimizes violence as a way of solving conflicts. In keeping with this dimension of change, it is important to make the public aware that the quest for family consensus, harmony, and stability must not take precedence over the well-being and security of the wife. Similarly, there is an urgent need for social change that will undermine values such as family privacy, family honor and reputation, and family unity. When these values and similar beliefs are challenged, victims of wife abuse and battering in the Arab society may be encouraged to stop keeping their plight to themselves and to enlist help from social and legal services to ensure their safety and well-being and break the pattern of violence against them. Efforts can be made to enhance public awareness to the dangerous consequences of preferring these traditional family values over the well-being, security, and safety of the wife.

An additional dimension that may be an essential part of any strategy for combating violence against women is to eliminate inequality based on gender and age. Such inequality is expressed by the dominance of males in the Arab family and the power relegated to senior family members and males over younger members and women. The social legitimacy for male dominance (particularly for husbands) is significantly related to justification of wife abuse and battering, and unwillingness to help battered women, as well as by absolving the husband of responsibility for his violent behavior and by the unwillingness to punish violent, abusive husbands (Haj-Yahia, 1991).

Conclusion

Finally, it is important to note that this chapter does not propose a specific model for prevention of family violence or for intervention in cases of wife abuse and battering in the Arab society in Israel. The main objective has been to highlight several observations and positions regarding wife abuse and battering in this society and to suggest some general directions for intervention, which may also be applicable in other societies where wife abuse is prevalent among minority populations. In addition, this chapter has emphasized the need to establish public programs for prevention of this problem and for community intervention settings. Clearly, there is an urgent need to continue this discussion in an attempt to find the most appropriate and culturally sensitive strategies for intervention with abused and battered women not only in the Arab society in Israel but also in other patriarchal and traditional minority societies as well as in other Arab societies throughout the world.

References

Aguirre, B. E. (1985). Why do they return? Abused wives in shelters. *Social Work, 30,* 350-354.

Al-Haj, M. (1987). *Social change and family processes.* Boulder, CO: Westview.

Al-Haj, M. (1989). Social research on family lifestyles among Arabs in Israel. *Journal of Comparative Family Studies, 20,* 175-195.

Al-Rifaee, H. H. (1994). *Marital rights in the Quran and Sunnah and the call for women's liberation.* Egypt: Islamic Awareness Press (Arabic).

Avitzur, M. (1987). The Arab family: Tradition and change. In H. Granot (Ed.), *The family in Israel* (pp. 99-115). Jerusalem: Council of Schools of Social Work in Israel (Hebrew).

Barakat, H. (1985). The Arab family and the challenge of social transformation. In E. W. Fernea (Ed.), *Women and the family in the Middle East: New voices of change* (pp. 27-48). Austin: University of Texas Press.

Bograd, M. (1984). Family systems approaches to wife battering: A feminist critique. *American Journal of Orthopsychiatry, 54*(4), 558-568.

Farrington, K., & Chertok, E. (1993). Social conflict theories of the family. In P. G. Boss, W. J. Doherty, R. LaRossa, W. R. Schumm, & S. K. Steinmetz (Eds.), *Sourcebook of family theories and methods: A contextual approach* (pp. 357-381). New York: Plenum.

Gelles, R. J. (1983). An exchange/social control theory. In D. Finkelhor, R. J. Gelles, G. T. Hotaling, & M. A. Straus (Eds.), *The dark side of families* (pp. 151-165). Beverly Hills, CA: Sage.

Haj-Yahia, M. M. (1991). *Perceptions about wife-beating and the use of different conflict tactics among Arab-Palestinian engaged males in Israel.* Unpublished doctoral dissertation, University of Minnesota.

Haj-Yahia, M. M. (1994). The Arab family in Israel: A review of cultural values and their relationship to the practice of social work. *Society and Welfare, 14*(3-4), 249-264 (Hebrew).

Haj-Yahia, M. M. (1995). Toward culturally sensitive intervention with Arab families in Israel. *Contemporary Family Therapy, 17*(4), 429-447.

Ibrahim, I. (1993). *The status of the Arab woman in Israel.* Jerusalem: Sikouy—The Association for the Advancement of Equal Opportunities. (Arabic).

Layish, A. (1975). *Women and Islamic law in a non-Muslim state.* New York: John Wiley.

Moghadam, V. M. (1992). Patriarchy and the politics of gender in modernizing societies: Iran, Pakistan and Afghanistan. *International Sociology, 7*(1), 35-53.

Roberts, A. R., & Roberts, B. S. (1990). A comprehensive model for crisis intervention with battered women and their children. In S. M. Stith, M. B. Williams, & K. Rosen (Eds.), *Violence hits home* (pp. 25-46). New York: Springer.

Schilling, R. D. (1987). Limitations of social support. *Social Service Review, 61*(1), 19-31.

Shokeid, M. (1993). Ethnic identity and the position of women among Arabs in an Israeli town. In Y. Azmon & D. N. Izraeli (Eds.), *Women in Israel* (pp. 423-441). New Brunswick, NJ: Transaction.

Sprey, J. (1979). Conflict theory and the study of marriage and the family. In W. R. Burr, R. Hill, F. I. Nye, & I. L. Reiss (Eds.), *Contemporary theories about the family: Vol. II. General theories/theoretical orientations* (pp. 130-159). New York: Free Press.

Strube, M., & Barbour, L. (1983). The decision to leave an abusive relationship: Economic dependence and psychological commitment. *Journal of Marriage and the Family, 45,* 785-793.

PART III

INTERVENTION WITH SURVIVORS, PERPETRATORS, AND THEIR CHILDREN

7

Battered Women's Strategic Response to Violence

The Role of Context

Mary Ann Dutton

The future of intervention with battered women and their families lies in better understanding battered women's efforts to resist, escape, avoid, and stop the violence against them and their children. Although important, merely identifying the battered women's strategic responses to violence, for example, calling the police, going to a shelter, leaving home, fighting back (Bachman, 1994; Bowker, 1983; Gondolf & Fisher, 1988), is not sufficient. We need to understand better what explains the differences in strategic response among battered women as well as within the same battered women across time. Why do some women repeatedly call the police and others never do? Why do some women seek help from a shelter, but others do not? Why does a battered woman begin to fight back after years of having not done so? What explains why some women fight back at the first threat of violence but later stop? Why do some women seek help from health professionals, and other women turn to the courts, and still others never seek help outside the family?

The answers to these questions are important because they can potentially lead to better interventions for assisting battered women in increasing their own and their children's safety. This information is also needed because, without it, misinterpretation of battered women's actions has important consequences to the battered woman and her family. Certain efforts to resist violence (e.g., fighting back in self-defense, verbal and physical expressions of anger) have been used to define battered women as hostile or aggressive. Other efforts (e.g., compliance, staying in the battering relationship) have been cited as evidence of their passivity or dependence when, in fact, they were strategic choices about safety. Many decisions made about battered women's lives (e.g., availability of the protection of the court, custody, criminal culpability for actions taken, distribution of property in marital dissolution, right to claim damages for violence) are influenced by others' appraisal of their strategic response to domestic violence. For these reasons, a more complete understanding of battered women's strategic response to violence is needed.

To date, two predominant theories have been developed to explain battered women's strategies for responding to violence. The learned helplessness theory of depression (Seligman, 1975) was adapted by Walker (1984) to explain battered women's apparently passive, helpless response. For example, the theory has been used to explain why some battered women do not leave the battering relationship. However, application of learned helplessness theory to battered women's inaction, in the face of actual physical threat, has been challenged by the authors of the original theory as a misapplication of the theory (Peterson, Maier, & Seligman, 1993). Furthermore, the theory of learned helplessness applied to battered women fails to account for the active efforts many battered women make to resist, avoid, or escape violence.

The survivor theory suggests that battered women respond to abuse with help-seeking methods that are largely unmet and that women increase their help seeking as the danger to themselves and their children increases (Gondolf & Fisher, 1988). Thus, the survivor theory emphasizes battered women's active help-seeking behavior. An empirical test of the model (Gondolf & Fisher, 1988) incorporated dimensions of the domestic violence (e.g., physical abuse, verbal abuse, injury), economic resources (e.g., victim's income), children (e.g., number of children), other types of violence in the family (e.g., child abuse), and batterer's other behavior (e.g., substance abuse, general violence, arrests, batterer's response to violence) to explain the number of types of battered women's help-seeking behavior. A major contribution of this model is that it demonstrates the importance of contextual variables, in addition to violence, for understanding battered women's help-seeking behavior.

The major purpose of this chapter is to present a comprehensive model for incorporating social and individual context toward a better understanding of battered women's efforts to resist, escape, avoid, or stop the violence against them and their children (Dutton, 1993). The model can explain differences in battered women's strategic responses to violence. The nested ecological model presented here provides a contrast to the *battered women's syndrome* analysis of women's responses to violence. The nested model offers a mechanism for explaining observed variability in battered women's responses to violence. The battered women's syndrome not only suggests a singular condition but also gives the appearance of pathology. The second purpose of this chapter is to discuss related intervention, research, and policy implications that follow when social and individual context are included in an analysis of battered women's responses to the violent behavior directed against them and their children.

Omission of Context: An Illustration

Common stereotypes of battered women are based on an omission of the social and individual context. Battered women are often thought of as a group defined only by their experience of battering and a singular response to it, often a helpless or passive one. Although the common experience of battering is a crucial one for understanding battered women's experience, there are also important differences among battered women's experiences that are not often considered. Yet, these differences among battered women's strategic responses to violence and abuse are evident with even a cursory glance. The fact of these differences has important implications for intervention, research, forensic practice, and policy. Case examples below—constructed from real battered women's lives, with details modified to protect anonymity—illustrate how a disregard for social and individual context can contribute to the distortion in understanding of battered women's strategic responses to violence.

> Joanne is a battered woman whose responses to violence included reporting her husband's domestic violence and the sexual abuse of her daughter to his employers, seeking help from a psychiatrist, contemplating suicide many times, and attempting to kill herself by drowning on one occasion.

Consider the following social and individual contextual factors. First, the abuse Joanne experienced was repeated physical violence, along with intimidation, emotional abuse, and coercive threats, over a 30-year period, beginning early in the marriage. Second, Joanne's reporting of her husband's abuse toward both her daughter and herself, in the early years of their marriage, was responded to by her husband's employer, the military, with a warning that her husband's job would be jeopardized if she took the matter further. Joanne held the belief that this was a consequence for which she felt she could not take responsibility. Third, Joanne was financially dependent on her husband, in terms of both his income and her employment position in his professional office. Although she possessed employable skills and took a great deal of responsibility in running her husband's office, Joanne believed that she was not competent to work independently of him. Finally, the psychiatrist's response to Joanne's reaction to her violent situation was to prescribe medication for her depression and anxiety. At no time did he express concern about the safety of herself and her children.

These are but a few examples of the social and individual context in which Joanne experienced domestic violence. But, without a recognition of the military's response to Joanne's reporting of both domestic violence and child sexual abuse, one might question why she never reported these to the police. But knowing that the person to whom Joanne turned for the most personal assistance, her psychiatrist, chose to treat Joanne's depression as the primary intervention; that Joanne was financially dependent; and that she lacked the self-confidence to seek independent living contributes to an understanding of why Joanne never chose to leave the relationship.

Another example is of a Hispanic woman's experience:

> In responding to the physical and sexual violence against her, Margarite told no one directly about it. She begged her husband to stop when he raped her and repeatedly asked him why he was doing this to her. Margarite moved away from her husband once in order to get away from him, but he followed her and moved in with her in spite of her resistance. Margarite routinely slept on the couch in an attempt to reduce the

opportunities for sexual assault. Margarite planned to return to her home country, but only after she obtained her citizenship, which would allow her to return to work when it became necessary to do so.

Consider the following contextual variables: First, when Margarite moved away from her husband early in their marriage, his extended family encouraged her to let him stay, saying he couldn't get along without her. Margarite had no social contact other than people she knew at work and his family. Second, Margarite had frequent respites from the violence when her husband spent days or weeks away from the home with other women. During these times, Margarite's life was more peaceful. Third, Margarite sent much of the money she earned in her full-time job to family members in her home country. Her sister's husband left his family with three children to raise and only her sister to support them. Fourth, Margarite's husband was not only violent to her but he also knocked down a policeman on one occasion, when a neighbor called because Margarite's husband was holding her over a balcony and threatening to drop her. Observation of her husband's violence against the police reinforced her belief in her husband's omnipotence. Finally, consider Margarite's immigrant status.

These contextual variables provide a basis for understanding Margarite's long-term plan for ending the violence. She attempted more short-term strategies, such as moving away from her husband, but that did not work to keep him away from her. Thereafter, she engaged in a much more long-term plan. Without considering Margarite's immigration status, one may not appreciate the importance of her remaining in the United States. Without U.S. citizenship, she had no guarantee of returning and would face economic hardship like her sister did. Without recognizing Margarite's belief that no one could control her husband's violence (reinforced by her husband's violence to the police), one might not understand why she didn't call the police, why she lied to victim's advocates in the prosecutor's office on the one occasion when criminal charges were made (the balcony incident), or why she didn't physically resist the sexual assaults.

Defining the Context of Battered Women's Experience

All human experience is situated in a configuration of events and circumstances that reside both inside and outside the individual. The perspective of understanding behavior as a function of both social and individual context (individual differences) is clearly situated within the social science literature. For example, the interactionist view (Endler & Magnusson, 1976) considers behavior as a function of personality variables, situational variables, and the interaction between the two. Social learning theory explains individual behavior as a function of situational and individual variables (Goldfried & Sprafkin, 1976; Kanfer & Saslow, 1965; Meichenbaum, 1977). Family systems theory focuses on family interaction as a context for understanding an individual's behavior within the family (see Bograd, 1984, for a feminist critique of family systems theory for explaining battering).

Previous work in a related area provides an important precedent for a contextual analysis of battered women's experience of violence. Several authors have applied a nested ecological model of human behavior (Brofenbrenner, 1977, 1979, 1986) to the problem of intimate violence (Belsky, 1980; Carlson, 1984; Dutton, 1988, 1995; Edleson & Tolman, 1992). The key element of an ecological approach to understanding battering is the notion of nested social and psychological factors that exert direct and indirect influence on the batterer's behavior—toward either desistance or continued violence. These factors, individually and in combination, determine their overall impact.

Although the model can appear complex, a simple illustration focusing on a batterer's behavior can show how a nested ecological model makes common sense and gives meaning to the phrase, "It all depends on the circumstances." In one example, a man hits his pregnant wife for the first time. She leaves to stay with a friend, calls the police, and files for a civil protection order wherein the man is arrested and ordered to vacate the home and attend batterer treatment. When he tells of his plight to a friend, his buddy cautions him that repeat occurrences will mean jail time and reminds him of his responsibilities to the unborn child.

In a contrasting example, when the police arrive, they chat with the batterer for a while, suggest that perhaps his wife is a bit oversensitive because she's pregnant, and casually suggest that he take it a bit easy. The woman does not file for a civil protection order, believing that it would do no good because the police appear to be on his side anyway. The man's friend jokingly suggests that he has to keep a rein on things because he is, after all, the man of the house.

The different circumstances of each scenario define the extent to which the batterer's violent behavior was negatively or positively sanctioned. That is, the contrasting responses send quite different messages to the batterer about what he can expect if violence were to continue. Predicting whether the man would again use violence could be argued to depend on the circumstances of this first occurrence.

Although this example is oversimplified, it illustrates that predicting the man's behavior is a function of the circumstances or context that surround the situation. In this case, the context included the response (or lack thereof) of police, courts, peers, and his partner, as well as the interaction of one type of response (police indifference to the violence) with another (a battered woman's decision to not seek a civil protection order).

Context, as it applies to battered women's experience, is defined by the social and individual factors that are comprised in the situation in which the violence occurs. It is necessary to consider these factors both singly and in combination with each other. Contextual analysis of human behavior is neither new nor specific to one set of theories. Application of the nested ecological model, an integrated approach to contextual analysis, is also not new for understanding violent behavior. However, in this chapter, a nested ecological model is used to organize existing knowledge about battered women's experience with violence and to provide the basis for a comprehensive contextual analysis of battered women's strategic responses to violence. Following is an elaboration of the nested ecological model for classifying contextual variables for the purpose of explaining battered women's experience with violence.

Classification of Contextual Variables

The formal nested ecological model used for explaining intimate violent behavior includes five overlapping systems (Edleson & Tolman, 1992). By adapting the nested ecological model to battered women's experience, the five systems can be defined as follows:

1. the *individual battered woman,* her individual personal history, and the meaning she makes of it (i.e., ontogenetic);
2. family, friendship, workplace, and other *personal networks* in which the battered woman interacts, the developmental history of each, and the meaning she makes of them (i.e., microsystem);
3. the *linkages between the networks* or systems defining the battered woman's social environment, the history of those linkages, and the meaning she makes of them (i.e., mesosystem);

4. the *larger community networks* in which the battered woman doesn't interact directly but which, nevertheless, influence her indirectly (i.e., exosystem), the developmental history of those networks, and the meaning she makes of them; and
5. the *society and cultural blueprint* defined by the cultural, ethnic group, and social class factors, the historical development of the blueprint, and the meaning she makes of it (i.e., macrosystem).

At each level, the influence of contextual variables is considered along with the meaning attached to them by the battered woman. This allows for a recognition of the influence of social and environmental factors per se as well the unique meaning attached to them by different people. For example, a coworker's inquiry about a visible bruise is an exosystem factor that may have considerable influence on a battered woman's response to violence. But, depending upon whether the woman takes her coworker's comment to be one of support and an offer to provide needed assistance or as an invasive, rude comment, the coworker's inquiry may serve to encourage the battered woman to either talk about the violence or deny it.

The developmental history of the ecological system (i.e., chronosystem) is also included in each level of the nested model. With reference to the above example, depending upon whether the battered woman's previous employer had fired her because of battering or had provided support and refuge, the history of workplace networks may also influence the battered woman's response to the present coworker's inquiry. The model presented here also includes an *economic and tangible resources* variable.

A nested ecological model for understanding battered women's experience of domestic violence allows for the classification of social and individual contextual variables at each ecological level. Table 7.1 is an illustration of the nested ecological model for explaining battered women's responses to violence. For each of the five levels of the model, relevant contextual variables are identified along with questions useful for interpreting the influence of the variable.

Economic and Tangible Resources

Economic and tangible resources are needed by the battered woman and her children for daily living. These include access to money or credit as well as access to housing, transportation, food, and

text continues on p. 116

Table 7.1 Nested Ecological Model of Battered Women's Response to Violence

Level of Analysis	*Contextual Variables*	*Relevant Questions (Examples)*
Economic and tangible resources	• money, credit	• To what amount of economic resources does the battered woman have immediate access, regardless of her social class or the resources of her partner?
	• housing, food, transportation, clothing	• To what essential, tangible resources necessary for daily living does the battered woman have access?
The ontogenetic (individual personal history)	• significant historical events	• What have been significant historical events during the battered woman's lifetime, and what are her attitudes and beliefs about them?
	• emotional strengths and limitations	• What are the battered woman's emotional strengths and limitations and what are her attitudes and beliefs about them?
	• physical strengths and limitations	• What are the battered woman's physical strengths and limitations and what are her attitudes about them?
	• behavioral strengths and limitations	• What are the battered woman's behavioral strengths and limitations and what are her attitudes about them?
The microsystem (personal networks)	• family network	• What interactions, including but not limited to the violence, occur between the battered woman and the batterer? What are the battered women's attitudes and beliefs about all of the batterer's behavior?
	• friendship, workplace, social and other networks (e.g., children's school)	• What other family members, including children, comprise the battered woman's family network and what interactions occur with them? What are the battered woman's related attitudes and beliefs?

(continued)

Table 7.1 Continued

Level of Analysis	*Contextual Variables*	*Relevant Questions (Examples)*
		• Who comprises the battered woman's social, friendship, workplace, and any other personal networks, and what interactions occur within them? What are the battered woman's attitudes and beliefs about these networks and the interactions she has within them?
The mesosystem (linkages between microsystem networks)	• linkages between the battered woman's microsystem networks (e.g., the relationship with the batterer and the battered woman's workplace, children, or extended family) • linkages between the microsystems that comprise the exosystem (e.g., connection between the police department and the prosecutor's office, emergency department, or courts) • linkages between the battered woman's microsystem networks and the microsystems that comprise the exosystem (e.g., the extended family's involvement with the court system; the school system's involvement with the local domestic violence coordinating council)	• What interactions occur between the microsystems that comprise the battered woman's exosystem and what is the battered woman's attitudes and beliefs about them? • What interactions occur between the battered woman's microsystems and the microsystems that comprise the battered woman's exosystem? What are the battered woman's attitudes about them?

The exosystem (the larger community networks)	• institutional policies and practices concerning violence	• What policies and practices characterize law enforcement, the courts, mental health agencies, health agencies, schools, corporations, and other agencies in the battered woman's community concerning the problem of domestic violence? What is the battered woman's view of these policies or practices?
The macrosystem level (societal and cultural blueprint)	• attitudes about violence toward women	• What are the prevailing attitudes and beliefs in the battered woman's cultural or ethnic group and social class about intimate male violence toward women and what is the battered woman's view of these attitudes?
	• sex-role beliefs	• What are the prevailing attitudes and beliefs about the role of women in the family, in the workplace, and in the community and what is the battered woman's view of these attitudes?
	• beliefs related to battered woman's and batterer's culture and ethnicity, class, and other status characteristics (e.g., sexual preference, age)	• What are the prevailing societal attitudes and beliefs about both the battered woman's and the batterer's cultural, ethnic, or social class status? What is the battered woman's view of these attitudes?

clothing. Even when a woman has lived her life in a middle- or upper-class lifestyle, she may not have personal and ready access to these necessary resources. This depends on who actually holds ownership of bank accounts, credit cards, and property, and the extent of economic control throughout the battering relationship. A battered woman may be economically dependent on her partner even though she has enjoyed the benefits of a nice home, expensive cars, and an extravagant lifestyle during the course of the relationship.

For battered women of lower socioeconomic means, the lack of economic and tangible resources may mean that she does not have the available resources to provide herself or her children with shelter, food, diapers, or transportation to work and school, even during a time of transition. Further, if she is without the resources to maintain a life independent of the batterer, the act of leaving the relationship may accomplish little in her struggle for safety. Some women know that they are in greater danger if they leave but are forced, out of necessity, to return. Thus, the economic and tangible resources available to a battered woman contribute to defining the options available to her and the children for responding to domestic violence.

Individual Battered Women

Factors at the individual level include the battered woman's emotional, physical, behavioral, interpersonal, and cognitive strengths and limitations. There are numerous individual variables that are potentially important to examine, such as emotional (e.g., self-esteem), physical (e.g., injuries, illness, disability), behavioral (e.g., employment skills, skill in the use of weapons, independent living skills, special skills such as karate), interpersonal (e.g., assertiveness), and cognitive (e.g., appraisal of danger, intelligence) factors. Personal history is important, for example, including such events as prior traumatization, significant losses, and prior significant relationships.

Finally, the meaning the battered woman attaches to any of these individual factors is also considered. For example, a malignant breast tumor may lead one woman to think that her life is almost over and so there is little use in attempting to leave the battering relationship, but another may see the same illness as a motivation to leave the violence at whatever cost. The event itself, although powerful, cannot be interpreted without the context of meaning attached to it.

Personal Networks

The battered woman is potentially involved in numerous personal networks, at the center of which (for this analysis) is the relationship with the intimate abusive partner. The family, including children, form another of these networks. The extended family, friendship circles, workplace networks, neighborhood or community groups, exercise or sports groups, religious groups, and the children's school (e.g., parent organizations, relationships with teachers) are networks in which the battered woman may interact. These networks may be extensive or they may be minimal. The developmental history of the networks is another dimension that cannot be ignored. Having been part of the same workplace network over an extended period of time, one in which coworkers have consistently provided support, is quite different from being in a new workplace situation with little established personal history. Finally, the meaning attached to personal networks influences their contextual role.

Larger Community Networks

Numerous larger community networks, ones in which the battered woman does not have direct interaction, nevertheless have an impact on battered women. Policies and procedures that govern law enforcement, prosecutor's offices, courts, hospital emergency departments, and child welfare agencies, for example, define the community response to violence. The historical development of these networks (e.g., police officers have only been recently trained about handling domestic violence cases; prosecutor's offices routinely drop most domestic violence cases) can also play an important role. Finally, the meaning attached to these networks, and their policies and procedures, by the battered woman must also be considered.

Societal and Cultural Blueprint

General acceptance of violence against women in mainstream culture (e.g., as portrayed in court decisions, the media, entertainment, advertising) cannot be ignored as one blueprint that potentially influences battered women's experience of violence. The historic tradition of women as men's property, both literally and figuratively, is also influential. Blueprints identified with subcultural or ethnic groups (e.g., unacceptable to go outside the family with family problems) must also be recognized as potentially influential. The meaning attached to these blueprints is also important. A woman who has internalized the culturally sanctioned blueprints for her life may respond differently from the woman who has rejected them.

The nested ecological model provides a framework to guide the contextual analysis of battered women's experience with violence. The contextual configuration does not assume the role of causation in explaining a battered woman's behavior. Rather, it establishes a mechanism to explain individual differences in battered women's behavior through an understanding of factors that serve as either obstacles or supports in the battered woman's life situation—as either mediators or moderators in the relationship between the violent behavior and battered women's strategic response to it.

Implications of a Contextual Analysis

A contextual analysis of battered women's strategic responses to violence holds implications for research, intervention, forensic practice, and policy. Each of these areas is addressed below.

Research

An important implication of contextual analysis for research on battered women's experience is the necessity of multivariate models. By this approach, it is possible to examine not only individual factors but also their interactions in combination with each other. The complexity of contextual analysis may also require qualitative models of research (Patton, 1990).

A second implication of a context-sensitive approach to research concerning battered women is the inclusion of women from groups outside the mainstream culture. Results of research including only Anglo American women cannot be assumed to apply to women of color, women living in poverty, or women whose native language is other than English. Research on battering and its effects for disenfranchised women, such as the homeless, the seriously and chronically mentally ill, and the immigrants, is necessary to capture the unique contextual influences that define the life circumstances of these groups of battered women.

Although no single study can include all, or even most, relevant contextual variables, a greater emphasis on the role of context in research would imply an inclusion and recognition of these factors routinely across studies and researchers. Where specific studies are unable to vary contextual factors for purposes of statistical analyses (e.g., due to small sample sizes), the context for which the research applies can be clearly identified (e.g., description of research subjects by ethnicity, age, relationship status, length of time away from relationship; subject selection method; prior victimization) to better enable interpretation of research results.

Gondolf's (Gondolf & Fisher, 1988) research is one example of incorporating contextual variables (e.g., income, number of children, child abuse, injury, nature of violence) in research on battered women's help-seeking behavior. Other researchers (Foa, Steketee, & Rothbaum, 1989; Follingstad, Brennan, Hause, Polck, & Rutledge, 1991) have developed similar models for examining battered women's traumatic response to violence (e.g., post-traumatic stress disorder). Research that extends this previous work is needed.

The contextually sensitive study of battered women's strategic response to violence also requires attention to change over time. The context of time is a particularly important one, because battered women's strategies vary across time, influenced by a continually changing social context (e.g., children are born, leave home; serious illnesses develop; families relocate to areas without support for the battered woman; the violence escalates over time or begins to involve children as direct victims). Thus, not only is time an important contextual variable itself, but change in battered women's strategies over time is also a dependent variable for which there has been relatively little previous attention. Research by Campbell (Campbell, Miller, Cardwell, & Belknap, 1994) is one example of studying the impact of time on battered women's responses to violence.

Attention to these research issues can begin to capture the complexity in battered women's strategic response to violence. Social science research provides an important foundation for interventions with and policies that affect battered women and their children. Accountability in research related to battered women requires that our research models adequately reflect their real lives and actual needs.

Intervention

Mental health, physical health, and advocacy interventions with battered women are informed, in part, by social science research. One application of that research is toward informing case analysis. A case formulation that incorporates a contextual analysis is one for which the focus, by definition, is less on the individual battered woman and more on the interaction of the battered woman with the environment in which she lives. Conclusions about factors that influence the battered woman's behavior take into account the impact of the surrounding social context on her attitudes and behaviors. Social learning (Goldfried & Sprafkin, 1976; Kanfer & Saslow, 1965; Meichenbaum, 1977), family systems (see Boss, Doherty, LaRossa, Schumm, & Steinmetz, 1993), and feminist theories (Brown & Root, 1990) of psychotherapy strongly emphasize social context as essential for case analysis and intervention. Thus, the idea of contextual analysis is not new for mental health intervention.

Most basically, a formulation about a battered woman's psychological condition cannot be understand apart from the essential context of the domestic violence and abuse to which she has been exposed (Dutton, 1992). Prior traumatic experiences provide a similar context that is also associated with level of current psychological distress or well-being (Briere, 1992; Courtois, 1988). Thus, intervention targeted at a battered woman's depression must consider the recurrent violence to which she is exposed, resultant social withdrawal, lack of economic resources, and ineffective police response as important elements. Attempting to reduce depression without attention to these factors would likely be ineffective.

Consider the following factors in designing an intervention appropriate for a battered woman's alcohol problem: history of severe violence with the current boyfriend, including threat with a weapon; prior history of battering from previous boyfriend; alcohol use exacerbated by a recent escalation in violence severity; woman's ability to support herself financially; social support from family for leaving this relationship, but with little tangible support for doing so; and prior attempts to report violence to police failed to provide even short-term protection. Effective intervention would require attention to these factors.

Of course, a contextual analysis does not eliminate individual responsibility for the battered woman's behavior. The influence of a particular battered woman's social context is filtered through her perceptions, appraisal, attitudes, expectations, and beliefs. Nevertheless, even within the most egregious of abusive circumstances, some personal choices remain. Although some behaviors are clearly limited by obstacles and events beyond the battered woman's control, one of the goals of advocacy and mental health intervention with battered women should be to increase the range of those choices.

A contextual analysis also influences work with battered women by encouraging a more holistic approach to intervention. Thus, all aspects of the individual, including strengths and vulnerabilities, are considered. The battered woman's physical, emotional, behavioral, cognitive, and spiritual selves are considered necessary for understanding and helping to change any aspect of herself. For example, knowing that a woman's cognitive style was one that relied on reason and logic may suggest that a cost-benefit analysis of decisions about the battering relationship may be an effective intervention strategy. Alternatively, understanding that a battered woman felt emotional support from talking with others about her situation may suggest that a support group would be a useful intervention modality.

Contextual analysis for intervention means, at minimum, that social and individual factors are considered together in terms of their influence on the battered woman. In many cases, it also means that interventions are targeted at changing some aspect of the social (e.g., social support) or individual (e.g., increase hope about escaping violence) context in order to achieve the desired results (e.g., reduce alcohol intake).

Forensic Practice

There is some precedent in the law generally for understanding context in relation to behavior. For example, self-defense statutes justify violent behavior when it is in response to the reasonable perception that someone is about to cause great bodily harm or death to oneself or to someone else. Furthermore, statutes and case law that allow testimony concerning domestic violence and its effects have recognized the added importance of understanding the dynamics of the domestic violence in determining such factors as reasonable perception (e.g., Cal. Evid. Code §1107), temporal proximity as it relates to the perception of danger (e.g., Cal. Evid. Code §1107), and proportionality of force used to respond to the perception of danger (Mass. Gen. Laws Ann. ch. 233 §23E).

Nevertheless, many aspects of social context are functionally invisible in the legal system. Until the recent passage of the Violence Against Women Act, recognition of immigrant status was missing from legal protection of immigrant battered women in their efforts to report the battering. Although recommended by the American Bar Association (ABA, 1994, p. 15), not all states have adopted a presumption against a domestic violence perpetrator with regard to custody decisions.

In part, this lack of emphasis has been encouraged by conceptualizing battered women's response to violence from the perspective of the battered woman syndrome (Walker, 1984). Although important for having achieved acceptance of testimony concerning battered women in the courtroom, battered woman syndrome as a concept allows little room for consideration of social context (Dutton, 1993). Social framework testimony (Vidmar & Schuller, 1989; Walker & Monahan, 1987), in which the expert testifies about general conclusions from the social science research in order to assist the fact finder, usually a jury, is defined by "information about the social and psychological context in which adjudicative facts occurred" (Vidmar & Schuller, 1989, p. 133). The application of social context analysis when testimony is offered about a particular case (Dutton, 1993) provides the fact finder with a basis to evaluate the battered woman's behavior in order to determine the ultimate issue.

Policy

Contextual analysis of battered women's experience can inform public policy in important ways. For example, consideration of the impact of welfare reform in relation to battered women is informed by an understanding of economic context on battered women's ability to extricate themselves from a violent relationship. A context-sensitive examination of the impact of health care reform on battered women highlights the essential nature of access to health care for women and their children without reliance on a husband's insurance plan. The recently enacted Violence Against Women Act illustrates a consideration of context in the provision that allows battered immigrant women to petition for a green card independently of their husbands when there is indication of battering. These and other examples illustrate the central role of context in public policy matters.

Conclusion

Analysis of social context in understanding battered women's experience provides a challenge for the next decade of work with battered women. Social context analysis is not new to the social sciences. However, it's influence has yet to be fully integrated in work with battered women, whether in research, intervention, forensic practice, or public policy. Comprehensive social context analysis dramatically changes the way in which battered women's experience is understood, whether it be their strategic behaviors designed to resist violence and increase their and their children's safety or their traumatic responses to violence (e.g., post-traumatic stress disorder). The next decade of work with battered women is compelled to address the real complexity and diversity of battered women's experience—across women who vary from each other according to race, ethnicity, social class, age, sexual preference, and physical ablebodiness. Social context analysis is one tool easily accessible for the task.

References

American Bar Association (ABA). (1994). *The impact of domestic violence on children: A report to the president of the American Bar Association.* Chicago: Author.

Bachman, R. (1994). *Violence against women: A national crime victimization survey report* (BJS Publication No. NCJ-145325). Washington, DC: U.S. Department of Justice.

Belsky, J. (1980). Child maltreatment: An ecological integration. *American Psychologist, 35*(4), 320-335.

Bograd, M. (1984). Family systems approaches to wife battering: A feminist critique. *American Journal of Orthopsychiatry, 54,* 558-568.

Boss, P. G., Doherty, W. J., LaRossa, R., Schumm, W. R., & Steinmetz, S. K. (Eds.). (1993). *Sourcebook of family theories and methods.* New York: Plenum.

Bowker, L. H. (1983). *Beating wife beating.* Lexington, MA: Lexington.

Briere, J. (1992). *Child abuse trauma: Theory and treatment of the lasting effects.* Newbury Park, CA: Sage.

Brofenbrenner, U. (1977). Toward an experimental ecology of human development. *American Psychologist, 32,* 523-531.

Brofenbrenner, U. (1979). *The ecology of human development: Experiments by nature and design.* Cambridge, MA: Harvard University Press.

Brofenbrenner, U. (1986). Recent advances in research on the ecology of human development. In R. K. Silbereisen, K. Eyferth, & G. Rudinger (Eds.), *Development as action in context: Problem behavior and normal youth development* (pp. 287-308). New York: Springer.

Brown, L. S., & Root, M. P. P. (1990). *Diversity and complexity in feminist therapy.* New York: Harrington Park.

Campbell, J. C., Miller, P., Cardwell, M. M., & Belknap, R. A. (1994). Relationship status of battered women over time. *Journal of Family Violence, 9,* 99-111.

Carlson, B. E. (1984). Causes and maintenance of domestic violence: An ecological analysis. *Social Service Review, 58,* 569-587.

Courtois, C. (1988). *Healing the incest wound: Adult survivors in therapy.* New York: Norton.

Dutton, D. G. (1988). *The domestic assault of women: Psychological and criminal justice perspectives.* Boston: Allyn & Bacon.

Dutton, D. G. (1995). *The domestic assault of women: Psychological and criminal justice perspectives* (Rev. ed.). Vancouver: UBC Press.

Dutton, M. A. (1992). *Empowering and healing the battered woman: A model of assessment and intervention.* New York: Springer.

Dutton, M. A. (1993). Understanding women's responses to domestic violence: A redefinition of battered woman syndrome. *Hofstra Law Review, 21*(4), 1191-1242.

Edleson, J. L., & Tolman, R. M. (1992). *Intervention for men who batter: An ecological approach.* Newbury Park, CA: Sage.

Endler, N. S., & Magnusson, D. (1976). Toward an interactional psychology of personality. *Psychological Bulletin, 83,* 965-974.

Foa, E. B., Steketee, G., & Rothbaum, B. U. (1989). Behavioral/cognitive conceptualizations of post-traumatic stress disorder. *Behavior Therapy* (20), 155-176.

Follingstad, D. R., Brennan, A. F., Hause, E. S., Polck, D. S., & Rutledge, L. L. (1991). Factors moderating physical and psychological symptoms of battered women. *Journal of Family Violence, 6*(1), 81-95.

Goldfried, M. S., & Sprafkin, J. N. (1976). Behavioral personality assessment. In *Behavioral approaches to therapy.* Morristown, NJ: General Learning Press.

Gondolf, E. W., & Fisher, E. R. (1988). *Battered women as survivors: An alternative to treating learned helplessness.* Lexington, MA: Lexington.

Kanfer, F. H., & Saslow, G. (1965). Behavioral analyses. *Archives of General Psychiatry, 12,* 529-538.

Meichenbaum, D. (1977). *Cognitive-behavior modification: An integrative approach.* New York: Plenum.

Patton, M. Q. (1990). *Qualitative evaluation and research methods* (2nd ed.). Newbury Park, CA: Sage.

Peterson, C., Maier, S. F., & Seligman, M. E. P. (1993). *Learned helplessness: A theory for the age of personal control.* New York: Oxford University Press.

Seligman, M. E. P. (1975). *Helplessness: On depression, development, and death.* San Francisco, CA: W. H. Freeman.

Vidmar, N., & Schuller, R. A. (1989). Juries and expert evidence: Social framework testimony. *Law & Contemporary Problems, 52,* 113-176.

Walker, L. E. (1984). *Battered woman syndrome.* New York: Springer.

Walker, L. & Monahan, J. (1987). Social frameworks: A new use of social science in law. *Virginia Law Review, 73,* 559-598.

8

"Secondary" Victims No More

Refocusing Intervention With Children

Einat Peled

In an article on children's problems, published in *The Survey* in 1924, the pediatrician Ira S. Wile wrote the following:

> It is undoubtedly true that the brawling home has little advantage compared with the equable atmosphere secured by divorce. Yet, so long as cruelty and animosity are not directed upon the children, they are at least free from the internal stresses that exist when divorce breaks up the home or tears those intangible ties termed home influences. (Wile, 1924, p. 474)

Wile may have been one of the first professionals to understand and to comment on the predicament of children from "brawling homes," though he failed to fully appreciate the negative effects of violence for the witnessing child. Wile did not recommend direct intervention with child witnesses, but rather suggested that "the child is not the problem; the solution to his difficulties is only attainable through a modification of the social milieu" (Wile, 1924, p. 473).

The 70 years that have passed since the publication of Wile's article have brought significant changes in the social awareness of and response to the plight of child witnesses of violence. Nonetheless, Wile's recommendation as to the steps to be taken in order to help the suffering children seems to be a major principal still guiding societal response to children of battered women; namely, regarding child witnesses of woman battering as secondary victims of the violence. This chapter starts with a brief review of advancements made in research and intervention in this domain in the past two decades. Presented next are three factors I suggest currently hinder adequate, widespread response to the needs of children of battered women: (a) the secretive nature of domestic violence; (b) lack of required knowledge, skills, and commitment among relevant social services; and (c) the perception of children as secondary victims by the battered women's movement. Finally, regarding each of these factors, I examine current efforts to provide adequate services to children of battered women and outline some suggestions for future refocusing and change.

Children as a Focus of Research and Intervention

Following the construction of woman battering into a social problem in the 1970s (Loseke, 1987), children of battered women first became a direct focus of both research and intervention in the 1980s (Peled, 1993a). The number of children witnessing domestic violence in the United States each year was estimated to be between 3.3 million (Carlson, 1984) and 10 million (Straus, 1991). Data indicate that extremely high numbers (ranging from 28% to 70%) of child witnesses are themselves physically abused, sexually abused, or both (Bowker, Arbitell, & McFarron, 1988; Gayford, 1975; Giles-Sims, 1985; Hughes, 1988; Layzer, Goodson, & deLange, 1986; Petchers, 1995; Roy, 1977; Stark & Flitcraft, 1988; Straus, 1983; Suh & Abel, 1990; Tutty, 1995; Walker, 1984; Washburn & Frieze, 1980).

Research also provides convincing evidence for an array of behavior problems suffered by children of battered women. Child witnesses were reported to experience post-traumatic stress (e.g., Black & Kaplan, 1988; Burman & Allen-Meares, 1994; Malmquist, 1986; Pynoos & Eth, 1984) and to have more social, cognitive, emotional, and behavioral problems than children from nonviolent homes (e.g., Christopherpoulos et al., 1987; Forsstrom-Cohn & Rosenbaum, 1985; Hinchey & Gavelek, 1982; Holden & Ritchie, 1991; Hughes, 1988; Jaffe, Wolfe, Wilson, & Zak, 1986; Westra & Martin, 1981; Wolfe, Zak, Wilson, & Jaffe, 1986). To date, however, evidence is less conclusive regarding factors mediating the presumed causal relationship between witnessing violence and behavior problems (Fantuzzo & Lindquist, 1989; Jaffe, Wolfe, & Wilson, 1990; Peled & Davis, 1995, pp. 5-11).

Qualitative research and clinical observations added to the quantitative data an understanding of the complex life circumstances experienced by children of battered women (Ericksen & Henderson, 1992; Jaffe, Wolfe, & Wilson, 1990; Peled, 1993b; Roy, 1988). In a study of the experience of violence for preadolescent children of battered women (Peled, 1993b), I found that children's experience of the violence was multidimensional, reflecting not only the impact of direct exposure to violence but also factors such as separation from a parent, frequent moves, relationships with each of their parents, involvement of others in the family's life, and, of course, the child's personality. Children experienced the violence and its effects over a prolonged period of time, under changing family and violence-related circumstances. Some children related their experience of being locked in a family secret, having to cope with fear, anger, and confusion alone. Others were struggling to figure out how to maintain a relationship with their father without hurting or betraying their mother, or how to keep on loving and caring for their father while witnessing his violent behavior.

Both quantitative and qualitative research on child witnesses suggests that the experience of violence and surrounding stress-inducing family circumstances prevent children from achieving an adjusted, well functioning childhood. Intervention models specifically designed for children of battered women were developed throughout the 1980s as a response to children's observed and documented difficulties. These models consist mainly of post-traumatic individual therapy (e.g., Silvern & Kaersvang, 1989; Silvern, Karyl, & Landis, 1995) and, more commonly, psychoeducational group treatment (Alessi & Hearn, 1984; Cassady, Allen, & Lyon, & McGeehan, 1987; Frey-Angel, 1989; Gentry & Eaddy, 1980; Gibson & Gutierrez, 1991; Grusznski, Brink, & Edleson, 1988; Hughes, 1982; Johnson & Montgomery, 1990; Peled & Davis, 1995; Ragg & Webb, 1992; Wilson, Cameron, Jaffe, & Wolfe, 1986). Recently, in-depth descriptions and analyses of intervention with children of battered women within a variety of other social contexts have started to appear (e.g., Davidson, 1994; Peled, Jaffe, & Edleson, 1995).

As this century comes to a close, an evaluation of societal response to children of battered women reveals significant developments in professional awareness of the problem, in knowledge about difficulties experienced by children, and in services provided to children. We now know that millions of children each year suffer a multiplicity of problems following their exposure to violence; we understand some of the complex dynamics involved in creating barriers for normal development for these children; and we have developed some interventions to provide children with the professional support they need. Still, it seems that most children of battered women do not get the help and support they desperately need. For example, new research conducted by Peled and Edleson (1996), at the Domestic Abuse Project in Minneapolis, shows that although a large number of the battering men and battered women receiving services are parents, only about 15% of their children are at some point connected with the agency for services, and only about 66% of these complete services. Schechter with Mihali (1992) reported that only 12 paid child advocates provided services to more than 2,500 children residing in Massachusetts' shelters for battered women in 1991. Only approximately 80 children of battered women in this state were reported to have received support group services outside shelters in 1991.

The three following major factors seem to prevent intervention efforts from reaching more children of battered women: (a) the secretive nature of domestic violence, (b) lack of adequate knowledge and skills among professionals in settings where child witnesses can be identified and supported, and (c) the perception of children as "secondary" victims by part of the battered women's movement. In the remainder of this chapter, each of these obstacles will be carefully examined. Although the discussion of the secretive nature of violence and of functional shortcomings in service systems will be descriptive in nature, the examination of the battered women's movement's response to child witnesses of violence will take the form of a critical analysis, raising possibly controversial issues.

Obstacle I— The Secretive Nature of Domestic Violence

Many children of battered women cannot be identified by service providers because they live in a secret. The emotional, physical, and sexual violence children witness may be kept as a secret by abuser, or victim, or both. Parents may try to hide the violence from the outside world, from their families, from their children, and, sometimes, from themselves. The "fights" the child witnesses may not be defined as violence or hardly discussed at all between the child and his or her parents, or between parents and people outside the family. As a consequence, the child may not be fully aware of the extent or severity of the abuse (Peled, 1993b). Nonetheless, children who witness violence at home commonly report feelings of fear and terror (Blanchard, Molloy, & Brown, 1992; Ericksen & Henderson, 1992; Jaffe, Wolfe, & Wilson, 1990, Peled, 1993b). Children may be afraid for their mother, of getting hurt themselves, and of undesired changes in their lives as a result of the violence or of their mother's response to it (e.g., separating from their father). Other feelings experienced by children who live with the secret of violence are anger, confusion, guilt, shame, hopelessness, and helplessness (Cottle, 1980). Because the secret is kept both inside and outside the family, the child who wants to alleviate the bad feelings he or she is experiencing often has to do it alone.

Until the secret of violence is broken by a family member or others who are aware of it and decide to report or intervene, it may not be possible to individually help children in these families. Although the difficulties of some child witnesses are visible to those around them through external symptoms such as academic difficulties or behavior problems, others contain their secret inside, showing no discernible symptoms. Thus, efforts to reach children locked in this terrible situation can be made through available indirect means such as school programs and media publicity.

Violence Prevention in Schools

In the past decade, a variety of violence prevention strategies and programs have been instituted in some elementary, middle, and high schools (e.g., Gamache & Snapp, 1995; Sudermann, Jaffe, & Hastings, 1995). The main goal of these programs is to not only identify the ways violent behavior may be reinforced through victimization and witnessing violence during a child's development but also encounter this social learning before negative patterns are established. Violence prevention programs usually include one or more of the following strategies: (a) affective education, (b) skills education, (c) values education, (d) family life education, and (e) violence education (Gamache & Snapp, 1995).

Child witnesses participating in such programs may discover that their experience is shared by many others and that there are people who can help them and their parents. Raising awareness and empowering all students to respond to violence in their community and in their own lives possibly represents one of the most effective actions a community can take to reduce the incidence of violence and to ameliorate its effects (Sudermann et al., 1995). Hence, domestic violence education in schools (Grades K-12) should be encouraged. Simultaneously, school personnel need to be trained to adequately respond to children who may reveal their experience of violence following participation in such a program.

Media and Community Programs

A major goal in therapeutic intervention with children of battered women is to lessen their feelings of loneliness and shame by helping them understand that they are not the only ones living in a family where the mother is being abused (Peled & Davis, 1995). This goal is commonly achieved by working with child witnesses in a group format, facilitating children's discussions of their experiences with violence, and exposing them to books and movies whose protagonists are children of battered women. The discussion of violence in these groups usually leads to a discussion of ways in which children can take care of themselves during and after violent events (Peled & Davis, 1995).

Children who live in families where the violence is still a secret do not have the opportunity to benefit from such interventions. These children, however, are likely to watch TV, may borrow books in their school or local library, and are exposed to information displayed in public places. TV programs, children's books, and advertisements are all potential channels for communicating to children who live with the secret of violence that (a) they are not the only ones who experience such a family situation and (b) there are ways to take care of themselves and places to turn to for help. Hence, communities should ensure that children's books on domestic violence (e.g., Bernstein, 1991; Davis, 1984; Paris, 1985) are included in each school and public library, that movies and programs about children of battered women (e.g., Tri-State Coalition, 1986; National Film Board of Canada, 1988) are featured as part of children's programming on local and national TV channels, and that ongoing information on places children can turn to for support and help is displayed in public places such as school buses, school toilet doors, shopping centers, and the like.

Media publicity should also be directed toward the general public to create an awareness of the widespread and ongoing nature of the trauma experienced by child witnesses of violence (Blanchard et al., 1992). Because neighbors and relatives living nearby appear to be the most effective source of crisis support for children, it is important that they understand child witnesses' experience, and be willing and know how to help them when required.

Obstacle II— Lack of Adequate Knowledge and Skills

Domestic violence may be disclosed, and symptoms indicating domestic violence may be presented within a variety of social systems, schools being but one example. Professionals who work within the medical, welfare, and criminal justice systems encounter battered women and their children who have never before identified themselves as victims of violence nor been provided with protection, support, and advocacy services by domestic violence agencies. The opportunity to help child witnesses of violence within these settings is often missed, because the professional who encounters the children (or their parents) lacks the knowledge and skills required to provide them with the support, information, and referrals they need. This section focuses on two social systems, the police and child protective services, which are often socially mandated to intervene in cases of domestic violence but are not always successful in responding to the specific needs of children of battered women. Following a description of current practices, suggestions for improving police and child protection response to child witnesses will be outlined. A discussion of health care interventions with children of battered women can be found in Schechter's chapter in this volume (see also Davis, 1988; Groves, Zuckerman, Marans, & Cohen, 1993; Henderson, 1993; Hoffman, Sinclaire, Currie, & Jaffe, 1990).

Police Intervention

Police officers called to intervene in cases of domestic violence are often the first social agents to directly witness the impact of the violence on the children. They may be the first adults ever to try talking with the child about the violence he or she witnessed. The position of police officers responding to domestic disputes when children are present is a delicate one: They can provide a meaningful crisis intervention for the children or, by an inappropriate response, they can fail to protect the child and increase his or her feelings of fear, stress, guilt, and confusion. The latter may be especially true when children are asked by police officers to report or give testimony on the violence they witnessed, and thus, feel forced to break the family secret, incriminate the abuser, who happens to also be their parent, or both. Buzawa and Buzawa (1990) suggest that children may also be traumatized by the arrest of the abuser or the stigma associated with the arrest. They believe that most children who identify closely with their abusive parent would not benefit from seeing him led out of the house in handcuffs any more than they would from seeing him beating their other parent. Police officers may also fail to meet the needs of children by not inquiring of them or their parents regarding children's needs for safety and protection and by not providing the woman with information on available protection for her children (Davidson, 1994).

Surprisingly little has been written about direct police intervention with child witnesses of domestic violence. Available literature on police policies and procedures regarding domestic violence mention the fact that children may be present in the scene but neither discusses the role of the police officer vis-à-vis the child nor regards child witnesses as victims needing assistance (e.g., Buzawa & Buzawa, 1990; Goolkasian, 1986; see Davidson, 1994, for an exception). Children seem to be regarded as an extension of their mother and thus are assumed to be taken care of through the same interventions delivered to her—mainly victim advocacy services. A somewhat different approach is demonstrated by the London (Ontario) Police Force which, together with hired social workers, provides unique crisis services (Jaffe & Thompson, 1984). The service, known as Family Consultant Service, offers immediate support to the police in handling a complex situation with conflicting needs of family members, especially child witnesses to violence. The consultant staff, members of which are available around the clock, 7 days a week, can offer immediate assistance to victims and their children and provide an important bridge to other community agencies.

Another important contribution to an adequate police response to child witnesses is provided as part of the Community Intervention Projects (CIPs) established in several cities in the United States (Edleson, 1991; Gamache, Edleson, & Schock, 1988). CIPs coordinate criminal justice and social service intervention, with the goal of maximizing the immediate protection available to victims while empowering them and minimizing further danger or victimization. As part of the procedures in communities where CIPs exist, once an arrest has been made, the police department immediately notifies the local CIP office, and a battered women's advocate is sent to visit the victim at home and offer support and information. Time permitting, advocates also attempt to contact and provide services to women at home where police intervened but did not make an arrest (Edleson, 1991). It is not clear whether women advocates are specifically trained to help child witnesses or what part of their effort is devoted to helping the children. Moreover, an appropriate response of an advocate cannot replace an appropriate response of a police officer, but rather should supplement it.

Child-sensitive police intervention with children of battered women requires officers to be knowledgeable about the impact of domestic violence on witnessing children and the difficulties experienced by these children. Police officers should be further trained to address the immediate safety, shelter, and medical assistance needs of both the victim's children and the victim herself (Davidson, 1994). Specific procedures promoting the safety and emotional well-being of the children need to be designed and followed by law enforcement officers who respond to an emergency call. These procedures include the following (Davidson, 1994, Jaffe, Finlay, & Wolfe, 1984): (a) ask to see and speak with the children in the home in order to ensure their safety; (b) inform victims about their right to seek and obtain a protection order on their own and their children's behalf, including arrangements for removal of the abuser from home, child custody, possession of their residence, child support, and appropriate safe visitation; and (c) call to the scene an advocate who can offer immediate assistance to child witnesses and refer the victims to agencies that can protect them and help them with court assistance and other urgent needs.

Child Protection Services

Subjecting children to the victimization of their mothers is a severe form of psychological maltreatment. Children of battered women grow up terrorized by having witnessed violent and sometimes self-destructive behaviors and are influenced by negative and limiting role models (Brassard, Germain, & Hart, 1987; Garbarino, Guttmann, & Seeley, 1986). This section examines the role of child protection services in responding to children's witnessing of domestic violence as a form of child maltreatment. As mentioned above, children of battered women are also at an increased risk for being physically and sexually abused. Intervention with child witnesses who are also physically and sexually abused will be discussed later in this chapter.

Whether child protection services should at all intervene in cases of woman abuse is very controversial. The fact is that child protection services do not protect millions of children from the damaging effects of the violence they witness at home (Echlin & Marshall, 1995). There are at least four explanations for the failure of child protection services to respond appropriately to the needs of this population: (a) insufficient and ambiguous legislation; (b) lack of specialized knowledge; (c) an underfunded, overwhelmed, and overworked system; and (d) resistance by advocates of battered women (Echlin & Marshall, 1995; Peled, 1993a). Accordingly, the improvement of the child protection response to child witnesses depends on affecting changes in each of these four domains, as briefly discussed below.

Currently, there are no specific laws regarding child witnesses of woman battering at both the federal and the state level in the United States, though virtually all states include emotional abuse, mental injury, or impairment of emotional health as a reportable condition in their child abuse laws (Younes & Besharov, 1988). Although there appears to be common agreement that a child who witnesses woman abuse is emotionally maltreated, most state legislatures have failed to develop comprehensive statutory definitions instructing when and how child protection services should intervene in those cases. Even when such definitions exist, child witness cases are hard to substantiate in court and rarely go to trial. In Canada, 6 of the 10 provinces stipulate that a child who has witnessed woman abuse can be found to be in need of protection (Echlin & Marshall, 1995). However, these laws are problematic and rarely used, because the definitions they contain are too vague, too broad, or not inclusive enough.

Some advocates for battered women have resisted the development of specific legislation regarding child witnesses. They worry that such legislation will include mandatory reporting, which could harm battered women, especially those from minority populations, and may deter women from disclosing their abuse for fear of losing their children (Peled, 1993a). Mandatory reporting of child witnessing seems to be particularly dangerous for battered women and their children in light of the current knowledge base of many child protection workers. Battered women's advocates claim that most child protection workers have limited or no training on the issue of woman abuse and on its impact on children who witness violence. This is reflected in an inconsistent response to child witnesses that, at times, fails to recognize the battered woman's history of victimization and minimizes or ignores the responsibility of the violent parent (Echlin & Marshall, 1995).

Appropriate laws, an adequate knowledge base, and sensitivity to the rights and needs of the adult victim will not suffice to ensure that child witnesses of woman abuse are well protected by child protection services. Child protection systems in the United States and Canada are underfunded, overworked, and overwhelmed (Zellman & Antler, 1990). Under these conditions, child abuse cases are being triaged, and priority is given to cases that show visible and severe signs of neglect and abuse (Kamerman & Kahn, 1991). Presently, child witnesses of violence whose wounds are not physically visible and whose cases are harder to document and to prove in court are not likely to access the child protection system.

Child protective services are socially mandated to protect maltreated children and to prevent abusive adults from further abuse. Child witnesses of violence are emotionally maltreated and their needs for protection and support must be recognized by society and effectively met by its mandated agents. Hence, child protective services should support and collaborate with the efforts of battered women's advocates to protect battered women and their children from further abuse. The perpetrator of violence must be held accountable not only for the abuse of his partner but also for the emotional abuse of the witnessing children. The battered woman's struggle to protect her children from further exposure to violence should be supported in an empowering manner.

Sensitive and effective response of child protection workers to child witnesses of domestic violence demands the establishment of (a) mandatory training programs on woman abuse and its impact on children; (b) protocols for the identification, treatment, and referral of cases in which woman abuse is occurring; and (c) procedures for cooperative and effective work with battered women and their advocates, and with children's advocates in domestic violence agencies. Appropriate legislation may further support the protection of child witnesses' rights by child protective services and may facilitate the allocation of earmarked funding for intervention with this population. Battered women's advocates and child protection workers should work together on the drafting of such legislation to ensure its sensitivity to the needs and rights of both children and women. The willingness of battered women's advocates to collaborate with child protection services will partially depend on their conception of appropriate intervention with child witnesses of battered women.

Obstacle III—
Child Witnesses as "Secondary" Victims

Staff in shelters for battered women were the first to report the emotional and behavioral problems exhibited by child witnesses of violence (e.g., Alessi & Hearn, 1984; Haffner, 1979; Hughes, 1982). In 1981, only 172 of the 325 shelters for battered women allowed children to stay with their mothers, and only 3 provided children with counseling (Alessi & Hearn, 1984). A decade later, the U.S. national directory of domestic violence programs (National Coalition Against Domestic Violence [NCADV], 1991) reported that two thirds of the existing 1,200 shelters for battered women listed a children's program. These children's programs range widely in sophistication and complexity (Hughes & Marshall, 1995).

Presently, intervention with children of battered women is most closely associated with the battered women's movement. Children are usually identified as witnesses of domestic violence in battered women's shelters and community domestic violence intervention programs. These agencies provide the majority of domestic-violence-related advocacy, shelter, and counseling services for battered women and hence, also provide initial support to their children.

The battered women's movement not only has the advantage of immediate accessibility for many children of battered women but, more important, also provides a socially unique context within which intervention can be sensitive to the needs and rights of both child witnesses and their battered mothers (see Peled, 1993a). These make battered women's programs the natural and most fitting leader of a societal response to the plight of child witnesses of domestic violence, and a major partner in service provision to these children. However, current priorities and ideologies held by many in the movement seem to interfere with the realization of this mandate, that is, providing all children of battered women with the protection and support they need.

At least three issues need to be reconsidered by child-minded members of the battered women's movement: (a) the movement's commitment to the protection of children; (b) woman battering and child abuse; and (c) battering men as fathers. A critical analysis of these issues is offered in the hope of stimulating discussion that, in turn, will lead to an expansion and improvement of services to child witnesses of domestic violence.

The Movement's Commitment to Protecting Children

The battered women's movement was created to respond to the needs of battered women, both as a collective and as individuals. A definition given by Dobash and Dobash (1992), in a book analyzing British and American responses to woman battering, reflects the movement's mandate:

> Stripped to the barest level . . . the central goals concern the protection of abused women and change for all women: that is, to provide assistance to abused women and their children and to change gender inequalities in the domestic, economic and political arenas that form the foundation of and provide support for male violence. (p. 28)

Dobash and Dobash, mirroring a common view, present children as a secondary target group for the movement, victims by association; their mothers are seen as the primary victims of male violence. Another example of this approach is the introductory chapter to Yllo and Bograd's (1988) book on feminist perspectives on wife abuse. Children of battered women are omitted altogether in their suggested feminist analysis of woman battering. The child-minded reader gradually realizes that children are perceived by large parts of the movement as secondary victims, and as secondary clients. This perception of children's status within the movement is not only theoretical but also has direct impact on service provision. Putting it gently, the battered women's movement has not always been able to divert its limited resources toward the children; putting it more bluntly, some children of battered women do not get the services they desperately need, because priority is given to women's services (see also Jaffe, Wolfe, & Wilson, 1990; McLoed, 1987).

The secondary priority assigned to children may reflect a basic ideological commitment of the feminist movement in general, and the battered women's movement in particular, to women's (rather than children's) rights. Since its inception, the feminist movement has aimed to counteract the patriarchal presumption that women's responsibilities as wives and mothers supersede their personal needs and social rights, including their needs for independence and physical safety (Stark & Flitcraft, 1988). In accordance, the battered women's movement struggled to mobilize societal support for battered women as adults whose rights and safety have been violated, rather than as mothers of children at risk (Dobash & Dobash, 1992). This important and just cause seems to have led the movement to an ambivalent and, at times, detached treatment of children's issues. Nowhere is this more evident than in the movement's approach to child witnesses of violence who are also abused.

Woman Battering and Child Abuse

Subjecting children to the victimization of their mothers is a severe form of psychological maltreatment. As mentioned earlier in this chapter, children of battered women are also much more likely than children from nonviolent homes to be physically and sexually abused. Physically and sexually abused child witnesses have been found to have more behavioral problems than unabused child witnesses (Davis & Carlson, 1987; Fantuzzo et al., 1991; Hughes, 1988; Hughes, Parkinson, & Vargo, 1989; Jaffe et al., 1986; Jouriles, Murphy, & O'Leary, 1989; Pfouts, Schopler, & Hanley, 1981).

Findings from a nationally representative survey (Straus, 1983) suggest that 50% of the men who battered their wives also abused a child more than twice a year, a rate about seven times that for nonviolent husbands (7%). About half as many battered women (24%) reportedly abused a child more than twice a year, a rate about twice that of unbattered women (10%). Several other studies found that more battering men than battered women abuse their children (e.g., Gayford, 1975: 54% men, 37% women; Stark & Flitcraft, 1988: 50% men, 35% women) or use more severe violence more frequently against a child (Giles-Sims, 1985). Still other studies inquired only about the battering men's abusive behavior to their children (numbers are for physical abuse; Bowker et al., 1988: 70%; Layzer et al., 1986: 67%; Suh & Abel, 1990: 40%; Tutty, 1995: 52%).

Though most studies of domestic violence that also explore child abuse have serious methodological shortcomings (Saunders, 1994), and although several of these studies gathered data *only* regarding the man's abusive behavior, a common conclusion (and often, initial assumption) of writers is that it is mostly the battering men who are responsible for the strong association between woman battering and child abuse (e.g., Bowker et al., 1988; Hotaling & Sugarman, 1986; National Center on Women and Family Law, 1991). Such a definitive conclusion may be more appropriate when grounded in methodologically rigorous studies. What is more disturbing, however, is the tendency of most writers to minimize or even completely ignore data (and clinical observations) regarding battered women's abusive behavior toward their children (but see Petchers, 1995; Saunders, 1994; Stark & Flitcraft, 1988).

Battered women all too often are victimized both by their intimate partners and by social systems that not only fail to protect them but also blame them for being dysfunctional parents who neglect to protect their children. Lacking an understanding of the context and dynamics of woman abuse, service providers find it hard to accept that many of the behaviors of battered women cannot be adequately evaluated clinically in the midst of crisis and post-traumatic stress (Bograd, 1988). Stark and Flitcraft (1988), in an in-depth analysis of the relationship between child abuse and women abuse, conclude that battered women abuse their children because they are entrapped. They suggest that once battered women are empowered and feel that way, they will cease to abuse their children; in their words, "female empowerment is the best means to prevent child abuse" (p. 115) (see also Layzer et al., 1986; Walker, 1984).

Although agreeing with much of the above analysis and conclusions, I think it is problematic (though good intentioned and convenient) to assume that all battered women are potentially good mothers, and that the most effective way to protect children is always by protecting and empowering their mothers. By holding these assumptions, possibly justified in most cases, we are neglecting the emotional and physical safety of those children whose protection cannot be achieved, in the short or the long run, just through the protection and empowerment of their mothers. Because children are not an extension of their mothers, and because children's and mothers' interests do not always overlap, looking at battered women's parenting only through the lens of women's rights can lead to a sacrifice of children's rights. For example, Stark and Flitcraft (1988) recommend that practitioners support battered women's empowerment even when their children are known to be abused in the process:

> The battered mother can select the options she feels best suits her situation, even when she has abused the child. A woman may chose to remain in a violent relationship of course, but in general, empowerment is impossible while the woman and child are accessible to the batterer. . . . Extraordinary ethical and liability issues are involved in the decision to support a battered woman, even when she has previously put the child at risk or may do so, in a shelter environment, e.g., during the process of empowerment. *Even in the worst case, however, this is preferable to the present practice of sacrificing the battered mother to rescue the child* (often to a worse fate), and so restricting the mother's options that further child abuse and battering are virtually ensured. (p. 115, emphasis added)

We can no longer ignore, minimize, or define away the reality of child abuse perpetrated by battered mothers. As phrased succinctly by Ash and Cahn (1994),

> feminism is limited to the degree that it fails to give some account of the aspects of women which seem ugly or undesirable . . . if feminist theory is an "outsider" criticism, "bad mothers" are an example of an "outsider" to feminist theory. (p. 191)

Ash and Cahn further emphasize the need for feminist research to illuminate the contexts of the so-called bad mothers' lives and to confront difficult and yet unanswered questions, such as whether the civil and criminal law should treat battered women who abuse their children differently from male child abusers or other abusive mothers. Although we are asking and answering difficult questions about battered women's abusive behavior, we need to avoid the common injustice done to women by attributing to them solely the responsibility for children's protection and well-being. If we believe women and men are to share responsibility for the well-being of their children, we can no longer ignore the role of battering men as fathers.

Battering Men as Fathers

Feminist domestic violence researchers criticize protective services for focusing their attention and intervention efforts solely on mothers, the available, more manageable clients, and for making the abusive fathers invisible, not accountable for their abuse. Paradoxically, the alternative approaches they offer for protection of and intervention with children of battered women fail to include a reference to the role of battering men as fathers, and to their responsibility for their children's well-being (e.g., Bograd, 1988; Bowker et al., 1988; Dobash & Dobash, 1992; Stark & Flitcraft, 1988). This is also reflected by the common terminology *children of battered woman*—never children of battering men. Thus, abusers' responsibility and accountability as fathers is made invisible by the same people who point at the damage of such invisibility.

Current practice and ideology in the battered women's movement to a large extent let battering men off the parenting hook and regard women's needs for safety, protection, and validation as precluding parenting work with their abusive partners. Further, present intervention with child witnesses, whether in shelters or in community agencies, rarely aims at fostering better relationships between children and their fathers. Still, the empowerment of women as mothers entails an egalitarian distribution of parenting rights and responsibilities between men and women. As responsible parents, we should expect battering men who didn't lose their rights to parent to sustain a supportive and nurturing relationship with their children and to take part in the enormous effort required to heal their children from the effects of their exposure to and experience of violence. Supporting the role of battering men as fathers is important not only for reasons of justice and equality but also may contribute to the children's well-being.

Little has been written about the relationship of child witnesses of domestic violence with their abusive fathers. Recent qualitative research suggests that at least some child witnesses find their relationship with their fathers to be a source of pain, resentment, disappointment, and confusion. Children were described as being caught between two opposing emotions concerning their father: On the one hand they feel the violence is wrong, damaging, and frightening; on the other, they love and are attached to their father, the man who behaved abusively, hurt their mother, and violated social rules and norms (Blanchard et al., 1992; Ericksen & Henderson, 1992; Peled, 1995). Further, like other children in families of discord and divorce (e.g., Wallerstein & Kelly, 1980), child witnesses often find themselves in a conflict of loyalties, having to choose sides between their mother and their father (Peled, 1995). The difficulties child witnesses experience might be greater than those of children in nonviolent families, because the violence raises stronger emotions, poignant moral questions, and unbridgeable schisms between family members. A mother's pain and suffering may raise the child's empathy and anger at the abuser, but siding with the person who has the power and control in the family can be attractive as well. Moreover, in some situations, the child may perceive his or her mother's efforts to end the abuse as the cause of family separation and disruption, and identify with the father who had to leave the family, is all alone, and may go to jail.

It seems that tremendous emotional work may be required by children of battered women to make sense of and maintain their relationship with their fathers (Peled, 1995). Unfortunately, many children have to face this difficult task alone, receiving little guidance or support from the adults surrounding them. People concerned with the well-being of children of battered women can help them establish the best relationship possible with their fathers. Although some forms of intervention with some battering fathers will be impossible without violating the safety of the mother and children, much can be improved in current practices of both shelters and domestic violence community agencies.

Improving Existing Intervention

The foregoing critique notwithstanding, I believe children of battered women can be best supported by intervention designed and carried out by practitioners and advocates working within the battered women's movement. Based on the above discussion, recommendations for improving intervention fall into the four following service domains: children's programs, child abuse intervention (protecting children), visitation, and parenting intervention.

Children's Programs. Battered women's shelters provide children with safety, rest, and support but, at the same time, may be experienced by the child as a highly stressful environment within which painful memories are digested and difficult issues need to be confronted (Alessi & Hearn, 1984; Carlson, 1984; Cassady et al., 1987; Layzer et al., 1986). The needs of children in battered women's shelters are great and often require crisis intervention and ongoing emotional support, medical attention, interaction with educational systems and academic help, interface with the legal and child protection systems, and work with mothers on parenting issues (Hughes & Marshall, 1995).

Although growing recognition of the needs of children has resulted in more shelters developing special services for children, such programs exist in only two thirds of U.S. shelters and vary greatly in the quality of service provided. On the one end of the continuum might be a staff member who meets with the children occasionally in a child care role. At the other end might be a children's advocate with advanced training in child and family therapy who oversees a well-funded, secure program (Hughes & Marshall, 1995). Child witnesses of violence will not get the support they need in times of crisis until each and every battered women's shelter includes a quality children's program suited to support women's parenting skills and answer children's individual needs. This requires both the allocation of sufficient funding by public and private funding resources and the designation of children's programs as a high priority by shelter staff.

Most children of battered women do not reside in shelters at any given point in time but are living at home. Some of them continue for years to witness violence or live with the threat of violence. Others live with the memories of witnessed violence and its aftereffects, such as emotional and physical scars, separation and divorce, and financial deterioration. The cessation of violence is not sufficient for healing from its effects and related difficulties. Child witnesses of violence need emotional support both during and after witnessing the violence. Some children of battered women are traumatized by the violence they witnessed and require intensive, short- or long-term individual therapy (see Arroyo & Eth, 1995; Silvern et al., 1995). The needs of others may be answered through small psychoeducational groups in which children can "break the secret" of family violence (e.g., Johnson & Montgomery, 1990; Peled & Davis, 1995; Ragg & Webb, 1992; Wilson et al., 1986). Specialized individual and group treatment programs that are available and accessible to all child witnesses of violence should be a part of each community's social services.

Protecting Children. Because the interests of mothers and children may be in conflict, it is crucial that children be represented in the shelter by a children's advocate. A major challenge faced by children's advocates is the protection of abused children and coordination with child protection agencies. All staff members of a domestic violence program, but particularly children's advocates, must be clear about the appropriate policy and procedures for reporting abuse and neglect and protecting children from further abuse. An appropriate response to child abuse includes protecting the child from further abuse while also understanding the abuse in the context of woman battering, and empowering the woman by highlighting her strengths and capacities and allowing her maximum control over her own and her children's lives.

Any effort should be made to prevent a mother from removing (or returning) her children to a severely abusive environment, even if such an act interferes with her empowerment. This may imply helping a mother who chooses to remain with a partner, who abused her and her children, to find an alternative safe living arrangement for her children. In cases where children are abused by the mother, a careful assessment should be made to determine the likelihood the abuse will cease once the woman is safely away from her abuser (Saunders, 1994). Collaborative efforts of child protection services and shelters are essential in securing the safety and the empowerment of both battered women and their children. Such collaboration may include professional development workshops, case conferences, and joint client interviews (Cummings & Mooney, 1988).

Visitation. Separation increases the danger of abuse for battered women (Pagelow, 1984). Separated battered women reported being battered 14 times as often as women still living with their partners (Harlow, 1991). Children who were once witnesses of violence at home may become central to the conflict between separating couples (Henderson, 1990; Shepard, 1992). Separated battered women protect themselves from being abused and their children from witnessing this abuse through custody orders, protective orders, criminal proceedings, and tort suits (Zorza, 1995). Abusive men, however, were found to be far more likely to fight for custody and not pay child or spousal support than nonabusive men (Liss & Stahly, 1993; Taylor, 1993). Abusive men tend to construct fatherhood in terms of "rights" to children and may be more concerned with maintaining control over their children than with nurturing them (Arendell, 1992; McMahon & Pence, 1995). Enabling children of separated battered women to maintain a positive relationship with the perpetrator is extremely complex in light of conflicting needs, interests, and rights of family members.

Visitation centers, designed as safe places through which parental visitation is facilitated, were created in a response to this need. So far, such centers exist only in some communities, and the services they provide range from overseeing visits and child exchanges only, to a complex multidisciplinary organization leading a coordinated community response to issues of custody and visitation. An example of the latter is the Duluth Visitation Center, established and operated by battered women's advocates (McMahon & Pence, 1995). The center's ideology states that the harm done to child witnesses of violence cannot be separated conceptually or empirically from the harm done to their battered mothers. It is part of the center's role to intervene in and influence the process of reordering family relationships from the standpoint of those who had been harmed by violence. This puts the children's viewpoint at the center of the program's focus, but in a way that does not treat the children as separable from their primary relationships (McMahon & Pence, 1995). Visitation centers should be available to every woman who wants to protect herself while enabling her children to maintain a safe relationship with their father. A thoughtful and critical perspective is required to ensure that visitation centers' procedures and operation do not reproduce gender inequality and its destructive consequences for children (McMahon & Pence, 1995).

Parenting Intervention. Domestic violence and its impact on family members and family relationships raise significant parenting challenges for both victim/survivors and abusers. Many abused women find themselves in an almost impossible situation where, on the one hand, their emotional and physical resources are depleted while, on the other, they are aware of their children's growing needs for support following their exposure to the violence (Henderson, 1990, 1993; Hilton, 1992). It is not surprising, then, that maternal stress was found to be significantly related to behavior problems of child witnesses (Wolfe, Jaffe, Wilson, & Zak, 1985, 1988). Battering men are often less aware than battered women of the effects of violence on their children. Many perpetrators also see less of their children following the exposure of violence and parental separation. Nonetheless, efforts should be made to help battering men develop and strengthen their parenting skills.

Structured parenting intervention for battered women and battering men is usually done through parenting groups (e.g., Mathews, Matter, & Montgomery, 1990; Peled & Davis, 1995; Pence, Hardesty, Steil, Soderberg, & Ottman, 1991). These can take place at a shelter, at a domestic violence agency, through a community social service, or through a visitation center. Child rearing may be one of the few things a battered woman may perceive herself as having control over and, hence, any parenting intervention with battered women needs to be respectful, empowering, and acknowledging of their struggle to be the kind of parents they wish to be (Hughes & Marshall, 1995). Bilinkoff (1995) suggests the following four main parenting issues that need to be discussed and resolved by the victim/survivor: (a) using power and control, (b) making up for the absent father, (c) using the children as confidants or allies, and (d) dealing with her perception of her children's similarity to their father.

Although some battered women receive help with their parenting as part of their shelter stay or women's group, an often missed opportunity for assisting child witnesses of domestic violence is working with the perpetrator of violence (Mathews, 1995). Separate parenting groups should be made available and offered to all perpetrators of domestic violence who have children. Even "reformed" abusers should not be included in groups with victim/survivors, because their presence may intimidate and block participation by some victim/survivors (Peled & Davis, 1995). Perpetrators are likely to confront different parenting issues than those of battered women, among which are the following: (a) limited knowledge of child development, (b) shame and how to cope with it, (c) ability to have empathy for their children's experience of their violence, (d) stepparenting, and (e) willingness to make a commitment to nonviolent parenting (Mathews, 1995).

Both parents and children will also benefit from allocating time in groups for battered women and battering men to discuss the influence of witnessing violence on children and to encourage parents to participate in parenting groups. Parents' involvement in their children's individual and group treatment is important for facilitating their support and understanding of the child's needs and also to prevent possible tensions between parents and children as a result of the treatment (James, 1989; Peled & Edleson, 1992). Children's feelings and thoughts about their abusive parent are an important focus for intervention and children should be allowed to express them in a nonjudgmental environment. The (past) abusive parent's involvement in the child's treatment should be encouraged, and positive relationships between children and their abusive parents should be facilitated if that does not lessen in any way the safety of the mother and the children (Peled, 1995; Peled & Edleson, 1992). Such involvement may help child witnesses, who often seem to be struggling with continuing or recreating their relationship with the abusive parent.

Coordinated, Multisystem Responses

Stopping violence and healing from its effects are possible only through a coordinated, multisystem response (Peled et al., 1995). A multisystem community response to child witnesses of woman battering consists of efforts to prevent future violence from happening, to teach both victims (women and children) how to survive it while it occurs, to teach perpetrators how to end their violence, and to help all heal from the aftereffects. Although regarding the child witness as a direct, primary victim of the observed violence, a multisystem response maintains a perspective that situates the child within his or her family and larger social networks. Hence, intervention is provided not only to the child but also to the parents and others who take part in shaping the child's life. Finally, a multisystem response must attempt to change society's attitude toward violence and help victims/survivors of violence within a multitude of relevant social settings. These settings include but are not restricted to shelters, schools, community centers and youth clubs, religious and spiritual centers, health and mental health organizations, child protection services, police, courts, and the legislative system.

References

Alessi, J. J., & Hearn, K. (1984). Group treatment of children in shelters for battered women. In A. R. Roberts (Ed.), *Battered women and their families,* (pp. 49-61), New York: Springer.

Arroyo, W., & Eth, S. (1995). Assessment following violence-witnessing trauma. In E. Peled, P. Jaffe, & J. L. Edleson, (Eds.), *Ending the cycle of violence: Community responses to children of battered women* (pp. 27-42). Thousand Oaks, CA: Sage.

Arendell, T. (1992). The social self as gendered: A masculinist discourse of divorce. *Symbolic Interaction, 15,* 151-181.

Ash, M., & Cahn, N. R. (1994). Child abuse: A problem for feminist theory. In M. A. Finema & R. Mykitiuk (Eds.), *The public nature of private violence: The discovery of domestic abuse* (pp. 166-194). London: Routledge.

Bernstein, S.C. (1991). *A family that fights.* Morton Grove, IL: Albert Whitman.

Bilinkoff, J. (1995). Empowering battered women as mothers. In E. Peled, P. Jaffe, & J. L. Edleson, (Eds.), *Ending the cycle of violence: Community responses to children of battered women* (pp. 97-105). Thousand Oaks, CA: Sage.

Black, D., & Kaplan, T. (1988). Father kills mother: Issues and problems encountered by a child psychiatric team. *British Journal of Psychiatry, 153,* 624-630.

Blanchard, A., Molloy, F., & Brown, L. (1992). *"I just couldn't stop them"—Western Australian children living with domestic violence: A study of the children's experience and service provision.* Report prepared for the Western Australia Government Office of the Family.

Bograd, M. (1988). Consultant's response. In R. M. Tolman (Ed.), Case conference: Protecting the children of battered women. *Journal of Interpersonal Violence, 3,* 476-483.

Bowker, L. H., Arbitell, M., & McFarron, J. R. (1988). On the relationship between wife beating and wife abuse. In K. Yllo & M. Bograd (Eds.). *Feminist perspectives on wife abuse* (pp. 158-174). Newbury Park, CA: Sage.

Brassard, M. R., Germain, R., & Hart, S. N. (Eds.). (1987). *Psychological maltreatment of children and youth.* New York: Pergamon.

Burman, S., & Allen-Meares, P. (1994). Neglected victims of murder: Children's witness to parental homicide. *Social Work, 39,* 28-34.

Buzawa, E. S., & Buzawa, C. G. (1990). *Domestic violence: The criminal justice response.* Newbury Park, CA: Sage.

Carlson, B. E. (1984). Children's observations of interparental violence. In A. R. Roberts (Ed.), *Battered women and their families,* (pp. 147-167), New York: Springer.

Cassady, L., Allen, B., Lyon, E., & McGeehan, C. (1987, July). *The Child-Focused Intervention Program: Program evaluation for children in a battered women's shelter.* Paper presented at the Third National Family Violence Researchers Conference, Durham, New Hampshire.

Christopherpoulos, C., Cohn, A. D., Shaw, D. S., Joyce, S., Sullivan-Hanson, J., Kraft, S. P., & Emery, R. E. (1987). Children of abused women: I. Adjustment at time of shelter residence. *Journal of Marriage and the Family, 49,* 611-619.

Cottle, T. J. (1980). *Children's secrets.* Garden City, NY: Anchor.

Cummings, N., & Mooney, A. (1988). Child protective workers and battered women's advocates: A strategy of family violence intervention. *Response, 11,* 4-9.

Davidson, H. (1994). *The impact of domestic violence on children: A report to the president of the American Bar Association.* Washington, DC: American Bar Association.

Davis, D. (1984). *Something is wrong in my house—A book about parents' fighting.* Seattle, WA: Parenting Press.

Davis, K. E. (1988). Interparental violence: The children as victims. *Issues in Comprehensive Pediatric Nursing, 11,* 291-302.

Davis, L. V., & Carlson, B. E. (1987). Observations of spouse abuse: What happens to the children? *Journal of Interpersonal Violence, 2,* 278-291.

Dobash, R. E., & Dobash, R. P. (1992). *Women, violence and social change.* London: Routledge.

Echlin, C., & Marshall, L. (1995). Child protection services for children of battered women: Practice and controversy. In E. Peled, P. Jaffe, & J. L. Edleson, (Eds.), *Ending the cycle of violence: Community responses to children of battered women* (pp. 170-185). Thousand Oaks, CA: Sage.

Edleson, J. L. (1991). Coordinated community responses. In M. Steinman (Ed.), *Woman battering: Policy responses* (pp. 203-219). Cincinnati, OH: Anderson.

Ericksen J. R., & Henderson, A, D. (1992). Witnessing family violence: The children's experience. *Journal of Advanced Nursing, 17,* 1200-1209.

Fantuzzo, J. W., DePaola, L. M., Lambert, L., Martino, T., Anderson, G., & Sutton, S. (1991). Effects of interparental violence on the psychological adjustment and competencies of young children. *Journal of Consulting and Clinical Psychology, 59,* 258-265.

Fantuzzo, J. W., & Lindquist, C. U. (1989). The effects of observing conjugal violence on children: A review and analysis of research methodology. *Journal of Family Violence, 4,* 77-94.

Forsstrom-Cohn, B., & Rosenbaum, A. (1985). The effects of parental marital violence on young adults: An exploratory investigation. *Journal of Marriage and the Family, 47,* 467-472.

Frey-Angel, J. (1989). Treating children of violent families: A sibling group approach. *Social Work With Groups, 12,* 95-107.

Gamache, D. J., Edleson, J. L., & Schock, M. D. (1988). Coordinated police, judicial, and social service response to woman battering: A multiple-baseline evaluation across three communities. In G. T. Hotaling, D. Finkelhor, J. T. Kirkpatrick, & M. A. Straus (Eds.), *Coping with family violence* (pp. 193-209). Newbury Park, CA: Sage.

Gamache, D., & Snapp, S. (1995). Teach your children well: Elementary schools and violence prevention. In E. Peled, P. Jaffe, & J. L. Edleson, (Eds.), *Ending the cycle of violence: Community responses to children of battered women* (pp. 209-232). Thousand Oaks, CA: Sage.

Garbarino, J., Guttmann, E., & Seeley, J. W. (1986). *The psychologically battered child: Strategies for identification, assessment, and intervention.* San Francisco: Jossey-Bass.

Gayford, J. J. (1975). Wife battering: A preliminary survey of 100 cases. *British Medical Journal, 1,* 194-197.

Gentry, C. E., & Eaddy, V. B. (1980). Treatment of children in spouse abusive families. *Victimology, 2-4,* 240-250.

Gibson, J. W., & Gutierrez, L. (1991). A service program for Safe-Home children. *Families in Society: A Journal of Contemporary Human Services, 72,* 554-562.

Giles-Sims, J. (1985). A longitudinal study of battered children of battered wives. *Family Relations, 34,* 205-210.

Goolkasian, G. A. (1986). *Confronting domestic violence: A guide for criminal justice agencies.* Washington, DC: National Institute of Justice, U.S. Department of Justice.

Groves, B. M., Zuckerman, B., Marans, S., & Cohen, D. J. (1993). Silent victims: Children who witness violence. *Journal of the American Medical Association, 13,* 262-264.

Grusznski, R. J., Brink, J. C., & Edleson, J. L. (1988). Support and education groups for children of battered women. *Child Welfare, 68,* 431-444.

Haffner, S. (1979). Victimology interview: A refuge for battered women: A conversation with Erin Pizzey. *Victimology, 4,* 100-112.

Harlow, C. W. (1991). *Female victims of violent crimes.* Washington, DC: Bureau of Justice Statistics.

Henderson, A. (1990). Children of abused wives: Their influence on their mothers' decisions. *Canada's Mental Health, 38,* 10-13.

Henderson, A. D. (1993, March). Abused women's perceptions of their children's experiences. *Canada's Mental Health,* 7-11.

Hilton, Z. N. (1992). Battered women's concerns about their children witnessing wife assault. *Journal of Interpersonal Violence, 7,* 77-86.

Hinchey, F. S., & Gavelek, J. R. (1982). Empathic responding in children of battered women. *Child Abuse and Neglect, 6,* 395-401.

Hoffman, B. F., Sinclaire, D., Currie, D. W., & Jaffe, P. (1990, July). Wife assault: Understanding and helping the woman, the man and the children. *Ontario Medical Review,* 36-44.

Holden, G. W., & Ritchie, K. L. (1991). Linking extreme marital discord, child rearing, and child behavior problems: Evidence from battered women. *Child Development, 62,* 311-327.

Hotaling, G. T., & Sugarman, D. B. (1986). An analysis of risk markers in husband to wife violence: The current state of knowledge. *Violence and Victims, 1,* 101-124.

Hughes, H. M. (1982). Brief interventions with children in a battered women's shelter: A model preventive program. *Family Relations, 31,* 495-502.

Hughes, H. M. (1988). Psychological and behavioral correlates of family violence in child witnesses and victims. *American Journal of Orthopsychiatry, 58,* 77-90.

Hughes, H. M., & Marshall, M. (1995). Advocacy for children of battered women. In E. Peled, P. Jaffe, & J. L. Edleson, (Eds.), *Ending the cycle of violence: Community responses to children of battered women* (pp. 121-144). Thousand Oaks, CA: Sage.

Hughes, H. M., Parkinson, D., & Vargo, M. (1989). Witnessing spouse abuse and experiencing physical abuse: A "double whammy"? *Journal of Family Violence, 4,* 197-209.

Jaffe, P., Finlay, J., & Wolfe, D. (1984). Evaluating the impact of a specialized civilian family crisis unit within a police force on the resolution of family conflicts. *Journal of Preventive Psychiatry, 2,* 63-73.

Jaffe, P., & Thompson, J. (1984). Crisis intervention and the London family consultant model. *R.C.M.P. Gazette, 46,* 12-17.

Jaffe, P., Wolfe, D. A., & Wilson, S. (1990). *Children of battered women.* Newbury Park, CA: Sage.

Jaffe, P., Wolfe, D., Wilson, S., & Zak, L. (1986). Similarities in behavioral and social maladjustment among child victims and witnesses to family violence. *American Journal of Orthopsychiatry, 56,* 142-146.

James, B. (1989). *Treating traumatized children: New insights and creative interventions.* Lexington, MA: Lexington.

Johnson, R. J., & Montgomery, M. (1990). Children at multiple risk: Treatment and prevention. In R. T. Potter-Efron & P. S. Potter-Efron (Eds.), *Aggression, family violence and chemical dependency* (pp. 145-163). New York: Haworth.

Jouriles, E. N., Murphy, C. M., & O'Leary, D. K. (1989). Interspousal aggression, marital discord, and child problems. *Journal of Consulting and Clinical Psychology, 57,* 453-455.

Kamerman, S. B., & Kahn, A. J. (1991). Social services for children, youth and families in the United States. *Children and Youth Services Review, 12,* 1-184.

Layzer, J. I., Goodson, B. D., & deLange, C. (1986). Children in shelters. *Response to Victimization of Women and Children,* 9(2), 2-5.

Liss, M. B., & Stahly, G. B. (1993). Domestic violence and child custody. In M. Hansen & M. Harway (Eds.), *Battering and family therapy: A feminist perspective* (pp. 175-187). Newbury Park, CA: Sage.

Loseke, D. R. (1987). Lived realities and the construction of social problems: The case of wife abuse. *Symbolic Interaction, 10,* 224-243.

Malmquist, C. P. (1986). Children who witness parental murder: Posttraumatic aspects. *Journal of the American Academy of Child Psychiatry, 25,* 320-325.

Mathews, D. J. (1995). Parenting groups for men who batter. In E. Peled, E., P. G. Jaffe, & J. L. Edleson (Eds.), *Ending the cycle of violence: Community responses to children of battered women* (pp. 106-120). Thousand Oaks, CA: Sage.

Mathews, D., Matter, L., & Montgomery, M. (1990). *Wilder parenting manual.* Minneapolis, MN: Wilder Foundation.

McLoed, L. (1987). *Battered but not beaten . . . Preventing wife battering in Canada.* Ottawa: Canadian Advisory Council on the Status of Women.

McMahon, M., & Pence, E. (1995). Doing more harm than good? Some cautions on visitation centers. In E. Peled, P. Jaffe, & J. L. Edleson, (Eds.), *Ending the cycle of violence: Community responses to children of battered women* (pp. 186-206). Thousand Oaks, CA: Sage.

National Center on Women and Family Law. (1991). *The effects of woman abuse on children.* New York: Author.

National Coalition Against Domestic Violence (NCADV). (1991). *1991 national directory of domestic violence programs: A guide to community shelters, safe home, and service programs.* Washington, DC: Author.

National Film Board of Canada. (Producer). (1988) *The crown prince* [film]. San Diego, CA: The Media Guild.

Pagelow, M. D. (1984). *Family violence.* New York: Praeger.

Paris, S.(1985). *Mommy and daddy are fighting.* Seattle: Seal.

Peled, E. (1993a). Children who witness woman battering: Concerns and dilemmas in the construction of a social problem. *Children and Youth Services Review, 15,* 43-52.

Peled, E. (1993b). *The experience of living with violence for preadolescent witnesses of woman abuse.* Unpublished doctoral dissertation, University of Minnesota.

Peled. E. (July, 1995). *Children of battering men: Living in conflicts of loyalties and emotions.* Paper presented at the 4th International Family Violence Research Conference, Durham, NH.

Peled, E., & Davis, D. (1995). *Groupwork with children of battered women: A practitioner's manual.* Thousand Oaks, CA: Sage.

Peled, E., & Edleson, J. L. (1992). Multiple perspectives on groupwork with children of battered women. *Violence and Victims, 7,* 327-346.

Peled, E., & Edleson, J. L. (1996, June). *Predicting children's domestic violence service participation and completion.* Paper presented at the First National Conference on Children Exposed to Family Violence, Austin, TX.

Peled, E., Jaffe, P., & Edleson, J. L. (Eds.). (1995). *Ending the cycle of violence: Community responses to children of battered women.* Thousand Oaks, CA: Sage.

Pence, E., Hardesty, L., Steil, K., Soderberg, J., & Ottman, L. (1991). *What about the kids? Community intervention in domestic assault cases—A focus on children.* Duluth, MN: The Duluth Domestic Abuse Intervention Project.

Petchers, M. K. (1995, July). *Child maltreatment among children in battered mothers' households.* Paper presented at The 4th International Family Violence Research Conference, Durham, NH.

Pfouts, J. H., Schopler, J. H., & Hanley, H. C. (1981). Deviant behavior in child victims and bystanders in violent families. In R. J. Hunner & Y. E. Walker (Eds.), *Exploring the relationship between child abuse and delinquency* (pp. 79-99). New York: Allaheld, Osman.

Pynoos, R. S., & Eth, S. (1984). The child as witness to homicide. *Journal of Social Issues, 40,* 87-108.

Ragg, D. M., & Webb, C. (1992). Group treatment for the preschool child witness of spouse abuse. *Journal of Child and Youth Care, 7,* 1-19.

Roy, M. (Ed.) (1977). *Battered women: A psychosociological study of domestic violence.* New York: Van Nostrand Reinhold.

Roy, M. (1988). *Children in the crossfire: Violence in the home—How does it affect our children?* Deerfield Beach, FA: Health Communications.

Saunders, D. (1994). Custody decisions in families experiencing woman abuse. *Social Work, 39,* 51-59.

Schechter, S., with Mihali, L. K. (1992). *Ending violence against women and children in Massachusetts families: Critical steps for the next five years.* Boston: Massachusetts Coalition of Battered Women Service Groups.

Shepard, M. (1992). Child-visiting and domestic abuse. *Child Welfare, 71,* 357-365.

Silvern, L., & Kaersvang, L., (1989). The traumatized children of violent marriages. *Child Welfare, 68,* 421-436.

Silvern, L., Karyl, J., & Landis, T. Y. (1995). Individual psychotherapy for the traumatized children of abused women. In E. Peled, P. Jaffe, & J. L. Edleson, (Eds.), *Ending the cycle of violence: Community responses to children of battered women* (pp. 43-76). Thousand Oaks, CA: Sage.

Stark, E., & Flitcraft, A. H. (1988). Women and children at risk: A Feminist perspective on child abuse. *International Journal of Health Services, 18,* 97-118.

Straus, M. A. (1983). Ordinary violence, child abuse, and wife-beating: What do they have in common? In D. Finkelhor, R. J. Gelles, G. T. Hotaling, & M. A. Straus (Eds.), *The dark side of families: Current family violence research* (pp. 213-234). Beverly Hills, CA: Sage.

Straus, M. A. (1991). *Children as witnesses to marital violence: A risk factor for lifelong problems among a nationally representative sample of American men and women.* Paper presented at the Ross Roundtable on "Children and Violence," Washington, DC.

Sudermann, M., Jaffe, P. G., & Hastings, E. (1995). Violence prevention programs in secondary (high) schools. In E. Peled, P. Jaffe, & J. L. Edleson, (Eds.), *Ending the cycle of violence: Community responses to children of battered women* (pp. 232-254). Thousand Oaks, CA: Sage.

Suh, E., & Abel, E. (1990). The impact of spousal violence on the children of the abused. *Journal of Independent Social Work, 4,* 27-34.

Taylor, G. (1993). Child custody and access. *Vis a Vis: National Newsletter on Family Violence, 10,* 3. Canadian Council on Social Development.

Tri-State Coalition. (1986) *It's not always happy in my house* [Film]. Deerfield, IL: MTI Film & Video.

Tutty, L. M. (1995, July). *Research connections between spouse abuse and child abuse.* Paper presented at The 4th International Family Violence Research Conference, Durham, NH.

Walker, L. E. (1984). *The battered woman syndrome.* New York: Springer.

Wallerstein, J. S., & Kelly, J. B. (1980). *Surviving the breakup: How children and parents cope with divorce.* New York: Basic Books.

Washburn, C., & Frieze, I. H. (1980, March). *Methodological issues in studying battered women.* Paper presented at the Annual Research Conference of the Association for Women in Psychology, Santa Monica, CA.

Westra, B., & Martin, H. P. (1981). Children of battered women. *Maternal Child Nursing Journal, 10,* 41-54.

Wile, I. S. (1924). Children and this clumsy world. *The Survey, 51,* 471-486.

Wilson, S. K., Cameron, S., Jaffe, P. G., & Wolfe, D. (1986). *Manual for a group program for children exposed to wife abuse.* London, Ontario: London Family Court Clinic.

Wolfe, D. A., Jaffe, P., Wilson, S. K., & Zak, L. (1985). Children of battered women: The relation of child behavior to family violence and maternal stress. *Journal of Consulting and Clinical Psychology, 53,* 657-665.

Wolfe, D. A., Jaffe, P., Wilson, S. K., & Zak, L. (1988). A multivariate investigation of children's adjustment to family violence. In G. T. Hotaling, D. Finkelhor, J. T. Kirkpatrick, & M. A. Straus (Eds.), *Family abuse and its consequences: New directions in research* (pp. 228-241). Newbury Park, CA: Sage.

Wolfe, D. A., Zak, L., Wilson, S., & Jaffe, P. (1986). Child witnesses to violence between parents: Critical issues in behavioral and social adjustment. *Journal of Abnormal Child Psychology, 14,* 95-104.

Yllo, K., & Bograd, M. (Eds.). (1988). *Feminist perspectives on wife abuse.* Newbury Park, CA: Sage.

Younes, L. A., & Besharov, D. J. (1988). State child abuse and neglect laws: A comparative analysis. In D. J. Besharov (Ed.), *Protecting children from abuse and neglect: Policy and practice* (pp. 353-490). Springfield, IL: Charles C Thomas.

Zellman, G. L., & Antler, S. (1990). Mandated reporters and CPS: A study of frustration. *Public Welfare, 48,* 30-37.

Zorza, J. (1995). How abused women can use the law to help protect their children. In E. Peled, P. Jaffe, & J. L. Edleson, (Eds.), *Ending the cycle of violence: Community responses to children of battered women* (pp. 147-169). Thousand Oaks, CA: Sage.

9

Controversy and Change in Batterers' Programs

Jeffrey L. Edleson

A recent high-profile case involving the murder of a battered woman by her estranged husband has brought a deluge of inquiries, asking, Do batterers' programs work? Most of those asking have sought simple sound bites that can explain a complex issue to a startled public. Unfortunately, there are no easy answers to this question. In fact, most people who have studied batterers' programs hold mixed opinions on their usefulness and on future changes that might bridge the gaps between differing views.

This chapter examines the complexities of any attempt to answer the question, Do batterers' programs work? It starts by examining the term *works* and the various meanings people attach to this term when evaluating batterers' programs. It then looks at the published outcome data on batterers' programs and examines their results through the various lenses of the public debate on treatment effectiveness. The chapter concludes with suggested policy and program directions for the future of intervention with men who batter.

When Does a Program Work?

It is not uncommon to hear a practitioner, policymaker, or researcher stridently claim that "this program really works" and then hear an equally qualified and strident critic argue that the same program "doesn't work at all." Sometimes it almost feels as if one is listening to competing political advertisements. When discussing programs aimed at rehabilitating or reeducating men who batter, it is hard not to hear such divergent claims pertaining to a single program or to all such programs. One of the reasons for such divergent opinions lies in the fact that there has never been agreement among major stakeholders in this area about what may be defined as a program that works. How we answer hinges to a great degree on what changes we expect in violent men's behavior in order for a program to be deemed successful.

Criteria of Success

The literature is full of essays and published program evaluations that each use quite different success criteria. Most such discussions focus on outcome studies, and that will be the focus here. It should be noted, however, that many people judge a program's success on a variety of criteria other than outcomes. These include theoretical, ideological, moral, and political factors, with measured outcomes often accorded less importance.

A range of perspectives is identifiable even within the narrower focus of outcome studies. At one end of the continuum, some researchers have used *typically significant positive change* or statistically significant changes in a desired direction among participants (Neidig, 1986; Neidig, Friedman, & Collins, 1985) to claim program success. At the other end, others have advocated for nothing short of a transformation of program participants "until men are prepared to take social action against the woman-battering culture" (Gondolf, 1987, p. 347) and become an "accountable man" (Hart, 1988). These positions illustrate the ends of the continuum along which there are many positions concerning what signals a program that works.

The use of *statistically significant decreases* in violent behavior, or increases in other behaviors without linking them to violence can be very problematic as criteria for success. A group of men could, under such criteria, be successful participants if they have decreased their average violence from five to three beatings a week or similarly increased their average ratings on a measure of marital satisfaction. Or a large group of program participants, who decrease their violence by a few percentage points more than a comparison group, could also be judged successful under this criterion.

The problem with using statistically significant change as a criterion of success is that it may have little *practical significance* (see Bloom, Fischer, & Orme, 1995) for victim/survivors. That is, percentage decreases in violent behavior or similar increases in martial satisfaction or communication may make little difference to those who continue to receive or witness repeated assaults each week, albeit fewer than before.

Considering practical significance, most experts working in interventions with batterers agree that *ending* violent behavior is an important success criterion. Many also agree that ending threats of violence is a worthy goal. Most program evaluators have attempted to measure the degree to which men's programs end violent behavior, but only a few have examined a range of direct and indirect threats of violence (cf. Edleson & Syers, 1990, 1991; Tolman & Bhosely, 1991). It is more likely that greater attention will be paid to some classes of threatening behavior as states and localities adopt laws expanding the definition of illegal actions to include behaviors such as stalking.

A related debate concerns the almost exclusive reliance of most studies on the Conflict Tactics Scales (CTS) (Straus, 1979). This measure—and the many adaptations of it—is by far the most commonly used instrument in batterer program evaluations. Critics have argued, however, that the CTS measures only a narrow band of perpetrator behavior, to the exclusion of the effects that such tactics have on victimized women and children (see Straus & Gelles, 1990). Why are measures of the physical, psychological, and social effects a perpetrator's violence creates in women's and children's lives so frequently missing from program evaluations?

An expanded version of the CTS, which attempts to measure sexual coercion and injuries resulting from physical abuse, and a related Tactics Correlates Inventory, measuring individual and relationship correlates of violence, have recently been released (Straus, Hamby, Boney-McCoy, & Sugarman, 1995). There is still a need to go well beyond even these new measures in future studies that examine broader indicators of success, such as women's and children's experience of safety. Yet, one must ask whether we truly expect batterers' programs to create legions of "accountable" men who will act to repair the world they have damaged. Do we expect such programs to end men's use of manipulative behaviors, ones that may be characteristic of many intimate relationships where violence does not occur? For example, a common definition of psychological maltreatment includes the category of "using male privilege," in which a man excludes his partner from major family decisions and expects her to fill traditional role expectations in support of him (Pence & Paymar, 1993). Do we expect successful male participants of batterers' programs to become partners in truly egalitarian relationships, as envisioned in Pence and Paymar's (1993) Equality Wheel? Is this a criterion for success in batterers' programs or does it represent our larger vision of social change, only part of which can be achieved through social services?

The degree to which one goes beyond acts of physical violence and threats to define the meaning of success is where most controversy surrounds evaluation of batterers' programs. Many strongly criticize or even reject batterers' programs as incapable of bringing about changes that have practical significance for women and child victims. Those most harshly criticizing batterers' programs argue that ending violence and some threats is insufficient to create true safety for women and children. They argue that other forms of manipulation often replace violence but maintain the same system of power and control by the man over his woman partner and children.

Role of Batterers' Programs

A subsidiary question that arises and was alluded to above is, What role do batterers' programs play in the larger effort to bring about major and lasting changes in the way society defines healthy intimate relationships? Some critics of batterers' programs would likely argue that these programs must be an active part of the transformation of male-female relationships and, at present, they fall far short of such a vision. On the other hand, many policymakers and most funders of batterers' programs are more likely concerned with ending illegal, violent behavior, regardless of the degree to which the participants are transformed. Many people are in between these two positions. On the one hand, they recognize that unfair power and control may well be maintained even after violence and threats have ended. On the other, it seems inappropriate to expect, or even mandate through the courts, that certain men identified by social agencies (often lower-income and racial minorities) attend a program to become transformed when others, who are not violent but who may be regularly applying unfair power and control in their own relationships, are not also required to attend programs to make similar changes in their behavior.

Another way of looking at this subsidiary debate is to ask, Where does the responsibility of batterers' programs end and a social movement to change all men's behaviors in intimate relationships begin? Similarly, when does a man's participation in a batterers' program end and participation in a men's change program begin?

In summary, the ways in which one defines the term *works* in relation to batterers' programs will greatly influence the degree to which one perceives these programs as effective. It appears that there is a limited social mandate from policymakers and funders to assist men in ending the use of illegal, violent, and threatening behaviors. Unfortunately, these same decision makers have yet to come to the point of supporting large-scale social interventions aimed at changing many nonviolent men's controlling behaviors toward women. If such a time should arrive, it is very *unlikely* that psychoeducational programs aimed at a targeted subgroup of men are alone the most effective way to bring about the desired social changes in all men's behavior toward women.

What Is the Best Format for Batterers' Programs?

Just as contentious as the debate concerning outcomes are current discussions regarding the input that creates these outcomes. What are the appropriate format, content, and provision of programming for batterers? A great deal of debate has occurred around the issue of *anger control* and its relative importance in batterers' programs (see Gondolf & Russell, 1986; Tolman & Saunders, 1988). Related to this debate is the rapid growth in *state guidelines* that set parameters for and, in some jurisdictions, official certification of the structure and content of batterers' programs as well as the qualifications of providers offering such programs.

Programs described in the literature vary a great deal, but the predominant format for offering services to men who batter is clearly small groups of 5 to 15 men, the leaders of which are often but not always male. Most programs described are highly structured, focused on teaching behavior and attitude change, and last from 10 to 36 sessions (see Edleson & Tolman, 1992; Eisikovits & Edleson, 1989).

Outcomes That Meet or Fall Short of Expectations

Over the past two decades, a number of batterers' programs have been evaluated and the results published. These studies, although limited in scope, offer a glimpse into the types of changes achieved by batterers' programs. Evaluations of these programs have been extensively reviewed elsewhere (Edleson & Tolman, 1992; Eisikovits & Edleson, 1989; Saunders & Azar, 1989; Tolman & Bennett, 1990; Tolman & Edleson, 1995). Here, the focus will be on men's groups and the degree to which current evaluations shed light on the question, Do they work?

Batterer Program Evaluations

A review of these summaries reveals a consistent finding that in varying programs, using various methods of intervention, a large proportion of men stopped their physically abusive behavior subsequent to involvement in the programs. Reports of successful outcomes ranged from 53% to 85%.

For example, in a study conducted at the Domestic Abuse Project, approximately two out of three men randomly assigned to receive either structured educational programs or those combining education with group processing were reported not violent by their woman partners during 6- and 18-month follow-up periods (ranged from 62.1% to 67.7%). Men in these groups achieved more stable outcomes than did those randomly assigned to a less structured, self-help program. The study also found that 12-session programs achieved outcomes similar to 32-session programs. Factors including a participant's education and involvement with the court also influenced outcomes (see Edleson & Syers, 1990, 1991).

Favorable evidence supporting the use of batterers' programs must be weighed in light of other explanatory factors, and with a high degree of caution, due to many methodological shortcomings evident in the studies thus far reported. For example, lower percentages of success tended to occur in programs with lengthier follow-up and when success was based on reports by women victims rather than official arrest rates or men's self-reports. A major methodological shortcoming of the existing literature on group treatment is the scarcity of experimental studies, leaving open the question of whether intervention itself is responsible for change in abusive men's behavior. Another shortcoming is the near absence of qualitative studies that might provide a greater understanding of how men who change proceed to nonviolence. The qualitative method could also provide a greater understanding of the types of changes required of a batterer for victims to feel that their environment is safe.

Program Dropout Rates

The evaluations cited thus far mostly concern the rate of recidivism among program completers. Unstated is the fact that these programs witness large numbers of men who contact the agency but never complete the prescribed program (see Deschner, 1984; Harrell, 1991). A graphic representation of this case flow would resemble a funnel or cone, with large numbers of men entering but fewer and fewer staying with the program at each point along the way to completion.

In one recent evaluation (Edleson & Syers, 1990, 1991), more than 500 men initially contacted the agency during a 12-month period. Of these, 283 completed the intake process and attended a first group session, and 153 completed the program. In addition, approximately two out of three of those men for whom follow-up data were available were reported to be nonviolent. These data indicate that approximately one third (30%) of the men who initially contacted the agency and slightly more than half (54%) of the men who entered the program ended up completing the 12- or 32-session programs to which they were assigned. Finally, because two thirds of those who completed the program were likely to be reported nonviolent during follow-ups, in the final analysis only one of five (20%) of those who originally contacted the agency made it all the way through the program and were reported not violent during follow-up periods.

Consistent with these findings are the results of two national surveys of batterers' programs. Feazell, Mayers, and Deschner (1984) reported, in their survey of 90 programs, that one third to one half of the men dropped out after the first session of a program. Similarly,

Pirog-Good and Stets-Kealey (1985) reported data based on a survey of 59 batterers programs where they found that 48% of the men starting a program did not complete it.

Here again, *success* is a relative term. Those who examine these data see many shades of success and failure. On the one hand, some see that approximately two thirds of program completers are reported not violent for periods ranging up to 18 months. These people conclude that such programs are successful. Others, however, see that only one in five men successfully completes a program and remains nonviolent over the relatively short period of 18 months. They often conclude that these programs are a failure and wasteful of scarce resources that could be spent elsewhere.

The Future of Intervention With Men Who Batter

It seems, given the above review, that batterers' programs are often viewed within the context of a larger social movement to alter historical inequities in intimate relationships between men and women. This is healthy because it holds such programs accountable to a high standard. It often seems, however, that achievement of many goals of a larger social movement are demanded of batterers' programs. This seems unrealistic and probably undesirable.

Batterers' programs can be only one part of a much larger network of intervention in men's inequitable treatment of women—both physical and psychological. They are not the cure-all that some therapists promise but they are also generally not the dismal failures that others see. Batterers' program appears generally successful in achieving very targeted and limited goals with some men. We should not overlook this contribution.

A Social Movement to Alter the Rules of Intimate Relations

The future of intervention with men who batter requires several changes at different levels of the social ecology (see Edleson & Tolman, 1992; Eisikovits & Edleson, 1989). At the most macro level, there is a large gap—especially in men's participation—in terms of an international movement to improve men's intimate relationships with women. It seems that progressive policy change in the United States and other democracies most often occurs when backed up by large-scale public pressure on decision makers. Women's movements have been successful in creating change and will continue to have successes in the future. It is sad to see a lack of comparative movement among men. Men's movements, for example, in the United States, appear frequently self-centered and often portray men as equal victims of a rigid social structure. Informally, there may be well-publicized shifts toward greater sharing of household and child rearing responsibilities, but there seems to be little organized movement among men to take responsibility for our share in the victimization of women and to examine and change the very foundations of male socialization. For example, few men are willing to examine the role that violent behavior and a winner-take-all mentality in amateur and professional sports play in male socialization (see Miedzian, 1991). It is not that men alone have to bring about these changes, but experience with current efforts to end violence against women shows that the greater the popular pressure for change, the more likely policymakers are to listen carefully.

Given this larger context, batterers' programs struggle for several hours a week over a short period to counterbalance much of what men learn over thousands of hours of exposure to a popular culture over their lifetime. The winner-take-all mentality and a lack of empathy for those with less power seem to be resurgent themes in the public life of America and other countries at mid-decade. What is needed, but not clearly on the horizon, is a major social movement in which men take responsibility for their abuses of power—both large and small—and in which they join with a more mature women's movement. Many men would probably welcome a movement that would lessen their emotional isolation from each other and from their intimate partners; ironically, that very isolation among men is probably one factor that inhibits such change.

Expanding the Definition of Battering and Batterer

Changes at the policy level also need to include a broadening of the definition of what behavior constitutes battering and who batters. First, it seems clear that most policymakers, as expressed in the laws they pass, consider only the most severe forms of abuse to be the realm of public policy and social intervention. This includes various forms of physical contact, some threatening behaviors, and sometimes also harassing behaviors such as stalking. We have not added a wide spectrum of psychological maltreatment to our legal definitions of abuse. Some women report that although their partners might end violent behavior, they shift some of their control tactics to ones less often defined as illegal, such as threats and harassment. Again, it will take much more than a persuasive argument to convince policymakers that nonviolent abuses, such as the abuse of financial power by a husband, should fall within the realm of legal definitions of violence against women. We have an even longer journey ahead if we hope to persuade policymakers to use women's and children's definitions of safety to drive our evaluations of program efforts.

A related definitional issue concerns the spectrum of people we define as batterers. In many locations where laws exist to aid battered adult women, they are restricted to women who are married or living with their partners. Some laws have been expanded to include couples who formerly lived together, who have a child in common, and increasingly those who have been dating. There is still a lack of attention to the younger and older victims and perpetrators of intimate violence, although cases of sexual harassment in primary and secondary schools and of elder abuse have raised awareness of these early and later forms of violence against women.

Our language in discussing battering is also primarily a white, heterosexist one. This chapter has spoken almost exclusively in terms of men's violence against women. This is where most of the programs and research exist. Lesbian women and gay men who batter are rarely discussed; only a few programs that address such violence exist; and program evaluations are nonexistent. In addition, few program evaluations have specifically examined differential outcomes based on race, disability, and ethnicity.

There is a need to find a new language to describe battering—one that doesn't lose the issues of gender, power, and control but is more inclusive of same-sex couples and sensitive to the cultural context of people of color. The danger in stripping our language of gender is that the road is paved for others to argue that gender has nothing to do with this issue and that "women are as violent as men." These debates rage in the field. For example, a set of exchanges during January and February 1995, on the electronic INTVIO-L (Interpersonal Violence List) operated by the University of Rhode Island, generated more than 100 hundred heated electronic messages from around the world. The debate concerned conflicting interpretations of research findings on women's use of violence. Those arguing that women were as violent as men argued that violence is committed by both genders, and used the existence of violence in same-sex couples as examples to support their somewhat questionable views. It will be important not to lose the gendered essence of this issue in the professional language that is evolving.

It will also be extremely important to find a terminology that allows differentiation between meanness and abuse. We need to be careful to not move so far toward expanding our definitions of abuse that all negative behavior becomes abuse, and the significance of beatings and terror that many now experience becomes just one of many abuses we live with. Violent men, in their first encounters with batterers' programs, often claim that "I may hit her, but she is verbally abusive to me." By expanding abuse to include heated verbal replies, we may offer violent men a powerful self-justification for their behaviors. This also feeds an "everybody is a victim" reaction that can lessen the motivation for others to help battered women.

Victim Safety as a Success Criterion

Somewhat related to definitional issues are criteria of success. It is clear that a great deal of the controversy about the success of batterers' programs revolves around the issue that many victims continue to feel threatened and unsafe despite the fact that some men do desist in their use of violence. Future evaluations of batterers' programs must develop measures that reflect a greater sensitivity to the experience of victims and such sensitivity must be made a greater part of the public policy debate.

In some cases, regardless of the change in a batterer's behavior, the survivor of his past violence will never feel safe. For the most part, however, there are many behaviors that world societies do not *socially construct* as problematic, for example, male entitlement, but that can often lead to victims experiencing an abuse of power, albeit not a physical one. If we obtain an in-depth understanding of how a terror-filled environment is constructed and deconstructed, program efforts might be able to teach men not only to change their violent behavior but also to help in rebuilding an environment of safety for his present or former woman partner. Evaluations that are more sensitive to victim perspectives may shed further light on these safety concerns and provide both policymakers and program developers with the ability to respond by refining interventions.

Programmatic Changes to Increase Effectiveness

There also appears to be a number of changes that might improve current programs for men who batter. These include greater selectivity in what types of violent men receive what types of services as well as the role of power, control, and affect in men's programs.

Targeted Programming. Most programs for men who batter run standardized curricula in which a large diversity of men participate. These curricula seldom offer tracking of particular subgroups of men; for example, first-time offenders, men reported only violent with intimate partners, men who are generally violent, or men who are thought to be most dangerous. For example, there is some research to suggest that first-time offenders respond more favorably to both police and social service interventions (see Edleson & Syers, 1991; Fagan, 1989). Should programs either focus resources on or create specialized services for different types of abusers?

Related to the notion of tracking are recent studies that have attempted to identify typologies of men who batter. These include attempts by Dutton (1988, 1995), Gondolf (1988), Holtzworth-Munroe and Stuart (1994), and Saunders (1992, 1993), among others to empirically classify batterers based on a number of factors. Gondolf, Holtzworth-Munroe, and Saunders each generated three similar types of batterers. Gondolf labeled his groups *sociopathic, antisocial,* and *typical.* Saunders's typologies included *family-only, generalized,* and *emotionally volatile.* Holtzworth-Munroe's were *family-only, dysphoric/borderline,* and *generally violent/antisocial.*

There is a need for more research on typologies and for studies that would evaluate the usefulness of such typologies in separating groups of batterers for different types of social responses (Saunders, 1993). The typologies currently available focus on grouping existing men on the basis of measurable psychological and social attributes. It might be more useful for future efforts to focus on empirically grounded categories of how men decide to change or how they respond to treatment (see Tolman, Edleson, & Fendrich, 1995; Tolman

& Edleson, 1995). There is also a severe shortage of culturally sensitive programming for men of color (Williams, 1992). Agency structures and program curricula must be refined so that they effectively address men of color.

The Role of Power, Control, and Affect in Batterers' Programs. It also seems that many batterers' programs use social power and control to coerce batterers into behavior change. The threat of court sanctions often hangs over a participant's head and, as a group leader, one often wonders how effective some confrontations with group participants are in modeling the type of behavior we hope men will practice outside the group. In short, is our use of power and control in the groups resulting in poor modeling?

In a recent proposal to the U.S. National Institute of Mental Health, Roffman et al. (1994) argue that individual change will not occur until denial and minimization by batterers can be overcome. They draw on a Stages of Change model (DiClemente & Prochaska, 1982; Prochaska & DiClemente, 1983) as a way of examining men's readiness for change. This model suggests that men would go through precontemplation, contemplation, and preparation stages before moving to action for change. Roffman and his colleagues argue that batterers must be brought to a preparation-for-action stage before engaging in the curricula that most programs currently offer. They suggest a preparatory program, using Motivational Interviewing techniques (see Miller & Rollnick, 1991), to move men from denial and minimization to readiness for change. Contrasting traditional approaches, Roffman et al. state that "motivational interviewing incorporates empowerment strategies intended to reinforce the individual's sense of personal control without the use of abusive tactics," (p. 59) suggesting that men must feel power over their personal decisions before they will be willing to change their abusive use of what power they do have.

There is room in current intake procedures and program curricula to reexamine the means for motivating men to change. There is also room for reexamining the types of relationships that program staff develop with program participants and how that increases or lessens men's sense of isolation and alienation.

It has always also seemed troubling that abandonment scenes are the ones to which violent men tend to react most aggressively (Dutton & Browning, 1988). Yes, abandonment represents a great loss of control over a partner, and within a power and control framework, there is a strong explanation for these findings. But it also may be true that abandonment represents a fear for some men of even greater isolation. Do batterers' programs really reach out to the fears these men may be experiencing and effectively help them overcome these fears in ways that might result in less of a desire to control others?

Conclusion

This chapter has attempted to bring the sometimes heated discussions about batterers' programs into focus in a way that might help us examine future policy and program changes. Most people do not want to hear a multilayered and complex answer to the question posed at the beginning of this paper, Do batterers' programs work? They often persist in seeking a clear-cut and simple response that can be easily digested—the so-called sound bite. Answering this question in an honest way, however, requires a complex examination of the meaning of the terms *work* and *success,* the underlying assumptions of policymakers, program providers, and evaluators. A recognition of the wide diversity of social agendas represented among those providing the answers is critical. Perhaps that question—the one most often asked by the general public, reporters, funders, and policymakers—is not even a question that can be answered at this time or at any time in the future. Batterers' programs do appear frequently successful in ending violent and the most threatening behaviors among the majority of participants who complete a prescribed program.

As we move toward a variety of changes in batterers' programs, our social construction of the problem, and a macro strategy for changing men's behavior toward women, we must be very careful not to lose our focus on providing models for healthy human interaction and a safer world in which surviving victims of violence and all others can live in peace.

References

Bloom, M., Fischer, J., & Orme, J. G. (1995). *Evaluating practice: Guidelines for the accountable professional* (2nd ed.). Boston: Allyn & Bacon.

Deschner, J. P. (1984). *The hitting habit: Anger control for battering couples.* New York: Free Press.

DiClemente, C. C., & Prochaska, J. O. (1982). Self-change and therapy change of smoking behavior: A comparison of processes of change in cessation and maintenance. *Addictive Behaviors, 7,* 133-142.

Dutton, D. G. (1988). Profiling of wife assaulters: Preliminary evidence for a trimodal analysis. *Violence and Victims, 3,* 5-29.

Dutton, D. G. (1995, July). *Personality predictors of cessation of intimate assaultiveness after group treatment, and long-term year criminal recidivism of treatment completers, partial completers, and non-starters.* Paper presented at the 4th International Family Violence Research Conference, University of New Hampshire, Durham, NH.

Dutton, D. G., & Browning, J. J. (1988). Concern for power, fear of intimacy, and aversive stimuli for wife assault. In G. T. Hotaling, D. Finkelhor, J. T. Kirkpatrick, & M. A. Straus (Eds.), *Family abuse and its consequences: New directions in research* (pp. 163-175). Newbury Park, CA: Sage.

Edleson, J. L., & Syers, M. (1990). The relative effectiveness of group treatments for men who batter. *Social Work Research and Abstracts, 26,* 10-17.

Edleson, J. L., & Syers, M. (1991). The effects of group treatment for men who batter: An 18-month follow-up study. *Research in Social Work Practice, 1,* 227-243.

Edleson, J. L., & Tolman, R. M. (1992). *Intervention for men who batter: An ecological approach.* Newbury Park, CA: Sage.

Eisikovits, Z. C., & Edleson, J. L. (1989). Intervening with men who batter: A critical review of the literature. *Social Service Review, 63,* 384-414.

Fagan, J. (1989). Cessation of family violence: Deterrence and dissuasion. In L. Ohlin & M. Tonry (Eds.), *Crime and justice, a review of the research: Vol. 11. Family Violence* (pp. 377-425). Chicago: University of Chicago Press.

Feazell, C. S., Mayers, R. S., & Deschner, J. (1984). Services for men who batter: Implications for programs and policies. *Family Relations, 33,* 217-223.

Gondolf, E. W. (1987). Changing men who batter: A developmental model for integrated interventions. *Journal of Family Violence, 2(4),* 335-349.

Gondolf, E. W. (1988). Who are those guys? Toward a behavioral typology of batterers. *Violence and Victims, 3,* 187-203.

Gondolf, E. W., & Russell, D. (1986). The case against anger control treatment programs for batterers. *Response, 9,* 2-5.

Harrell, A. (1991). *Evaluation of court-ordered treatment for domestic violence offenders: Summary and recommendations.* Washington DC: Urban Institute.

Hart, B. (1988). *Safety for women: Monitoring batterers' programs.* Harrisburg: Pennsylvania Coalition Against Domestic Violence.

Holtzworth-Munroe, A. & Stuart, G. L. (1994). Typologies of male batterers: Three subtypes and the differences among them. *Psychological Bulletin, 116,* 476-497.

Miedzian, M. (1991). *Boys will be boys: Breaking the link between masculinity and violence.* New York: Anchor.

Miller, W. R., & Rollnick, S. (1991). *Motivational interviewing: Preparing people to change addictive behavior.* New York: Guilford.

Neidig, P. H. (1986). The development and evaluation of a spouse abuse treatment program in a military setting. *Evaluation and Program Planning, 9,* 275-280.

Neidig, P. H., Friedman, D. H., & Collins, B. S. (1985, April). Domestic conflict containment: A spouse abuse treatment program. *Social Casework, 66,* 195-204.

Pence, E., & Paymar, M. (1993). *Education groups for men who batter: The Duluth model.* New York: Springer.

Pirog-Good, M., & Stets-Kealey, J. (1985). Male batterers and battering prevention programs: A national survey. *Response, 8,* 8-12.

Prochaska, J. O., & DiClemente, C. C. (1983). Stages and processes of self-change of smoking: Toward an integrative model of change. *Journal of Consulting and Clinical Psychology, 51,* 390-395.

Roffman, R., et al. (1994, October). *Motivating abusers to seek domestic violence counseling.* Proposal submitted for funding to the National Institute of Mental Health.

Saunders, D. G. (1992). A typology of men who batter: Three types derived from cluster analysis. *American Journal of Orthopsychiatry, 62,* 264-275.

Saunders, D. G. (1993). Husbands who assault: Multiple profiles requiring multiple responses. In N. Z. Hilton (Ed.), *Legal responses to wife assault* (pp. 9-34). Newbury Park, CA: Sage.

Saunders, D. G., & Azar, S. T. (1989). Treatment programs for family violence. In L. Ohlin & M. Tonry (Eds.), *Crime and justice, a review of the research: Vol. 11. Family Violence* (pp. 481-546). Chicago: University of Chicago Press.

Straus, M. A. (1979). Measuring intrafamily conflict and violence: The conflict tactics (CT) scales. *Journal of Marriage and the Family, 4,* 75-88.

Straus, M. A., & Gelles, R. J. (Eds.) (1990). *Physical violence in American families.* New Brunswick, NJ: Transaction.

Straus, M. A., Hamby, S. L., Boney-McCoy, S., & Sugarman, D. B. (1995, July). *The personal and relationship profile.* Paper presented at the 4th International Family Violence Research Conference, University of New Hampshire, Durham, NH.

Tolman, R. M., & Bennett, L. W. (1990). A review of quantitative research on men who batter. *Journal of Interpersonal Violence, 5,* 87-118.

Tolman, R. M., & Bhosely, G. (1991). The outcome of participation in shelter-sponsored program for men who batter. In D. Knudsen & J. Miller (Eds.), *Abused and battered: Social and legal responses to family violence* (pp. 113-122). Hawthorne, NY: Aldine.

Tolman, R. M., & Edleson, J. L. (1995). Intervention for men who batter: A review of research. In S. M. Stith & M. A. Straus (Eds), *Partner violence: Prevalence, causes and solutions* (pp. 262-273). Minneapolis: National Council on Family Relations.

Tolman, R. M., Edleson, J. L., & Fendrich, M. (1995, July). *The application of the theory of planned behavior to abusive men's cessation of violent behavior.* Paper presented at the 4th International Family Violence Research Conference, University of New Hampshire, Durham, NH.

Tolman, R. M., & Saunders, D. G. (1988). The case for the cautious use of anger control with men who batter. *Response, 11,* 15-20.

Williams, O. J. (1992). Ethnically sensitive practice to enhance treatment participation of African American men who batter. *Families in Society, 73,* 588-595.

10

Expanding Sanctions for Batterers

What Can We Do Besides Jailing and Counseling Them?

Richard M. Tolman

As a result of successful advocacy efforts by the battered women's movement in the United States, many jurisdictions now treat domestic violence as a crime. As a crime, the response of the criminal justice system is to arrest batterers, prosecute them effectively, and then sentence them appropriately when found guilty. Given the nature of the violent crime they commit, and the increasingly strident calls of many Americans for harsh treatment of violent criminals, one would expect courts to jail batterers for their crimes. However, although police arrest many more batterers than in the past, in most jurisdictions few batterers actually serve any jail time. Courts mandate many offenders to some type of batterer intervention program either as a condition of sentencing or as a condition of deferred prosecution. This chapter deals with sanctions other than counseling or treatment. Edleson discussed the issue of batterer intervention programs in the previous chapter.

Traditional Incarceration

Incarceration of offenders takes place in the United States in the following three basic systems: the federal prison system, the state prison system, and municipal (principally county) jails. Generally, persons convicted of misdemeanor charges would serve sentences in jails rather than prisons, which house felons. Many in the domestic violence field promote incarceration as a sanction for batterers for a number of reasons. First, incarceration gives the strongest message about societal disapproval of violence and may provide a strong deterrent message to batterers who serve sentences. The knowledge that a community has made incarceration a predictable outcome of battering may deter even those who have not had contact with the criminal justice system. The incarceration of perpetrators may also help change the views of others. For example, police may be more willing to take action against batterers if they believe it might result in actual jail time (though the opposite could also be true). Second, by separating the perpetrator from his victim for a period of time, incarceration provides time for a battered woman to pursue her options in safety. Incarceration prevents direct violence from occurring during the period of incarceration. However, incarceration might not be a completely safe option, either. For example, some incarcerated batterers have arranged for fellow gang members to rape or beat their partners (Jill Davies, personal communication, January 1994).

Although incarceration might be an effective deterrent to domestic violence, there are barriers to its increased use as a sanction for batterers. Many states and municipalities face overcrowded prisons and jails (Kinkade & Jenkins, 1994), sometimes resulting in early release of prisoners to reduce overcrowding. For whatever reason, many judges also appear to be reluctant to give jail sentences to batterers.

Some justification for considering alternative sanctions for batterers also comes from the limitations of incarceration as a sanction for batterers. Jail and prison cost society a great deal. They are costly in economic terms to the community and can exact high social costs not only on offenders but also on their families. Incarceration may increase the hostility of some batterers or potentially increase their criminality by increasing association with other offenders or stigmatization as criminals. Incarceration has economic ramifications as well: It interferes with offenders' jobs and may limit their employability when released. Incarceration of batterers may also be unacceptable to some battered women because of the loss of economic support, their reluctance to separate from their partners, or other reasons. Some fear that battered women might limit their use of the police for protection if they believe there is a high probability that the call will result in prosecution and incarceration of their partners. Finally, we cannot ignore charges that courts do not incarcerate equitably, but rather imprison a disproportionate number of racial minorities and those without adequate financial resources.

Despite the potential limitations of incarceration in some cases, we cannot reject it as a sanction for domestic violence perpetrators. On the contrary, given the potential for deterrent effects, as well as providing a period of brief or prolonged safety for victims, it is important that incarceration be a viable sanction for domestic violence perpetrators. One of the major difficulties in relying upon traditional incarceration is the reluctance of judges to impose it as a sanction, however warranted. Rather than arguing against traditional incarceration, my purpose here is to explore what else we might do instead of or in addition to traditional incarceration. We should consider any alternatives that might be effective in stopping violence against women by their male partners. In addition to deterrent sanctions, we should explore options for providing restorative justice to battered persons. Restorative justice might be promoted for battered women, for example, by arranging for restitution of damages done to them, or reducing impediments to their personal freedom by arranging for abusers to leave a geographic area.

A number of other sanctions could be considered for use with domestic violence perpetrators. The following sections evaluate a menu of options of alternative sanctions used with other crimes that could be implemented for batterers. Courts have applied some of the options to batterers. In others, there are no current reports of their use as sanctions for domestic violence.

Evaluating Sanctions

Sanctions may be viewed as fitting into one or more theoretical perspectives about the criminal justice system. Four theories or perspectives have wide acceptance in the criminal justice system: punishment, deterrence, rehabilitation, and justice (Allen & Treger, 1994). Punishment or retribution expresses societal disapproval by making offenders pay back society for the harm they have caused. Deterrence seeks to bring about conformity with the law through the threat of punishment or other means. Rehabilitation brings positive change in offender's behavior by provision of activities that help improve the psychological, educational, or other characteristics of the offender. The justice perspective seeks to promote fairness, equity, reconciliation, and a correction of the harm done by the criminal activity. These categories have been slightly modified, with an examination of each sanction in terms of six categories roughly corresponding to these theoretical perspectives. *Punishment* is considered by examining whether a sanction is likely to have significant social costs for the offender. This social cost may either contribute to *deterrence* of the individual offender or provide a message to others, general deterrence. Each sanction is examined as to whether deterrence of individual offenders may occur as a result of *monitoring* and surveillance of their activities, or by *incapacitation* of opportunities to commit those crimes. The contribution of sanctions to *rehabilitation* of the offender is also considered. Finally, the potential for each sanction to provide *restorative justice* to the survivors of battering is explored. Table 10.1 summarizes each sanction in terms of these categories. Also highlighted are some key aspects of the potential positive and negative effects of each sanction for batterers, summarized in Table 10.2.

Modified or Alternative Forms of Incarceration

One type of alternate sanction modifies traditional incarceration, either by changing the pattern of continuous prolonged incarceration or by changing conditions of the incarceration. Two alternative forms of incarceration are examined here: weekend or work release incarceration and home confinement.

Weekend Work Release Incarceration

An alternative to traditional incarceration is shorter, intermittent incarceration on weekends, or at times when the offender is not otherwise working. These incarcerations would have the advantage of not interrupting employment. This might make victims who depend on their batterers for support more amenable to following through

Table 10.1 Presumed Mechanisms of Influence

Sanction	*Punishment*	*Individual Deterrence*	*General Deterrence*	*Incapacitation*	*Surveillance/ Monitoring*	*Restoration*	*Rehabilitation*
Traditional incarceration	yes	yes	yes	yes	Not applicable	no	if linked to Tx
Day incarceration	yes	yes	yes	partial	partial	no	if linked to Tx
Weekend incarceration	yes	yes	yes	partial	partial	no	if linked to Tx
Home confinement	partial	yes	maybe	partial	yes	no	no
Intensive probation	limited	yes	limited	no	partial	no	if linked to Tx
Community service	partial	yes	low	no	no	not to victim	possible weak effect
Batterer programs	no	yes	no	no	limited	maybe if successful	yes
Restitution	no	maybe	maybe	no	no	yes	possible

NOTE: Tx = treatment.

Table 10.2 Some Possible Positive and Negative Effects of Sanctions

Sanction	*Short-Term Social Cost**	*Long-Term Social Cost**	*Victim Help-Seeking*	*Victim Vigilance*	*Negative Male Bonding/ Anti-Social Norms*
Traditional incarceration	High	High if significant sentence	May be improved during incarceration	Appropriately less while incarcerated	High potential
Day incarceration	Moderate	Moderate if significant sentence		May be reduced inappropriately	High unless milieu works actively
Weekend incarceration	Moderate	Moderate if repeated			High
Home confinement	Moderate to high	Moderate to high	Could be increased	May be decreased inappropriately	Low
Intensive probation	Low to moderate	Moderate	Could be increased with outreach and follow-through		
Community service	Low to moderate	Low to moderate			Moderate if in groups/ Could promote prosocial norms
Batterer programs	Low	Low	Could be decreased	Could be decreased	Depends on group
Restitution	Low to moderate	Low to moderate	Could be increased if restitution provides resources		Promotes prosocial norms

*Cost to the perpetrator.

with prosecution. The time spent incarcerated could be used to prepare offenders for participation in batterers' treatment, or to reinforce skills and attitudes that are the intended targets of batterer treatment. Two types of weekend incarceration might be considered: one-time "shock" incarceration, and repeated weekend incarceration.

Therapeutic shock incarceration is defined as a one-time, weekend incarceration as a precursor to ongoing treatment or education. This sanction incorporates both a deterrent and a rehabilitative function. Imposing the sanction of a weekend incarcerated gives a moderately strong message about the seriousness of the offender's actions. Weekend incarceration could provide educational intervention and also prepare offenders for participation in ongoing batterer counseling. The weekend incarceration needs careful structuring to minimize the opportunities for negative male bonding and the development of antisocial norms.

Tolman and Bhosely (1989) studied the effects of a weekend intensive workshop for batterers, many of whom were mandated by the court to attend batterers' treatment groups. They found that the intensive workshop reduced dropouts from the ongoing batterer intervention that followed the workshop. Requiring offenders to stay overnight would make a stronger statement regarding their behavior, presumably strengthening the deterrent impact of the sanction. Overnight incarceration would probably not be necessary for the educational/therapeutic dimension of the sanction.

Although the term *weekend incarceration* is used here, some offenders might be appropriate for alternative incarceration during the week. The critical elements include permitting the offender to continue to work and keeping incarceration to a relatively short period. Repeated weekend incarceration may serve as a more serious restrictive sanction, giving a deterrent message to offenders and incapacitating them during the weekend. This may be particularly effective for offenders who have a pattern of abuse on the weekends.

Home Confinement

Home confinement limits an offender to a residence, often by use of an electronic monitoring device that alerts authorities if the offender leaves the location. This method would clearly be inappropriate for any offender cohabiting with his victim. Domestic violence provides contraindication for use of electronic monitoring as an alternative sanction for offenders convicted of other crimes. Such confinement could contribute to risk for women and children living in the home with the offender.

On the other hand, electronic monitoring of offenders who do not live with their victims might be an effective alternative. It would have the advantage of decreasing access to the victim and also providing a negative sanction for the offense. Electronic monitoring systems should alert victims, as well as authorities, if the offender is not present at the specified location.

An alternative form of electronic monitor requires the offender to wear a bracelet that warns a potential victim that the offender is within a certain distance. This form of electronic monitoring has the advantage of giving information to a potential victim that the offender is nearby, giving her the chance to take protective action, including fleeing or contacting the police to provide protection. The monitor may also automatically alert police.

Existing systems have the limitation that the victim cannot move around with the monitor. The monitor, in effect, confines the victim by her desire to stay close to the monitored site. Electronic monitoring has other serious limitations. It may give a false sense of security to victims who believe the monitor will warn them if the offender is approaching. Because these systems are not foolproof, the promise of advance warning may be detrimental in that it provides false assurances, which might limit protective actions battered women would otherwise take without the monitoring system.

Both extensive preparation for victims who desire use of the monitors and close coordination of their use with other community resources address some of these limitations. Electronic monitoring of this type might be very useful in providing evidence that perpetrators have violated conditions of probation or parole, or orders for protection. This advantage must be weighed against any potential risk to victims. Because this type of monitoring does not confine the offender, social cost to him is low. Used as a sole sanction, this method may not convey the seriousness of the crime of domestic violence.

Options Separate From Incarceration

Several sanctions emphasize substantial monitoring of the offender in the community. These include day reporting, intensive probation, and electronic monitoring. The rationales, potential strengths, and limitations of each of these options for batterers are considered below.

Day Reporting Centers

Day reporting centers are highly structured, nonresidential programs utilizing supervision, sanctions, and services, coordinated centrally (Curtin, 1990). Day reporting centers have several potential advantages as alternative sanctions for batterers. First, monitoring is intensive. Typically, centers require attendance at least three times weekly, sometimes daily. Some centers require participants to submit an itinerary that details his daily schedule, whereabouts, and purpose for those daily activities. Centers often require offenders to call in several times a day, and the staff calls clients to verify their whereabouts (Diggs & Pieper, 1994). Second, day reporting centers entail substantial time commitment. This time commitment and the loss of personal liberty entailed by the intensive monitoring exact a social cost that could deter subsequent battering. In addition, they provide time for rehabilitative programming. Activities in day reporting centers often include literacy training, job skills and search, and other life skills training.

Abuse-specific programming maximizes the potential for a rehabilitative effect of day reporting on batterers. Day reporting centers could provide intensive abuser services themselves or could collaborate with abuser service programs to provide on-site programming. Centers providing alcohol and drug abuse services could also provide a mechanism for addressing those needs among batterers.

Although monitoring in day reporting centers might be intensive, a domestic violence perpetrator still has the opportunity to reabuse his partner. Day reporting centers could also have other unintended negative effects. To the extent that intensive contact with other criminals could foster antisocial or pro-violence norms, the contact batterers have with each other in these programs could support rather than inhibit their abusive behavior. The centers must create an environment that rejects aggression and encourages ways of relating that support nonviolent resolution of problems.

Data on day reporting centers is lacking. One study of 14 day reporting centers across the country provided descriptive data and evidence of effectiveness based largely on interviews with staff (Parent,

1990). There have been no studies to date that inform the use of day incarceration with domestic violence perpetrators.

Intensive Probation

Intensive probation has many elements that make it a suitable alternative sanction for batterers. Many batterers fit the profile often used to determine which offenders are in need of intensive probation rather than traditional probation supervision. These dimensions include the following:

1. They are violent criminals.
2. Many have extensive criminal histories or long histories of abuse.
3. Substance abuse among batterers is prevalent.
4. Batterers often rationalize their crimes; that is, they do not share the justice system's view that what they did was wrong or criminal.
5. A large proportion of batterers coming to the attention of the criminal justice system is generally violent.
6. Some batterers are unstable as a result of unemployment, family disruption, or change of residence.
7. Most important, they have easy access to their victims. (Klein, 1994)

Intensive probation can provide more extensive supervision and monitoring of the offender than can other forms of supervision. Offenders may, therefore, perceive an increased potential for further consequences resulting from reoffense. Intensive probation also offers multiple opportunities for criminal justice system contact with victims. Monitoring offender behavior through ongoing victim interviews provides multiple contact points to encourage victim cooperation with further court actions. These contacts may create opportunities to provide additional services and support to the victims. If the court empowers intensive probation officers to initiate further consequences for violations of probation, then offenders and victims alike will get a clear message of the court's resolve to hold offenders accountable. This means, of course, that additional sanctions must be available to the officer, and the courts must be willing to use them. Such sanctions could include weekend incarceration, day reporting, home confinement, and drug and alcohol treatment.

Some evidence suggests that offenders view intensive probation of some length and intensity as more punishing than more brief jail or prison sentences (Petersilia & Deschenes, 1994). However, studies of intensive probation on other populations have not uniformly supported its efficacy (Byrne et al., 1989; Petersilia & Turner, 1992). It is an essentially unstudied alternative for domestic violence perpetrators. A key to the safe and efficacious implementation of intensive probation with domestic violence perpetrators is likely to be frequent contact with victims by the probation officer, the special victim advocate within the probation department, or both.

Restorative Alternatives

The following options emphasize social costs to the offender and provide a benefit to the community or to the survivor of the criminal action. These options include community service and restitution.

Community Service

Community service is an attractive alternative sanction because it focuses on the provision of prosocial services as a consequence of antisocial behavior. Presumably, the community benefits from the provision of the services, and the offenders pay a social cost for their criminal behavior (California Department of Corrections, 1990). This social cost may have rehabilitative aspects, as the offender becomes involved in helping the community in some way. The provision of menial services, like cleaning trash off the highway, might have a deterrent effect because it is viewed as demeaning and shaming. Community service often includes public identification of the offender, which might deter some from subsequent violations. Some community service work assignments may also challenge offenders and enhance their social or vocational skills (Maher, 1994).

On the other hand, community service is usually used as a sanction for nonviolent crimes. A problem might be that this association would give the impression to the community and to the offender that the court does not view domestic violence seriously. In addition, it would be inappropriate to place violent offenders in service roles where they might endanger others. Using community service in conjunction with other sanctions could address some concerns. In addition, placing limitations on the types of community service roles assigned to batterers minimizes the risks.

Restitution

Restitution as a sanction requires actions that can repair the material and emotional damage caused by criminal actions. In practice, most restitution dispositions focus on payment of money for damages resulting from crime (i.e., medical bills, property damage, or lost wages). The use of material restitution as a sanction of battering might have several positive benefits. Restitution provides needed resources to battered women. The requirement to pay restitution also sends a message to the batterer that his actions are wrong and must be corrected. Loss of income might provide some deterrent effect for future behavior. Some also argue that restitution can serve a rehabilitative function, because it forces the offender to make reparation for the harm caused by his action (Roy, 1990).

Although restitution in criminal justice settings has been primarily material in nature, we might consider other forms of restitution in domestic violence cases. Hart's (1988) description of accountable behaviors provides some guidelines for the types of restorative actions batterers might take to repair the damage their behavior has caused. She suggests that a batterer becomes accountable when he, among other things, enumerates the losses suffered by the victim and her family; agrees to limit contact with her, her friends, and her family; agrees to avoid the places she frequents; and provides her with plenty of space away from him.

Specialized court programs might be set up to negotiate these restorative sanctions. The process of determining actions to be taken must be carefully considered. Victims would need to identify actions they desired a batterer to take. In some cases, the court would have clear authority to impose sanctions on batterers. In others, restitution would be a more complicated process, where a process of negotiation and clarification between the batterer and victim would be necessary.

In cases where a batterer is showing a willingness to engage in a restorative process, techniques of victim-offender reconciliation might be used (Umbreit, 1994). Although others use the terms *victim-offender reconciliation* and *victim-offender mediation* to describe this process (Umbreit, 1994), more appropriate terms might be *perpetrator accountability conferences* or *victim restitution conferences.*

Numerous safeguards for battered women would have to be implemented in this process. Some victim-offender reconciliation programs typically include direct meetings between the victim and offender, though many restitution programs do not (Hudson & Galaway, 1989). These meetings presumably can have an empowering effect for victims, because they face those who have victimized them and detail the ways the offender harmed them. In the case of domestic violence, face-to-face contact must not be required and would not be necessary or advisable in many—if not most—cases. Shuttle conferences, in which a staff member interviews the offender and the victim and relays information between them as necessary, could be substituted. To maximize safety, technology such as video conferencing might prove useful in this setting. Participation would have to be completely voluntary for the victim.

The restorative process could not include negotiation of any criminal penalties or of any issues that would diminish the victim's rights in criminal or civil actions. For example, it would be inappropriate to use such a process to negotiate child custody or support payments. If contact with the victim could be controlled by an order for protection, then limiting the batterer's contact with her would not be a proper subject for a restitution conference. However, discussion of limiting his contact with other friends or families, or avoiding places where she desires freedom from his presence, would be fitting. Such proceedings must not be used to exchange dropping charges or orders of protection in return for restitution. Additionally, no agreements should be made that require any interaction between the parties to carry out the agreement. Otherwise, the agreements run the risk of providing the batterer with an excuse for contact with his ex-partner. This alternative would only consider restitution that goes beyond other sanctions typically provided through criminal court or other civil proceedings.

Staff involved in such restitution meetings must be acutely aware of the power imbalance between offender and victim and must carefully structure the encounter to protect the victim. This power imbalance might be addressed by provision of advocacy for the battered woman, either by an attorney or a battered woman's advocate.

Restitution agreements might include actions that have an emotional or symbolic meaning for the victim, for example, a written apology and a statement acknowledging the batterer's responsibility for his violent behavior and a statement acknowledging the specific harm he has caused the victim, her family and friends. Restitution that includes social and emotional goals would be carried out most effectively after a batterer exhibits some willingness to be accountable for his actions. In that sense, it would be a sanction delayed, pending progress in batterer treatment. However, material restitution or restitution imposed by the court without a batterer's participation could proceed immediately. Participation in good faith and living up to the restitution sanctions imposed would serve as indicators that a batterer has become accountable.

Rehabilitative Options

Specialized court-ordered intervention programs have been the primary method of rehabilitation used with men who batter. An in-depth examination of these programs as sanctions is beyond the scope of this chapter, because they are examined in detail by Edleson earlier in this volume. Counseling or educational programs for batterers attempt to change batterers' abusive behavior by changing their attitudes, teaching skills, ameliorating psychological problems, or other mechanisms.

Batterer intervention programs, in addition to their rehabilitative aspects, provide some monitoring and surveillance of batterers. They may keep threat of other sanctions salient for batterers. Failure to comply with intervention mandates may sometimes result in other, more severe sanctions being applied.

Risks associated with batterer intervention include the potential for collusive male bonding that can occur in group settings (Pence, 1989). False hope, inspired by the promise of gains made in batterer programs, hampers some battered women's attempts to leave the relationship or follow through with other criminal justice system actions. Using batterer intervention as the sole sanction for the crime of domestic violence may also diminish perceptions of the seriousness of the crime by the batterer and others in the community.

Courts often use programs for batterers as the sole sanction provided. Alternative sanctions presented in this chapter may be used in combination with rehabilitative programs. Intervention programs alone may be helpful for some men, but clearly, additional options are necessary for some, because large percentages of men reoffend even after completion of mandated intervention programs (Tolman & Edleson, 1995).

Conclusion

This chapter covered various alternative sanctions one by one, but the sanctions might be most powerfully used in various combinations.

Langan (1994) suggests that felons receiving intermediate sanctions be closely supervised through electronically monitored house arrest, placed under probation with intensive reporting features, drug testing, and/or additional penalties that could include some jail time, a heavy fine and community service. Such combined approaches may maximize the impact of the criminal justice system on the offender and make desistance of abusive behavior more likely.

The effectiveness of sanctions depends on their enforcement. Unfortunately, the probability is low that the court will rigorously enforce sanctions for batterers in most jurisdictions unless there is vigorous effort by communities to hold systems accountable for enforcement. Little evidence exists to demonstrate that community sanctions are commonly enforced (Doob, 1990). Evidence on intermediate sanctions for convicted adult felons placed on state probation revealed that 49% had not complied with their sanctions fully at the time of discharge from probation (Langan, 1994). Studies on police and criminal justice system response to domestic violence suggest that ongoing intensive effort is needed to keep systems in compliance (Gamache, Edleson, & Schock, 1988).

This chapter explored some alternative sanctions developed in the context of the U.S. criminal justice system. To the extent that advocacy efforts in the United States focus so clearly on the criminalization of domestic violence, this emphasis is certainly justified. This focus is limited as well and options for sanctions not tied to the criminal justice system must be considered. The applicability of sanctions developed in the U.S. context may be limited in other countries. As we consider the future of interventions that seek to directly change the behavior of batterers, we must continue expanding this list of alternative sanctions, further explore the pros and cons of the sanctions listed here, and address the applicability of these sanctions to other countries and cultural contexts.

References

Allen, G. F., & Treger, H. (1994). Fines and restitution orders: Probationers' perceptions. *Federal Probation, 58,* 34-40.

Byrne, J. M., Lurigio, A. J., Baird, C., Markley, G., Cochran, D., & Buck, G. S. (1989). Effectiveness of the new intensive supervision programs. *Research in Corrections* (National Institute of Justice Monograph No. 2, pp. 1-48). Washington, DC: National Institute of Justice.

California Department of Corrections. (1990). Community services in corrections.
Curtin, E. L. (1990). Day reporting centers, a promising alternative. *IARCA Journal, 3,* 8.
Diggs, D. W., & Pieper, S. L. (1994). Using day reporting centers as an alternative to jail. *Federal Probation, 58,* 9-12.
Doob, A. (1990). Community sanctions and imprisonment: Hoping for a miracle but not bothering even to pray for it. *Canadian Journal of Criminology, 32,* 415-428.
Gamache, D. J., Edleson, J. L., & Schock, M. D. (1988). Coordinated police, judicial and social service response to woman battering: A multi-baseline evaluation across three communities. In G. T. Hotaling, D. Finkelhor, J. T. Kirkpatrick, & M. Straus (Eds.) *Coping with family violence: Research and policy perspectives* (pp. 193-209) Newbury Park, CA: Sage.
Hart, B. (1988). *Safety for women: Monitoring batterers' programs.* Harrisburg: Pennsylvania Coalition Against Domestic Violence.
Hudson, J., & Galaway, B. (1989). Financial restitution: Toward an evaluable program model. *Canadian Journal of Criminology, 31,* 1-18.
Kinkade, P. T., & Jenkins, D. A. (1994). Problems in establishing alternative programs in existing correctional networks. *Federal Probation, 58*(3), 37-44.
Klein, A. (1994). *The Quincy court: Model domestic abuse program.* Quincy, MA: Quincy Court.
Langan, P. A. (1994). Between prison and probation: Intermediate sanctions. *Science, 264,* 791-793.
Maher, R. J. (1994). Community service: A good idea that works. *Federal Probation, 58* 2, 20-23.
Parent, D. G. (1990). *Day reporting centers for criminal offenders: A descriptive analysis of existing programs.* Cambridge, MA: ABT.
Pence, E. (1989). Batterer programs: Shifting from community collusion to community confrontation. In P. L. Caesar & L. K. Hamberger (Eds.), Treatment for men who batter (pp. 24-50). New York: Springer.
Petersilia, J., & Deschenes, E. P. (1994). What punishes? Inmates rank the severity of prison vs. intermediate sanctions. *Federal Probation, 58*(1), 3-8.
Petersilia, J., & Turner, S. (1992). Evaluation of intensive probation in California. *Journal of Criminal Law and Criminology, 82*(3), 610-658.
Roy, S. (1990). Offender-oriented restitution bills: Bringing total justice for victims? *Federal Probation, 54,* 30-36.
Tolman, R., & Bhosely, G. (1989). A comparison of two types of pregroup preparation for men who batter. *Journal of Social Service Research, 13,* 33-44.
Tolman, R., & Edleson, J. (1995). Intervention for men who batter: A review of research. In S. Stith & M. Straus (Eds.), *Understanding partner violence: Prevalence, causes, consequences, and solutions* (pp. 262-274). Minneapolis: National Council on Family Relations.
Umbreit, M. (1994). *Mediating interpersonal conflicts: A pathway to peace.* Unpublished manuscript, University of Minnesota.

11

Toward a Phenomenological Intervention With Violence in Intimate Relationships

Zvi C. Eisikovits
Eli Buchbinder

Intervention with survivors and perpetrators of intimate violence is becoming increasingly professionalized. This is part of a process of growing recognition that the phenomenon is a serious social problem that needs to be given visibility and skilled attention. Some people believe this will enhance the quality of intervention but others feel it will tear its soul out. Whatever the outcome, professionalizing the intervention should be seen as part of a political struggle to define who "owns" the problem. This will no doubt result in tension between various claim-making groups (Kanuha, this volume; Loseke, 1987), and will bring the attempts to intervene and control woman battering to a new stage.

It is expected that the near future in this domain will be one of turmoil and anomie. At such junctures, one can expect an intensification of conflicts of interest, along with the rise and fall of various pressure groups, ideologies, and modalities of intervention with target groups. As priorities change, funding will be awarded to some approaches and not for others. For instance, the assertion that the criminalization of violent men will necessarily lead to a decrease in intimate violence is being increasingly questioned (e.g., Berk, 1993; Buzawa & Buzawa, 1993), but alternatives to criminal sanctions are slow to emerge (Tolman, this volume). The debate is heated both ideologically and professionally and is critical for the major stakeholders who are competing for funds throughout the debate.

A Rationale for a Phenomenological Model

Why is a phenomenological orientation timely at such a juncture? This paradigm is appropriate first of all because of its descriptive power. Such a descriptive approach is based on the assumption of the legitimacy of multiple perspectives and competing explanations; it encourages a reflective stance operationalized by an ongoing active and critical examination of the various approaches presented.

Second, a phenomenological constructivist approach focuses on the multiple ways in which a problem is constructed, framed, and presented by some actors in specific contexts. Once we accept a multiplicity of perspectives, we assume uncertainty about the legitimacy of a specific one and treat it in a manner that keeps us from being blinded by conflict, flux, and emergence.

Third, in the process of accounting to ourselves and others for our perspective as well as for the perspective of others, we explicitly legitimize the multiplicity of perspectives and make possible a continuous dialogue from heterogeneous and often conflicting positions. Thus, we can regard both clients and colleagues with divergent positions as creators of meaning and as resources.

Finally, this perspective enables us to adopt a *both/and* rather than an *either/or* attitude (Goldner, 1992). Given the complexity of the phenomena, polar thinking needs to be replaced by an ongoing search for a path among complex and seemingly contradictory options. For instance, intervention with battered women usually follows one of two modes: one focusing on the psychological consequences of abuse (e.g., learned helplessness or the battered woman syndrome, as proposed by Walker, 1993), and the other on the social and political context of abuse and the strategies of women for surviving it (Bowker, 1993). Usually, commitment to one approach precludes using the other. The phenomenological orientation recognizes the relative contribution of both modes and maintains that they feed each other and enhance our understanding of woman battering.

This model will enable us to present a humanistic, client-centered type of intervention and can incorporate much of what has been learned by clients and professional and activist groups. This knowledge can than be synthesized in our model with a contextualized approach that accounts for the ways in which various environmental factors interact in the construction of woman battering in a broader social context. Further, the model will allow us to use a distinct theoretical orientation heuristically—as a guiding framework—beyond the level of the lay person's tacit knowledge and understanding while still refraining from imposing a perspective that precludes others. The phenomenological framework will be used here in a heuristic fashion in order to develop the intervention model. Further enrichment of the model will be developed from practice by a method similar but not identical to what has been termed *analytic induction* (Manning, 1991). In this method, one develops *practice hypotheses* through descriptive information from the perspective of participants in real-life contexts. These are then examined in subsequent practice situations. If validated, they lead to abstractions and theoretical formulations that incorporate the multiple perspectives derived from field data. Throughout this process, there is an ongoing examination of the ways in which problems are described, framed, and accounted for. The models derived through this process can be applied carefully to elucidate analogous situations, bringing the level of generalization to that of *pattern analysis* or middle range theory (Dobbert, 1982).

The purpose of this chapter is to utilize the various tenets of the phenomenological approach to structurally map out an intervention model, examine some of its dynamics, and illustrate it in various practice situations. Although this chapter focuses on the clinical aspects of such a model, the social action and community intervention dimensions can and should be designed on the basis of similar principles,but taking into account the specific macro-social forces relevant for such a level of analysis.

A Phenomenological Approach to Understanding and Intervening

All concepts presented here have a double usage. First, they reflect a way of understanding intimate violence and second, they are suggestive of ways of intervening with victims and perpetrators. We intend to address both of these facets.

We are interested in understanding intimate violence in the everyday world of those who live it, *from their viewpoint.* We intend to break away from deterministic perspectives, which tend to decontextualize violent situations by presenting them as extreme and highly deviant. We assume that there is no one true way to understand intimate violence. Instead, we, the participants in various social situations, create our own ways of understanding by assigning multiple interpretations to experiences. Throughout this process, people may choose explanations that are harmful and painful for themselves or others. For instance, men who are violent may limit their interpretations of joint life by excluding positive elements and becoming trapped in such a partial view. On the other hand, this approach may benefit them by justifying their violence. Similarly, victims may assign meanings to violence that trap them within the boundaries of the family, so that they end up focusing on their perceived need to cope with and live in violence. Alternatively, they may redefine violence as unbearable, thus facilitating leaving an abusive relationship.

The intervention model to be presented here suggests ways to understand how people experience violent events, how they construct them into a violent life, and how they reinvent themselves and each other based on the meaning they choose to attribute to their experiences.

Working with violent men and battered women is based on the assumption that socially constructed interpretations are located in a constantly changing context of daily life. Intervention is essentially an attempt to provide alternative understandings and illuminate others' perceptions of various acts. Context-specific meanings are suggested by illuminating the relationship between interpretations provided and the social and interpersonal context.

Finally, a reflective stance is expected and encouraged, under which clients are expected to provide alternative accounts for the meanings they give to occurrences. Consider, for instance, the case of a woman who suggests that violence against her was the outcome of an argument that got out of control. In intervention, we will examine the ways she frames the concept of argument: its components, its boundaries, how things get out of control, when they are not out of control, and many similar questions.

In the process of reflecting to the client the multiple meanings she herself has provided, the worker introduces her to the concept of plurality of understandings and shows her that her emotional, social, and family situation arising from violence may have prevented her from seeing the possible alternative interpretations. By doing so, we are attempting to give the woman the message that she does have the freedom of choosing meanings, which violence can temporarily curtail but not deny.

Subsequently, the worker may use the interpersonal process that occurs between her or him and the client to clarify the interactive and subjective nature of constructing interpretations. For example, if the client's partner threatened her with a knife, she may view this as loss of control and frame it as an argument. For the worker, the situation is one of life and death. The worker needs to bring this interpretive gap to a metalevel of generalization and explain the ways in which the woman seems to develop specific meanings, the difference between her interpretations and the worker's, and how this may affect present and future negotiations between them.

The focus in this stage should not be on any specific explanation but rather on the epistemology: the way in which one makes sense of the world in general. The multiple understandings acquired can be applied subsequently to other contextual variables such as gender, class, culture, and religion. We can then see how meaning varies regarding these elements. By doing so, we achieve a double goal: First, the situation is freed from its specific clinical context in which it takes place in the client's psyche and the treatment room; second, we demonstrate the process of deriving meaning together by negotiating among the multiple understandings we bring to the situation.

Applying Key Concepts of Phenomenological Intervention

Several concepts are at the heart of developing practice hypotheses in a phenomenologically based intervention process, including experience, reflection, self-imposed naiveté, the interpersonal context of violence, the emotional content, the symbolic quality of language, and how all this is expressed in narratives.

Experience

Experience, reflecting our awareness at a given point in time, is the basis of how people know their world and how they behave. There is a widespread misconception that experience is *inside* us and as such is irrelevant to the *outside* world. But when one is violent, he or she does not experience it unidirectionally, that is, only inward, but rather simultaneously inward and outward (toward someone else).

Thus, the experience of being violent or being the target of violence is always *situated in the world.* Experiencing violence as a perpetrator, as a victim, or as both is a way of being present in the world, rather than a symptom or an isolated pathological behavior. Further, we cannot understand violence against women without *locating* it contextually within the social and political environment. As Denzin (1984a) stated, we must remember that violence occurs in the context of a taken-for-granted world of rituals, rules, and timetables, in which women are subordinate to men. When these taken-for-granted understandings are broken, violence may be the chosen course of action to reestablish what has been perceived as the previous, more desirable reality.

To clarify the implications for intervention of such an approach, let us examine the concept of loneliness characteristic of violent men. Loneliness is organized in men's phenomenology as part of the violent experience and is valued in male culture. It is perceived as being associated with toughness, self-determination, and control over one's destiny. The "lonely cowboy," who is unsupported and misunderstood but motivated by some inner sense of injustice, is very much present in men's role image. When alone, the violent man feels intentionally isolated, denied access by others. He reflects this feeling to the world by defining hostility and violence as a way of surviving or reconquering the world, a way of doing justice. Therefore, violence becomes a distorted way of expressing his need to survive in an unjust world that understands little about what is right and wrong.

The intervention process with violent men needs to break the chain of survival-hostility-loneliness and bring to the surface alternative ways of being with others while also providing the men with relevant skills and knowledge. The skills of communication, conflict resolution, negotiation, and empathic role taking are examples. It is essential to teach these skills while taking into account the broader existential and cultural contexts related to the ways in which violent men live in the world. One must also consider the societal attitudes they have acquired and the ways in which they view male ideal roles.

Reflection

Key to awareness and experience is reflection—an ongoing cognitive and emotional preoccupation with self, others, and the world. When we are alert to our awareness, we are self-reflective. We must ask, then, whether violence is a *reflective* act, and if it is not, whether we should aim our intervention toward making it such. We assume that reflection and self-reflection are preconditions for assigning meaning to violence for self and others and for being able to both take responsibility and consider alternatives.

Active reflection is associated with *intentionality.* That is, we consider violence an intentional act by which actors choose to give meaning to their lives. The targets of intervention are the choices made and the ways these came about. For instance, the perpetrator's possible interpretation of his violence as a reactive or automatic reaction will not be accepted as a point of departure in therapy. Rather, the role of violence in the perpetrator's overall existence will be illuminated and a reconstruction process will start in therapy, aimed at understanding the man's need for specific meanings in which violence was functional. Alternative avenues for the same interpretation or alternative interpretations will be jointly derived.

For the battered woman, the process will clarify the impact of gender roles on her ways of interpreting the occurrences. For instance, her view of loyalty to the batterer and commitment to the integrity of the family may keep her in a relationship with a violent partner. When such considerations are brought to the woman's awareness, she will have a better understanding of some reasons for remaining in the relationship. The concept of intentionality will, in itself, provide a sense of empowerment to substitute for emotional confusion and weakness.

Self-Imposed Naiveté

This intervention modality is based on an insider's view. The therapist's activities are guided by self-imposed naiveté, which allows her or him to relate to violence as it occurs in the client's perception. The worker is expected to temporarily suspend or *bracket* his or her own interpretations and develop grounded categories from the material presented by clients.

The worker structures the client's experience in terms of time, space, and living with others. These are seen as categories less stigmatizing than the conventional psychopathological labels. Hence, they are considered more expressive of a person's experiential world.

It should be stressed that although our model draws these categories from existential phenomenological psychology, it expands them to the social structural level. For instance, in trying to assess the attitudes of batterers, we use temporal or spatial categories to show how they impact on his ways of relating to his partner and also what they mean in terms of living in the world with other members of the opposite sex. These time- and space-related categories are useful in various stages of therapy. For example, a man may state that he "has no time left," that he is "running out of time," or that their relationship is running out of time. What is common among these statements is that the man experiences a sense of urgency associated with pressure to act, which can be expressed in violence. By working on the man's perception of time, his translation of his sense of urgency into pressure and violence, and the factors that may phenomenologically stretch his sense of time, the therapist may provide him with important experiential controls over his violence.

Interpersonal Context

Violence is experienced and related to others invariably in an interpersonal context. Meanings of violence are *coconstituted* in the dialectical process among the intimates. This is not to say that violence is necessarily the result of interaction, but rather that both perpetrators' and survivors' behavior is inherently interpersonal. There is a joint reality among all intimates that is created and recreated constantly in the process of negotiating their daily life. Their common routine is based on the interpretations that are agreed upon. In the process of creating their joint reality, they reaffirm each other.

When violence takes place, the need for a joint reality becomes even more acute on two levels: First, there is a need to come to a tentative agreement about each other's understandings of violence; and second, there is a need to agree on a joint framework for interpreting violence and the way it relates to their overall life. Many battered women describe feeling compassionate toward the perpetrator as a means to survive in violence, to attenuate its severity, and to balance it with positive feelings. A battered woman, who knows about her partner's either being witness to, or being a victim of violence in his family of origin, or both, and empathizes with him is able not only to identify with his story but also to accept it as her own in accounting for violence. In this way, the woman chooses to become part of his story and to make her present life continuous with his past history. His suffering is hers, and her suffering is attenuated by his and thus becomes bearable.

The couple needs to develop a joint explanation for the occurrence of violence that is acceptable to both partners. They may agree that there is a predictable sequence of events that leads to uncontrolled escalation and violence. For instance, they may agree that every time someone from the other's family interferes with their lives, the commitment of one partner to the joint meaning of the couple is broken and escalation becomes inevitable. By making violence predictable based on a joint explanation, the couple prepares for de-escalation and a solution: "Be more committed to our couplehood, place clear boundaries between ourselves and others, and violence will be avoided."

Intervention is geared toward understanding the processes. It should also be geared toward creating an active crisis in the jointly constructed meaning. For example, if she would stop empathizing with his plight, they would need to renegotiate the interpretation of his violence in a manner that clarifies his responsibility for being violent and hers to protect herself. This may address the issue of the boundaries of their mutual responsibility as a basis for living together. It is often difficult to deal with the element of responsibility, because most participants cannot relate to components of their experiences outside an interpersonal framework. It is in this context that we need to explore and expose men's accounts of their violence, such as "a response to her provocations," along with women's explanations of their decision to remain in violent relationships, such as, "he loves [her] and thus gets more angry at [her] than at others."

Violence as an Emotional Phenomenon

Violence is essentially an emotional phenomenon. For a more complete analysis of intimate violence as emotion, see Denzin (1984b),

Retzinger (1991), and Scheff and Retzinger (1991). It is associated with attempts to use physical or emotional force and coercion to *regain* something essentially emotional that is perceived as *lost* to the self (Denzin, 1984a). Four dimensions of emotions bear relevance to a phenomenological understanding of persons involved in intimate violence.

First, although emotions are at the heart of violence, there is little if any ongoing awareness and reflection on the part of those involved concerning their emotional states. Thus, emotions involved may be totally distorted and misinterpreted. For instance, when a battered woman behaves fearfully but excludes from her phenomenological field of experience the sense of fear, one has to understand how and for what purpose such exclusion was done. Also, there is a need to assess the potential risk, or benefit, or both of such emotional attitude. This information may guide the therapist concerning the ways in which fear can be made part of the battered woman's emotional context without producing harm. Such understanding is particularly important when the worker is encouraging a woman to apply for a restraining order. Her experiencing fear can be influenced in such instances by whether the man is violent in other contexts than the home, whether he has a history of general violence, and the like.

Second, when those involved in a relationship where violence exists do identify their emotions, they tend to oversimplify and point out one specific feeling or layer of emotionality without awareness of the complexity of their total emotional experience. For instance, when couples seek help for violence but want to remain together, they may expand on feelings that perpetuate the status quo and keep them together (e.g., loyalty and commitment) at the expense of negative feelings such as anger, jealousy, hatred, and fear. In such instances, intervention needs to address the whole range of feelings while helping the partners to contain them and showing them how accurate emotional communication may strengthen their bond rather than destroying it. In addition, this would both legitimize women's expression of negative feelings arising from being victimized and enhance a sense of strength by expressing them directly.

Third, emotions are gender-specific; that is, men and women have different emotions, which lead to attribution of different meanings to the same event and hence to different behavioral reactions. For instance, batterers have been known to experience "emotional funnel" (e.g., Long, 1987), with anger and rage as the core feelings experienced. These are accepted socially as masculine emotions and are thus seen as more normative than fear of abandonment, shame, and failure.

The role of the therapist in such instances is to help the man understand the whole range of feelings he experiences and be able to differentiate between them. Also, the man needs to legitimize such feelings in the context of gender socialization and reframe them as a process leading to positive power.

Fourth, emotions are simultaneously self- and other-directed and locate the protagonists in a field of emotional social interaction. For instance, much has been written lately about shame as a core feeling associated with intimate violence and its aftermath (e.g., Balcom, 1991). For batterers, shame is an emotional experience that places them in a position of inferiority and vulnerability on the personal, interpersonal, and social levels. The man judges himself as weak and a loser, and his partner as a source of his vulnerability. Socially, he experiences himself as a deviant who is emasculated by his acts. For the woman, shame is a source of her victimized position. She may judge herself as provoking the violence and feel guilty for staying in it. She may also perceive herself as incompetent and unable to protect her children and herself. To avoid the social consequences of her shame, she may keep the violence a secret and not turn for support or help to her environment.

In the process of forced self-evaluation, violence and its consequences always reflect, threaten, and diminish the self. Hence, there is an inherent failure in violence that produces escalation, as the violent person and his victim attempt repeatedly to establish control and by so doing destroy the relationship they intend to control.

It is essential that therapy break this vicious cycle. The sense of shame arising from the experience of failure will have to be brought to the surface, and the self-defeating pattern of attempting to achieve control by the use of force needs to be replaced by more positive and noncontrolling behavior. As a precondition for such substitution, therapy should be aimed at fostering self-affirmation based on valuing the ability to identify feelings and situations that are generating shame, and choosing alternative emotions and behaviors.

Symbolic Quality of Language

The key medium for the creation of meaning is language. By its symbolic quality, language enables people to organize, describe, and signify their experiences, behaviors, and overall existence (e.g., Berger

& Kellner, 1975). Language does not simply communicate but also creates reality. Thus, it is both descriptive and prescriptive of expectations. Through language, we label and frame experience and by so doing we direct and redirect them (Akillas & Efran, 1989; Efran, 1994).

A case in point is the way that couples who live in violence develop their individual and joint accounts for what takes place. In a study of cohabiting Israeli couples in which the man was violent (see Eisikovits & Edleson, 1986), spouses were interviewed separately and showed—in an unpublished analysis—a great deal of similarity in their accounts of the causes and the development of violence. There seems to be an ongoing negotiation, which ultimately brings about a joint language and categories of interpretations that reflect their life in violence. Another example is the development of a stable linguistic structure among batterers. In another study (Eisikovits & Buchbinder, 1995), we found that batterers use a metaphoric structure describing inward- and outward-directed wars, portraying the self as dangerous space, and subsequently signaling the end of violence by metaphors of de-escalation and balancing.

In light of the above, an in-depth understanding of the language used by clients is critical in therapy. Through language, we may both understand the subjective interpretations of the clients' world and attempt to induce change in these understandings. Achieving change in language may lead to new meanings, which may provide a whole new behavioral repertoire. Talking nonviolently or changing one's manner of interpretation in a way that recognizes the responsibility for violence is likely to lead to nonviolent behaviors.

Narratives

Clients' narratives of their life story are essential because they organize and integrate their experiences historically and thus influence what takes place in their present-day lives. In the ongoing process of creating and recreating their lives, people tend to present a *coherent and plausible* story line. One's life story is a valuable ecological tool, because it expresses the sense of self in a given social context, the strategies to communicate this sense to audiences, and a person's claims for membership in a social group.

Formulating a narrative about violence is intrinsically related to the teller's entire life, in which violence is but a part. When the story of violence is told, the person needs to adjust his or her entire life history to accommodate it. By the same token, when violence stops, the person involved will need to reframe his or her life history to make it plausible without it. The teller's account is time- and history-bound, and without these dimensions its specific parts cannot be understood. By attempting to present a coherent story, people are also implicitly describing the norms and values of the social groups in which they claim membership (Riessman, 1994).

Such reframings reflect the violent person's changing perceptions of his norms and attitudes during the intervention process. For example, if a man starts out by explaining how he became violent due to his wife's behavior and moves on to discuss his attitudes as he learned them at home, we need to locate his narrative historically on the basis of the expectations he learned concerning women's place in the family, and their role and position in the power structure of the family and society in general. For a man who believes in the subordinate position of his wife, her behavior may be interpreted as a breach of the social and interpersonal contract that he took for granted. This, along with a sense of injustice, provides ample grounds for violence as a tool to maintain the status quo.

The narrative and its structure are helpful intervention tools on several levels. First, the therapist needs to constantly be aware of the continuity and discontinuity between the specific narratives of violence and the teller's complete life story. The teller needs to be helped to generate an alternative life story in which there is no place for violence.

Second, we are often flooded by enormous amounts of information provided in the intervention process. The use of a structure in analyzing narratives may provide us with an opportunity to impose order on the clinical data without distorting or oversimplifying it. A good example is Labov's (1982) structural categories, which include an abstract or a summary; orientation regarding time, space, and participants; a typology of actions and events; an evaluative part, which gives us clues regarding the significance of a particular sequencing for the teller; and a solution and a coda, which return the whole narrative to the present. The worker should expect variation in the content and structure of the narratives and should use the orienting dimensions given above heuristically to refine his or her model of practice from case to case, following the logic of analytic induction.

Conclusion

In summary, phenomenological intervention, as suggested here, needs to address several dimensions simultaneously. First, the worker needs to place high emphasis on insiders' descriptions and acquire a set of listening skills permeated by an empathic and reflective attitude. By bracketing his or her preconceived ideas, theories, and values, the worker is expected to develop an interpretive openness. This will enable her or him to experience at least partially the subjective meanings attributed to events by clients. Also, specific events need to be placed in their context within the client's life story, which will help situate experiences historically. The worker needs to search for the ways in which the clients construct their intentionality. This can be done by understanding how clients direct and translate a range of emotions in their experiential world and how they use language to describe and prescribe their feelings, perceptions, and actions.

It is essential to understand violence as simultaneously self- and other-directed. Perpetrators and victims, although seemingly representing diametrically opposite interests, are inextricably tied together as they create interpretations that make sense to both.

References

Akillas, E., & Efran, J. (1989). Internal conflict, language and metaphor: Implications for psychotherapy. *Journal of Contemporary Psychotherapy, 19,* 149-159.

Balcom, D. (1991). Shame and violence: Considerations in couples' treatment. *Journal of Independent Social Work, 5,* 165-181.

Berger, P., & Kellner, H. (1975). Marriage and the construction of reality. In D. Brisset & C. Edgley (Eds.), *Life as theater* (pp. 219-233). Chicago: Aldine.

Berk, R. A. (1993). What the scientific evidence shows: On the average, we can do no better than arrest. In R. J. Gelles & D. R. Loseke (Eds.), *Current controversies on family violence* (pp. 323-336).Newbury Park, CA: Sage.

Bowker, L. H. (1993). A battered woman's problems are social, not psychological. In R. J. Gelles & D. R. Loseke (Eds.), *Current controversies on family violence* (pp. 154-165). Newbury Park, CA: Sage.

Buzawa, E. S., & Buzawa, C. G. (1993). The scientific evidence is not conclusive: Arrest is no panacea. In R. J. Gelles & D. R. Loseke (Eds.), *Current controversies on family violence* (pp. 337-356). Newbury Park, CA: Sage.

Denzin, N. K. (1984a). Towards a phenomenology of domestic family violence. *American Journal of Sociology, 90,* 485-511.

Denzin, N. K. (1984b). *On understanding emotion.* San Francisco: Jossey-Bass.

Dobbert, M. L. (1982). *Ethnographic research: Theory and application for modern schools and societies.* New York: Praeger.

Efran, J. (1994). Mystery, abstraction and narrative psychotherapy. *Journal of Constructivist Psychology, 7,* 219-227.

Eisikovits, Z., & Buchbinder, E. (1995, July). *Talking violent: A phenomenological study of metaphors battering men use.* Paper presented at the 4th International Research Conference on Family Violence, The University of New Hampshire, Durham, NH.

Eisikovits, Z., & Edleson, J. L. (1986). *Violence in the family: A study of men who batter.* Unpublished request for funding to the Harry Frank Guggenheim Foundation. Haifa, Israel: University of Haifa School of Social Work.

Goldner, V. (1992, March/April). Making room for both/and. *The Family Networker Therapy,* pp. 55-61.

Labov, W. (1982.) Speech actions and reactions in personal narratives. In D. Tannen (Ed.), *Analyzing discourse: Text and talk.* (pp. 219-247). Washington, DC: Georgetown University Press.

Long, D. (1987). Working with men who batter. In M. Scher, G. Good, & G. A. Eichenfeld (Eds.), *Handbook of counseling and psychotherapy with men* (pp. 305-320). Newbury Park, CA: Sage.

Loseke, D. R. (1987). Realities and construction of social problems: The case of wife abuse. *Symbolic Interaction, 10,* 224-243.

Manning, P. K. (1991). Analytic induction. In K. Plummer (Ed.), *Symbolic interactionism: Vol.2. Contemporary issues* (pp. 401-430). Brookfield, VT: Edward Elger.

Retzinger, S. M. (1991). *Violent emotions: Shame and rage in marital quarrels.* Newbury Park, CA: Sage.

Riessman, C. K. (1994). Making sense of marital violence: One woman's narrative. In C. K. Riessman (Ed.), *Qualitative studies in social work research* (pp. 113-132). Newbury Park, CA: Sage.

Scheff, T. J., & Retzinger, S. M. (1991). *Emotions and violence: Shame and rage in destructive conflicts.* Lexington, MA: Free Press.

Walker, L. E. A. (1993). The battered woman syndrome is a psychological consequence of abuse. In R. J. Gelles & D. R. Loseke (Eds.), *Current controversies on family violence* (pp. 133-153). Newbury Park, CA: Sage.

12

Couple Therapy With Battered Women and Abusive Men

Does It Have a Future?

Michal Shamai

Because the family constitutes both the locus and the context of domestic violence, one would expect family therapists to be at the cutting edge of intervention with such families, yet this is not the case. Moreover, family therapy has been widely criticized as a treatment approach for woman battering cases (Bograd, 1984; Goldner, 1985a, 1985b; Pressman, 1989). In this chapter, I will examine some of the reasons underlying this criticism. The impact of such criticism on the development of this field of practice will be addressed. This will be followed by a discussion of the possibilities offered by couple and family therapy in cases of woman battering.

Criticisms of Family Therapy

Whenever a family that experienced male violence enters therapy, questions arise concerning issues such as: Is family violence a crime or a family dysfunction? What is the therapist's role—to rehabilitate the offender's systems or see that he is punished? Are therapists committed to be active in a larger system than that of the family? (Bograd, 1992). These and other questions shape a controversy that has been growing in recent years among family therapists and between them and the activists who intervene in woman battering. The latter maintain that the field of family therapy has been ineffective in cases of male violence toward women.

The criticism is focused on several issues perceived as inherently rooted in family therapy. First, many family therapists have limited their systemic thinking to the family system alone. In cases of violence against women, one cannot ignore the social, political, and cultural contexts that allow this phenomenon to occur (Taggart, 1985). It is ironic that family therapists who have based their approach on the importance of the context and have criticized modes of individual therapy that disengaged the individuals from their context ignore the social context of the family, thereby limiting the intervention to the family system (Hansen, 1993; James & McIntyre, 1983; MacKinnon & Miller, 1987; Taggart, 1985). The avoidance of social contextual variables is one of the main charges feminist therapists make against traditional family therapy in cases of domestic violence (Avis, 1988, 1992).

Second, criticism has been directed against the systemic model—the prevalent theoretical approach guiding family therapy—and its possible implications for intervening in and understanding intimate violence. In the systemic model, phenomena are seen as interactive; therefore, any element of the system is determined and maintained by other elements in it. In other words, such theorizing may imply that causes of violence lie in the interaction among spouses and responsibility for it should be shared (Avis, 1992; Bograd, 1988, 1992; Goldner, 1992; Lamb, 1991). Clinical work based on such assumptions is likely to lead to blaming of the victim (Bograd, 1984; Hansen, 1993).

Third, much criticism focuses on the therapist's stance in the intervention process. Therapist neutrality regarding activities within the family system is an integral part of the education and training of family therapists, especially for those trained in the Milan systemic approach. This neutrality, based on the circular causality model of family interaction, hinders the ability of the therapist to deal with family violence. Situations of family violence require clear positions against the violence. The ability to focus on the man's responsibility for the violence is a prerequisite for developing effective intervention in cases of family violence (Avis, 1992; Willback, 1989).

Fourth, there is controversy surrounding the issue of whether violence is perceived as a symptom of dysfunction or as a total lifestyle. Family therapists have tended to perceive it as a symptom that functions to maintain the family homeostasis, for example, roles, hierarchy, values, and myths. Many family therapists believe that intervening in the system masks the actual issues that have to be dealt with and that are the actual reasons for the emergence of the symptom: violence. Without entering into the debate regarding the question of whether violence is a symptom or a lifestyle, it should be said that when working with violence, the therapist's primary focus must be to stop it. Only after it has been stopped should therapists look at the dysfunctional nature of the couple and family (Goldner, Penn, Sheinberg, & Walker, 1990; Hansen, 1993).

A fifth criticism of family therapy centers on the ways in which its assessment procedures lead to minimization of abuse, because of the tendency to maintain the power differential in the therapeutic situation (Cook & Frantz-Cook, 1984). Perpetrators tend to minimize the level of aggression, and the battered wives often are too afraid and embarrassed to either contradict their husbands or describe the real situation. Therefore, the women are likely to agree with and validate the men's descriptions (Goodstein & Page, 1981; Hansen, 1993; Rosenbaum & O'Leary, 1981).

Finally, therapists tend to enter family systems at the flexible end. The therapist may tend to enter the system via the women because, in many cases, they are likely to be more receptive to therapy than men. This may reduce the focus on the perpetrator and support the assumption that the wife is coresponsible for the phenomenon (Hansen, 1993). Therapists may also enter the system using the technique of joining. Minuchin and Fishman (1981) consider this a vital tool in challenging the family to enter the treatment process. The question then arises: How can a therapist join the feelings of terror and fear as they are expressed by the woman and at the same time join with the perpetrator? Furthermore, sometimes the initial joining with the family involves getting closer to the member with the most powerful position in the family in order to ensure continuation of the therapeutic process. What are the consequences of such an approach in cases where the strongest person is a man who perpetrates violence?

The family therapy literature has responded to this criticism in several ways. One response was to leave the field of woman battering to other therapeutic approaches. This was interpreted by Avis (1992) as therapist avoidance behavior at a time when awareness of the problem has reached monumental proportions. On the other hand, some therapists defend their abandonment of the field on the grounds that "political orthodoxy [is] stifling our treatment approaches" (Lipchik, 1991, p. 59). Thus, many family therapists avoid presenting publicly their interventions in cases of violence against women, even when they obtain effective results, for fear of being criticized if other issues, such as power, control, or role division involving gender differentiation, have not been treated using feminist philosophy (Erickson, 1992). Such defensive responses and the severe criticisms directed against family therapists were challenged by Bograd (1992):

> Important and potentially useful exchanges about the efficacy and assumptions of various treatment models of wife abuse often deteriorate into rigidified either/or positions that do not do justice to the richness of these models, to the integrity and thoughtfulness of most of us as clinicians, and to our shared desire to end violence in families. In our struggle for definitional control, we oversimplify—not only our own positions—but also the complexities and multidetermined nature of family violence. (p. 245)

This challenge leads us to the need to reexamine our modus operandi while incorporating ideas from feminist philosophy into family therapy (Cook & Frantz-Cook, 1984; Goldblatt & Shamai, 1994; Goldner, 1985a, 1985b; Goldner et al., 1990; Hansen & Goldenberg, 1993; Shamai, 1992, 1993). The criticisms of family therapy in cases of male violence toward women lead to the conclusion that the problematic issues are primarily in the domain of implementation, rather than in the conceptual or ideological field.

The family system, when wrongly perceived, may be seen as minimizing individual responsibility for violence and defining it as a systemic behavior, without differentiating between the respective roles and responsibilities of the aggressor and the victim. However, systemic thinking does not ignore the autonomy and self-determination of each individual in the system. On the contrary, in a functional family, there is enough space for every member and clear boundaries allowing togetherness as well as separation. There is also respect for the feelings, ideas, and desires of each member. A systemic approach to the family acknowledges different roles and responsibilities within the family. Therefore, it is not against the tenets of systemic theory to focus the responsibility for the violence on the abuser. It would be a skewed and simplistic interpretation of systems theory to relate to it as a simple arithmetical equation that divides the responsibility for every act equally among the members participating in it. Family therapy long ago adopted illustrative concepts, such as differential power and hierarchy (Haley, 1976; Madaness, 1981; Minuchin, 1974), which can also explain different responsibilities in various situations.

Systemic thinking and family therapy both look at the interactive variables that keep the couple together in spite of the violence. Are these variables related to the wider system? For example, it may be that the absence of an extended family or other support systems is related to either the wife's unwillingness to leave the dangerous system or the husband's purposeful isolation of the family. Intergenerational myths and values might also be at work, preventing acts against the husband and perpetuating messages about the role of a wife and the type of husband-wife relationship that is expected. Systemic thinking will examine how these variables interact with the abuser's reasons for staying in a relationship that causes him such anger: Are they related to intergenerational myths and values about the male role in the family or intergenerational messages about marital relationships? Or do they reflect fear of abandonment?

An examination of such variables does not necessarily translate into victim blaming, particularly when it is done within a context that clearly condemns the notion of violence and identifies the abuser as responsible for it. Rather, the search for these variables demonstrates the understanding that at least two people are involved in the violent episode, each having a different role and contribution in maintaining it. A systemic understanding of the violent interaction requires a careful examination of the behavioral, cognitive, and emotional position of each member, as well as the interaction of these positions, in order to implement every mode of therapy. Systemic understanding takes into account the larger system, including institutions and society as a whole (Minuchin & Elizur, 1989) and the way in which personal, interpersonal, social, and political factors interact in the creation of violence.

Family therapy does not depend on a specific way of implementing treatment or on one particular therapeutic approach. Family therapists can suggest to one or more of the family members a group therapy approach; it might include individual meetings, couple sessions, and sessions including the children or significant others from larger systems (extended family, school, health institute, etc.). Being open to various compositions of the system and its components is a basic requirement of the complicated therapy of battered women and their abusive husbands.

The supposed requirement that the therapist be neutral is an additional myth brought against family therapy. The work of some of the leading figures in family therapy, such as Minuchin, Whitaker, Haley, Andolfi, and others, shows their deep involvement in therapeutic sessions, including the expression of their own opinions in many cases. The Milan systemic approach requires neutrality, but it is not necessary to use this specific approach when working with this population.

Another criticism of family therapy relates to its goal. Family therapy is often attacked for its emphasis on keeping the family unit intact at the expense of individual rights and opportunities. Although the structural and technical features of couple therapy may lend themselves to such misunderstanding, it is known that most family therapy approaches seek neither to keep the family together in cases where the system is involved in unethical and immoral relationships, for example, violence (Boszormenyi-Nagi, 1981), nor to sacrifice individual rights to self-fulfillment (Satir, 1988; Whitaker & Keith, 1981).

Those family therapists who incorporate feminist principles into family therapy enhance the possibilities of working with intimate violence. They have also begun to change the language used by family therapists. Lamb (1991) comments that the family therapy literature used words like *spouse abuse, marital aggression, couples' violence,* and the like. We notice an increasing number of family therapists who are more and more often using specific language that indicates who is the perpetrator and who is the victim. Changes in language point to changes in thinking. As shown above, the changes needed in attempting to adapt family therapy to working with battered women and perpetrators of violence are mainly related to misuse and narrow implementation of theoretical concepts, which lead to unnecessary suspicions and resultant ostracizing of family therapists from this field of practice.

Couple Therapy Model for Treatment of Male Violence Against Women

When developing a therapeutic model, some basic questions need to be addressed: What is the rationale for developing it? To whom, how, and when can it be applied? What are the components of the model? How does it work? And what are its limitations? The answers to these questions can help us examine the potential contribution of couple therapy to this field.

Rationale for Applying Couple Therapy

Hansen and Goldenberg recognized that,

> Therapists are becoming increasingly concerned that many women remain in violent relationships in spite of the therapist's recommendation to leave (cite in Goldner, 1992). Indeed, even when women leave these relationships, they often return to them. . . . Often, when women attempt to leave, the risk for serious harm from their spouses increases (Walker, 1981). Moreover, given that batterers rarely perceive themselves as having a "psychological problem," most batterers are not responsive to individual psychological intervention (Walker, 1981). However, they may be encouraged by their wives to attend conjoint sessions. Thus a discussion of conjoint therapy is critical for a full consideration of therapeutic intervention. (Hansen & Goldenberg, 1993, pp. 82-83)

There are five major reasons for using couple therapy (Goldblatt & Shamai, 1994). First, the violent episode occurs within the couple system. Although the responsibility for it lies with the perpetrator, eliminating it requires changes in the aggressor, the victim, and the interaction between them. Second, 50% (more in some countries) of the couples continue their marriage or relationship in spite of repeated violence. There are couples who indicate that there are some positive aspects to their joint life in spite of the violence. Women consider leaving their spouses only when they feel that they are going to lose their sanity (Mills, 1985), or lose their lives (Browne, 1986), or when they can accept the fact that they are battered women and their justifications for staying with their spouses are not effective anymore (Johnson & Ferraro, 1984).

Third, spouses hold similar perceptions about the violence, the reasons that cause it, and the responsibility for it. Such perceptions help to maintain violence (Goldblatt, 1989). Therefore, creating change must involve both spouses. Fourth, many couples come to therapy due to marital problems that are perceived by them as more severe than violence. Many of them relate to the violence as one component of their marital dysfunction but not as the main one (Douglas, 1991; Goldblatt, 1989; Sela-Amit, 1992). And finally, there are couples who are either too afraid or too ashamed to deal directly with the violence. The label *couple therapy* or *marital therapy* can reduce the fear and shame and can thus be the first step in dealing with it.

Basic Principles of the Model

Based on Goldblatt and Shamai (1994), the basic principles for a sensitive approach to couple therapy in cases of violence include the following:

1. Because violence is being maintained by similar and complementary perceptions held by both spouses, therapy has to include both spouses in order to stop it.
2. The goal of couple therapy is to stop the violence. The intention is not to keep the relationship together. Couple therapy can result in a decision for separation. In that case, it is the role of the therapist to support the couple during the separation process, which in most cases is painful (Magill, 1989).
3. Couple therapy is not neutral. It is the task of the therapist to declare, at the first meeting, that he or she opposes and condemns violence, that there is never any justification for it. Furthermore, the therapist must make it clear that there is no joint responsibility for the violence.
4. The responsibility for the violence rests completely with the aggressor. However, the man in most cases can learn to control and overcome his violence.
5. The woman is responsible for her life; she is not responsible for the occurrence of the violence nor is she responsible for stopping it. The therapist must make it clear that even though the violence occurs within the family system, it is the abuser who is responsible for its existence and for stopping it. Applying for therapy is considered a

first step the woman takes to protect herself and get control over her life. The woman is responsible for learning how to identify behavior that can escalate to violence and for adopting new behaviors toward her husband while he is learning to control his violence.

6. The couple therapy is based on a written contract to which both parties are committed. The man is committed to stopping the violence, and the woman is committed to attending to her own safety.
7. The couple therapy includes behavioral, cognitive, and emotional variables, and its goal is to achieve changes on all levels.
8. The therapeutic process includes joint as well as individual sessions.
9. During the intake, there is at least one individual session with each spouse, which aims to reveal if there are issues concerning the violence that either spouse is afraid or ashamed to discuss in front of the other.
10. The therapy extends to larger systems beyond the couple as needed. This can include the children, who may be either witnesses to or victims of the violence. It can also include members of the extended family or others meaningful to the couple who can support them during the difficult process of change. If necessary, social institutions are also involved, such as police, attorneys, physicians, and the like.
11. Couple therapy is not a universal panacea and it cannot be used indiscriminately. It can work with couples who are willing to cooperate with the therapeutic process and with the therapists. It is most effective if there are some other aspects of the relationship that are perceived as positive elements in the marriage by both spouses. Couple therapy is not appropriate in cases where there are doubts as to the women's safety; for example, if there is a long history and high intensity of violence or if the man is not ready or able to stop the violence.
12. It is the right of each one of the partners to terminate the joint process and to meet the therapist individually.
13. In case of violence during the session itself, the therapist must terminate the joint therapy. The aggressor has to determine whether he can rejoin the therapy, with the understanding that therapy can work only when people can talk and control their behavior. If he decides he can accept these conditions, the spouses will renegotiate individually with the therapist about rejoining couple therapy, with the understanding that violence and couple therapy will not coexist.

Goals of Treatment

The main goal of treatment is to stop the violence and the threat of violence. Only when this goal is achieved can the therapist move on to other goals.

How can it be determined that this goal has been achieved? First of all, there must be an end to all violent episodes, including violent threats, such as "Hold me, otherwise I'll kill someone" or "Be careful, don't start with me." It requires that the former aggressor develop not only the cognitive and behavioral skills to control anger but also the skills to communicate anger and frustration in legitimate ways. To achieve lasting change, both spouses have to change their perceptions about gender roles. This requires not only cognitive change but also working through related emotions. The man will have to abandon and substitute some of his basic ideas and attitudes about manhood and family relations. This process will involve a feeling of loss and mourning. This may often be related to an enormous amount of anxiety about being abandoned by those who communicated to him this set of ideas. Furthermore, intrapsychic processes related to the type of his object-relation, such as insecure attachment or fear of being either overruled or abandoned by his partner, might raise feelings of sadness, fear, and pain that will have to be worked on in the therapeutic process.

The woman will have to change her self-perception about her rights and roles. This requires emotional changes that include mourning the loss of ideas and messages passed to her by previous generations and society. It also entails gaining an awareness that she has the right and power to take responsibility for her own life, desires, and behaviors. These changes are accompanied by various painful feelings, such as sadness for her unfulfilled dreams, anger at her husband, and fear of the unknown. To reach this therapeutic goal, it is necessary to intervene on the behavioral, cognitive, and emotional levels.

The second goal of treatment is to examine the marital relationship. If, at some point during the treatment process, the spouses decide to terminate their marriage, the therapist's goal shifts. The therapist must then help the spouses work through the process without violence.

If the couple decides to stay together, then work has to be done on the marital relationship, including such issues as the reason for choosing the spouse, intergenerational messages about marital relationships, communication patterns, problem solving, and role sharing. Both the therapist and the couple must accept that the marital history of the couple was chaotic and often traumatic and that it will be neither forgotten nor forgiven. Indeed, the history should be used to show how dangerous the violence is to all members of the family, including the abuser. These two treatment goals overlap to some extent.

Treatment Process

The length of this treatment process is at least 30 to 40 weekly sessions, which are followed by a long period of follow-up that includes one session per month. A short-term cognitive-behavioral approach can be effective for immediate cessation of physical violence but may not be sufficient for the complicated task of treating the associated psychological and sociological problems underlying the violent behavior.

Couple therapy can be accompanied by other types of treatment such as group therapy. It can also include individual sessions, as required, in situations where the man has stopped his violent behavior but his wife has just begun to express her anger toward him. A joint session might either discourage the husband who has finally given up violence or discourage the wife who has finally dared to recognize and express her feelings. Individual sessions may be needed to work on private issues or traumas such as incest.

The therapeutic process includes several stages, as follows:

Intake. This stage involves an assessment of the type and intensity of violence, a brief family assessment (power struggle, marital atmosphere, communication), information about types of treatment, including an evaluation of whether couple therapy is the appropriate approach, and a contract that creates hope concerning the possibility of cessation of the violence.

First stage. This stage focuses on teaching the couple cognitive and behavioral skills to either stop the violent behavior or defend against it and also to work on the emotions accompanying these changes.

Second stage. At this point, it is important to identify intergenerational and social messages affecting the type of marital relationship and to work through their emotional, cognitive, and behavioral consequences.

Third stage. Here, an examination of the marital relationship results either in working toward improving it or toward separating.

Resolution. The intensive treatment process comes to an end, and a long follow-up period begins. There is always the possibility of reentering another intensive stage if needed (for example, in an unpredictable stress situation involving new violence).

Various techniques are used by therapists, including supporting techniques, empowering, behavioral and cognitive tasks, genograms, narratives, rituals, and suggestive techniques (Shamai, 1992, 1993).

Unsolved Issues of the Model

In cases in which couple therapy seems appropriate, there are some issues that are still unsolved and call for special attention by the therapist. The first one is ideological. It cannot be denied that all societies, traditional as well as modern, value the institution of the family. Neither can it be denied that therapists who choose systemic thinking and a family therapy approach accept the value of a family. Yet, in some situations, preserving a family is damaging and dangerous. It is the responsibility of the therapist to recognize and accept that separation may become necessary when continuation of the relationship is dangerous or when one or both of the partners wants to terminate it.

The second unsolved issue is related to therapist loyalty. Feminist therapists call for special commitment to the battered woman and therefore perceive couple therapy as incompatible with such a commitment. A couple therapist cannot be loyal to one spouse but must be loyal to the goals of stopping the violence and helping each spouse—by helping the aggressor to stop being violent and helping the victim to defend herself against the violence. Being loyal requires a supportive attitude and behavior toward each member of the couple during this difficult process and includes, in addition to the therapeutic sessions, readiness to act as liaison with relevant social agencies (police, hospital, district attorney, public officer).

A third unsolved issue is the way in which the therapist uses power. This issue may be relevant to everyone dealing with domestic violence—individual, group and family therapists, feminist or otherwise. When he or she is working with domestic violence cases, the attitudes and behavior of the therapist should be to refrain from any form of the use of power or violence, including any directed against the aggressor. It is important to avoid misuse of authority and power so as not to create a threatening atmosphere. Therefore, therapists have to check continuously on how their clients understand the limits and rules they set. They must control their anger and frustration, both of which are invariably a part of working with this population. When such feelings are released, the form of the expression should be, at one and the same time, an assertive and supportive attitude.

These unsolved issues call for further implementation and evaluation of couple therapy with battered women and abusive men. Quantitative and qualitative evaluation of processes, outcomes, and therapist-client relationships will enrich the existing model.

The Future of Couple Therapy

Couple therapy is a potentially useful approach in the repertoire of interventions with battered women and abusive men. As I have tried to show in this chapter, systemic thinking incorporating couple therapy can be appropriate for intervention in cases of male violence against women. Most of the feminist critique of this method is related to implementation issues. Without ignoring the contribution of feminists to this domain of practice, it seems to me that they may be throwing the baby out with the bathwater. Rather than trying to encourage family therapists to further develop the method of couple therapy in order to increase the repertoire of interventions for stopping violence, much energy has been invested in fighting this approach (Avis, 1992; Erickson, 1992; Kaufman, 1992; Meth, 1992).

There is a place for couple therapy with this population. I would strongly advocate treatment programs that hold the man accountable for his violent behavior, confront issues of gender and power, and emphasize involvement with systems larger than the family involved, if needed. To this end, couple therapists should publish their work with this population both to help make explicit the potential contributions of their approach to the field and to clear up common misunderstandings of this approach. Couple therapists should also carry out systematic evaluations so the benefits and disadvantages of the approach can be studied for further development.

To resolve conflicts in this field, couple therapists should become the ones who call for exchanging knowledge between therapists, researchers, and politicians with different perceptions who are involved in the field. It is systems theory that insists on opening the system to information interchange rather than closing it, denying it, and opposing outside information. Couple therapists need to use their experience in conflict resolution to convert the conflict among those involved in the field into a dialogue. The dialogue should, aside from enriching the intervention repertoire, set itself up as a model of the respectful manner in which differences can be overcome. And finally, couple therapists need to explain to policymakers the importance of using couple therapy alongside social action and other therapeutic approaches. This should include specifying the rationale and the uniqueness of the couple therapy approach as well as the resources it requires for training and supervising therapists and ongoing evaluation.

References

Avis, J. M. (1988). Deepening awareness: A private study guide to feminism and family therapy. *Psychotherapy and the Family, 3,* 15-46.

Avis, J. M. (1992). Where are all the family therapists: Abuse and violence within families and family therapy's response. *Journal of Marital and Family Therapy, 18,* 225-232.

Bograd, M. (1984). Family systems approach to wife battering: A feminist critique. *American Journal of Orthopsychiatry, 54,* 558-568.

Bograd, M. (1988). How battered women and abusive men account for domestic violence: Excuses, justifications, or explanations? In G. T. Hotaling, D. Finkelhor, J. T. Kirkpatrick, & M. A. Straus (Eds.), *Coping with family violence: Research and policy perspectives.* Newbury Park, CA: Sage.

Bograd, M. (1992). Values in conflict: Challenges to family therapists' thinking. *Journal of Marital and Family Therapy, 18,* 245-256.

Boszormenyi-Nagi, I. (1981). Contextual family therapy. In A. S. Gurman and D. P. Kinskern (Eds.), *Handbook of family therapy.* New York: Brunner/Mazel.

Browne, A. (1986). Assault and homicide at home: When the battered kill. In L. Saxe & M. J. Saks (Eds.), *Advance in applied social psychology* (Vol. 3). Hillsdale, NJ: Lawrence Erlbaum.

Cook, D., & Frantz-Cook, A. (1984). A systemic treatment approach to wife battering. *Journal of Marriage and Family Therapy, 10,* 83-94.

Douglas, H. (1991). Assessing violent couples. *Families in Society, 72,* 525-535.

Erickson, B. M. (1992). Feminist fundamentalism: Reactions to Avis, Kaufman, and Bograd. *Journal of Marital and Family Therapy, 18,* 263-267.

Goldblatt, H. (1989). *Accounts—Reflection to violence between spouses.* Master's thesis submitted to the School of Social Work, University of Haifa.

Goldblatt, H., & Shamai, M. (1994). Couple therapy. In H. Goldblatt & Z. Eisikovits (Eds.), *Domestic violence: Towards a multi-model intervention.* Haifa: The Unit for Study, Treatment and Prevention of Domestic Violence.

Goldner, V. (1985a). Feminism and family therapy. *Family Process, 24,* 31-37.

Goldner, V. (1985b). Warning: Family therapy may be hazardous to your health. *Family Therapy Networker, 9*(6), 19-23.

Goldner, V. (1992). Making room for both/and. *Family Therapy Networker, 16*(2), 54-61.

Goldner, V., Penn, P., Sheinberg, M., & Walker, G. (1990). Love and violence: Gender paradoxes in volatile attachments. *Family Process, 29,* 343-364.

Goodstein, R. K., & Page, A. W. (1981). Battered wife syndrome: Overview of dynamics and treatment. *American Journal of Psychiatry, 138,* 1036-1044.

Haley, J. (1976). *Problem solving therapy.* San Francisco: Jossey-Bass.

Hansen, M. (1993). Feminism and family therapy: A review of feminist critiques of approaches to family violence. In M. Hansen & M. Harway (Eds.), *Battering and family therapy: A feminist perspective.* Newbury Park, CA: Sage.

Hansen, M., & Goldenberg, I. (1993). Conjoint therapy with violent couples: Some valid consideration. In M. Hansen & M. Harway (Eds.), *Battering and family therapy: A feminist perspective.* Newbury Park, CA: Sage.

James, K., & McIntyre, D. (1983). The reproduction of families: The social role of family therapy? *Journal of Marital and Family Therapy, 9,* 119-129.

Johnson, J. M., & Ferraro, K. J. (1984). The victimized self: The case of battered women. In J. A. Kotorba & A. Fontana (Eds.), *The existential self of society.* Chicago: University of Chicago Press.

Kaufman, G. (1992). The mysterious disappearance of battered women in family therapists' offices: Male privilege colluding with male violence. *Journal of Marital and Family Therapy, 18*(3), 233-243.

Lamb, S. (1991). Acts without agents: An analysis of linguistic avoidance in journal articles on men who batter women. *American Journal of Orthopsychiatry, 61,* 250-257.

Lipchik, E. (1991). Spouse abuse: Challenging the party line. *The Family Networker, 15,* 59-63.

MacKinnon, L. K., & Miller, D. (1987). The new epistemology and the Milan approach: Feminist and sociopolitical considerations. *Journal of Marital and Family Therapy, 13,* 139-155.

Madaness, C. (1981). *Strategic family therapy.* San Francisco: Jossey-Bass.

Magill, J. (1989). Family therapy: An approach to the treatment of wife assault. In B. Pressman, G. Cameron, & M. Rothery (Eds.), *Intervening with assaulted women: Current theory, research and practice.* Hillsdale, NJ: Lawrence Erlbaum.

Meth, R. L. (1992). Marriage and family therapists working with family violence: Strained bedfellows or compatible partners?: A commentary on Avis, Kaufman and Bograd. *Journal of Marital and Family Therapy, 18*(3), 257-261.

Mills, T. (1985). The assault on the self: Stages in coping with battering husbands. *Qualitative Sociology, 8,* 103-123.

Minuchin, S. (1974). *Families and family therapy.* Cambridge, MA: Harvard University Press.

Minuchin, S., & Elizur, J. (1989). *Institutionalizing madness: Families, therapy and society.* New York: Basic Books.

Minuchin, S., & Fishman, H. C. (1981). *Family therapy techniques.* Cambridge, MA: Harvard University Press.

Pressman, B. (1989). Wife-abused couples: The need for comprehensive theoretical perspectives and integrated treatment models. *Journal of Feminist Family Therapy, 1,* 23-43.

Rosenbaum, A., & O'Leary, K. D. (1981). The treatment of marital violence. In N. S. Jacobson, & A. S. Gurman (Eds.), *Clinical handbook of marital therapy.* New York: Guilford.

Satir, V. (1988). *The new peoplemaking.* Palo Alto, CA: Science and Behavior Books.

Sela-Amit, M. (1992). *Violence among spouses: Towards a theory of the violent episodes.* Master's thesis submitted to the School of Social Work, University of Haifa.

Shamai, M. (1992). *Using rituals in therapy of violent couples.* Paper presented at the International Conference on Families at Risk, London.

Shamai, M. (1993). *Using suggestions in therapy of violent couples.* Paper presented at the International Family Therapy Congress, Amsterdam, The Netherlands.

Taggart, M. (1985). The feminist critique in epistemological perspective: Questions of context in family therapy. *Journal of Marital and Family Therapy, 11,* 113-126.

Walker, L. E. A. (1981). Battered women: Sex roles and clinical issues. *Professional Psychology: Research and Practice, 12*(1), 84-94.

Whitaker, C. A., & Keith, D. V. (1981). Symbolic-experiential family therapy. In A. S. Gurman & D. P. Kniskern (Eds.), *Handbook of family therapy.* New York: Brunner/Mazel.

Willback, D. (1989). Ethics and family therapy: The case management of family violence. *Journal of Marital and Family Therapy, 15,* 43-52.

13

The Future of Intervention in Woman Battering

Common Themes and Emerging Directions

Zvi C. Eisikovits
Guy Enosh
Jeffrey L. Edleson

A reading of the previous chapters reveals common themes that run throughout the book. Each theme appears in varying ways among the positions taken by the authors. Sometimes, the authors reinforce one another's positions and sometimes they appear in opposition. As a result, the grounded themes generated in this book reflect both unifying ideas among the authors and points of departure. Overall, there is a great deal of agreement among the authors that multiple forms of intervention are needed—each making its unique contribution to an overall solution.

The purpose of this chapter is to identify these common themes and to compare and contrast variations among the authors. The following discussion is based primarily on a content analysis of the previous chapters. Tape recordings of discussions following each author's presentation in Haifa were also analyzed. Content analyses identified the following grounded themes along which a continuum of views were expressed: (a) variations in the definition of the problem and its scope; (b) ideological orientations, ranging from idealism to pragmatism; (c) dilemmas concerning political and organizational belonging; (d) a range of modus operandi between therapy and activism; (e) orientation to other social problems and agencies, ranging from cooperation to conflict; and (f) the types of metaphors used and the way in which each directs our cognitive orientation to understanding the problem. These themes represent a continuum along which the authors' individual positions fell.

We did not come to this analysis with the intent of imposing a specific theoretical orientation. After analyzing the data, however, it is hard to avoid the conclusion that the collected chapters of this volume are an illustration of the constructivist framework—almost independently of the topics addressed by specific writers. This is true whether the author was constructing history of a movement, the organizational and political issues involved in the emergence of woman battering as a social problem, the willingness to affiliate with other social problems, definitional issues, the language of discourse, or the level of intervention most desirable when dealing with woman battering.

The volume is constructivist because it addresses a variety of perspectives and presents the reality of the social movement on behalf of battered women as both *pluralistic* and *plastic* (Schwandt, 1994). Pluralistic in the sense that it uses a variety of symbols and language systems to address the subject matter in a specific and intentional way, and plastic because the various ways of presenting are stretched and shaped in a manner reflecting the intentions of the writers.

Each of the grounded themes that emerged from our content analysis will be discussed in detail below.

Variations in Problem Definition and Scope

Some authors have proposed a focused approach that advocates concentrating on various forms of woman abuse, with special emphasis on violence. The proponents of this approach suggest that broadening the issue beyond that of physical violence will bring about a loss of visibility and resources specifically dedicated to battered women and eventually lower the public priority assigned to this issue (Edleson). Similarly, a number of authors suggest direct intervention with battered women and batterers in specialized agencies with focused interventions (Eisikovits and Buchbinder, Shamai).

Other authors tend to broaden the definition of the problem and point out several interrelated directions: One is the effort to relate woman battering to other social problems that are faced by women, such as denial of human rights (Heise, Kanuha), economic discrimination (Dutton, Kelly), prostitution (Kanuha, Kelly), community-based exploitation (Kelly), racial discrimination (Kanuha), feminization of poverty (Kelly), and discrimination and labeling based on sexual orientation (Kelly, Kanuha). Broadening the problem definition also occurs by adding secondary victims of abuse—such as child witnesses—and viewing their victimization as equal to that of women themselves (Peled). The complex interactions between these multiple forms of oppression generate a different order of victimization, one that is structural in nature. This broadening of the problem definition and scope tends to enhance the connections between one form of victimization and another.

The same argument for broadening definition and scope has been suggested in the area of service provision. Proponents of this approach maintain that other more institutionalized service systems—such as child welfare, health care, general legal remedies, and criminal justice interventions—are likely to reach more battered women than do current specialized services. These other systems also offer the potential for greater material resources in supporting battered women and services to them (Schechter). Supporting this broadening of the service response are calls for considering other interventions with men who batter and with children (Peled, Edleson, Tolman).

Ideological Orientations: Idealism to Pragmatism

The authors vary in the degree to which they lean toward the idealistic or the pragmatic. These positions are matters of degree and not mutually exclusive or contradictory. In fact, all of the authors hold both idealistic and pragmatic thoughts but tend to emphasize one over the other in their writings for this book.

Those authors leaning toward idealism are far more broad in the scope of suggestions they raise and in their orientation toward a more distant future (Heise). Those leaning toward pragmatism are more specific and oriented to problem solving, with a clear emphasis on trying to address specific issues in the *here and now* (Tolman). Idealism is reflected in suggestions that previous approaches have to some extent failed, were atomized and partial, that there is an untried approach that promises a more comprehensive answer (Kanuha, Kelly). Pragmatism is reflected in more modest goals and a focus on adding another successful segment or building block to the handling of the problem (Shamai).

There is great variation even within these artificial categories of idealist and pragmatist. For instance, the chapters by Heise and Kelly each suggest idealist solutions at different ends of the social structure. Heise argues for intervention on the global level, and Kelly presents a community-based strategy located within informal social networks. Encompassing both is Dutton's framework that addresses all ecological levels.

Dilemmas of Political and Organizational Belonging

It is clear, in historical overviews, that the battered women's movement was essentially born as a response to the public's neglect of the plight of battered women and of women in general. The authors present a healthy tension between various positions regarding the extent of future rapprochement required with the established powers. Some authors recommend careful rapprochement, despite knowledge of the potential pitfalls (Schechter, Heise, Peled). Others believe that the price of such an approach would be too high in the context of structural arrangements presently available to women in most societies (Kelly). The latter recommends an emphasis on developing support and resources on a community level rather than counting on the establishment's helping hand.

A corollary of this discussion is the theme of professionalism versus voluntarism. There is a parallel between those who suggest locating activity at the community level and those who advocate for a focused approach using current institutional arrangements. This historical dilemma has a variety of ideological and political implications and is closely related to organizational and political affiliation. Those advocating increased professionalism and institutionalization within the present national and international health, welfare, and legal structures (Heise, Schechter) use reasoning such as the availability of more resources and the prospect of serving a larger number of women. Those uncomfortable in collaboration with existing institutions suggest that "selling out" will limit the movement ideologically, will curtail creativity and fervor, and will commit the members to institutionalized and professionalized ways of handling the problem. Moreover, it was argued that the entire perception of the problem will be limited to institutionalized interests and interpretations which, by default, will work against women's interests (Kelly).

Range of Modus Operandi: Therapeutic to Activist

Activist orientations among the authors advocate for social structural change and support to battered women from a partnership position (Kanuha). Therapeutically focused authors suggest interventions, such as couple therapy or phenomenological intervention, that are primarily micro in emphasis (Eisikovits and Buchbinder, Shamai).

The authors in this book do not take an *either/or* approach on this issue but rather attempt to complement each other. They take a *both/and* approach (Goldner, 1992) and present various options of these two extremes in a way that complements each other. For example, although Shamai is presenting a couple's therapy approach, she also emphasizes the systemic approach. Her approach assumes that therapy is not confined to the clinic and that advocacy and intensive work with additional social systems relevant to the problem is needed in various stages of the process. Coming at this from a different angle, Schechter suggests that systemic change of the health care and child welfare systems is required but offers this approach in the hope of providing more direct services to survivors of violence.

Cooperative to Conflictual Orientations

A common concern running through the chapters is the extent of collaboration or conflict with institutionalized social systems in the areas of law, health, and welfare. It should be noted that historically the battered women's movement was born out of conflict with these institutionalized social systems, which neglected the plight of the battered women. As one reflects on this history and reads the chapters, it appears that there is an evolution toward experimenting with expanded forms of cooperation. This willingness to cooperate—one that has always been present in the movement but is gaining strength—appears to be based on an assumption that the movement now has a solid identity from which it can reach out in ways that will benefit both battered women and the movement as a whole.

The trend toward cooperation with institutional powers is expressed in various forms. For example, Heise suggests international cooperation with a variety of world organizations in order to influence specific countries that are slow to assist battered women. Here, cooperation is suggested as a tactic in a strategic conflict. In other words, cooperation is expected to tip the power balance in favor of the women's interests in specific locations. Kelly's work presents the need for cooperation with community agencies but uses a conflict perspective to achieve this end. Dutton, Edleson, Shamai, and Schechter suggest that cooperative strategies will be conducive to reaching more women and will cover broader areas of helping them.

The conflict approach is seen as particularly useful in advocating for issues that have traditionally suffered from "selective inattention" and have been purposefully neglected over time. This is the case with race as it relates to violence against women. Kanuha suggests a conflict orientation vis-à-vis the battered women's movement itself. She points out that, in its quest for equality, the battered women's' movement forgot women of color, lesbians, and other groups marginalized within the movement. It is clear that although there is an overall tendency to find avenues of cooperation, many are still committed to the idea that conflict is useful in a social context based on power and conflicts of interests.

Use of Metaphors

Language and metaphors are an important symbolic medium by which authors express their ideological orientation, positions concerning practice issues, organizational affiliation, and the like. Writers construct a certain frame of mind that is conducive to their concepts by the use of certain kinds of metaphors. Metaphors thus describe and create reality.

The chapters in this book hold a number of examples of how metaphors are used to create a reality. For example, Dutton's metaphors create an ecological conceptualization of the entire topic presented and offer a framework that might be applied in organizing all that has been written. Similarly, the Eisikovits and Buchbinder chapter uses phenomenological metaphors, such as meaning and experience, to create a reading emphasizing personal meaning and an interpretive attitude to the text.

Heise's metaphors of rights and health bring us to two somewhat divergent worlds that represent wide spectrums of thought within the battered women's movement. One is legalistic and the other is public health. The legalistic orientation to battered women's individual rights is historically continuous with the advocacy movement's metaphors. Similarly, the public health metaphor directs our attention to medical definitions and a prevention orientation stemming from epidemiology as an ideology.

Conclusion

It is apparent from this analysis that the field of intervention in woman battering is tending to move toward broadened boundaries. This is expressed both in a tendency to broaden the definition of the problem and in a tendency to integrate it rather than separate it from other social problems. Although this tendency may be associated with a concern for loss of visibility and primacy, that will not necessarily be the case. It appears that the battered women's movement has reached the developmental stage whereby it can afford to contextualize its work and still preserve its primacy. It appears that activist fervor, which was highly functional in making woman battering into a social problem, will have to combine with increased professionalization in the field. Intervention modalities will have to range from grassroots activism and systems change to specialized individual, couple, and group activities, depending on the need and choice of clients.

This implies a *both/and* attitude rather than precluding certain intervention modalities on ideological grounds. Implicit to such an approach is an ideological orientation that seems to lean toward pragmatism. It is a kind of pragmatism that focuses on immediate, urgent needs of battered women without losing sight of needed structural and cultural changes. Such an orientation views pragmatic changes on the immediate level as building blocks of a larger plan, which has a clear, guiding ideology. These tendencies are symbolized by a language that is more inclusive. All these trends contribute to the construction of a field that is reaching out collaboratively after having successfully established a strong, independent identity.

References

Goldner, V. (1992, March/April). Making room for both/and. *The Family Therapy Networker,* 55-61.

Schwandt, T. A. (1994). Constructivist, interpretivist approaches to human inquiry. In N. K. Denzin & Y. S. Lincoln (Eds), *Handbook of qualitative research* (pp. 118-137). Thousand Oaks, CA: Sage.

Index

About the Editors

Photo by Marcie Stein

Jeffrey L. Edleson is a Professor in the University of Minnesota School of Social Work. He has published extensively on domestic violence, has served as director of Evaluation and Research at the Domestic Abuse Project in Minneapolis for the past 13 years, and is the Director of the Minnesota Higher Education Center Against Violence and Abuse. He has provided technical assistance to domestic violence programs and research projects across North America as well as in Israel and Singapore. Dr. Edleson is an associate editor of *Violence Against Women* and his books include *Intervention for Men Who Batter: An Ecological Approach,* coauthored with Richard M. Tolman, and *Ending the Cycle of Violence: Community Responses to Children of Battered Women,* coedited with Einat Peled and Peter G. Jaffe.

Zvi C. Eisikovits is an Associate Professor and Director at the Center for Youth Policy, Haifa University. He is the founding Co-Director and presently Research Director at the Haifa Center for Intervention, Research and Education on Domestic Violence. He has published widely on the topics of youth and deviance and, over the past decade, has focused on violence against women. He is the coeditor, with Jerome Beker, of *Residential Group Care in Community Context* and *Knowledge Utilization in Residential Child and Youth Care*. He was recently a Professor of Social Work at the University of Vermont, where he consulted with organizations working on violence against women and provided expert testimony in cases involving battered women and their children.

About the Contributors

Eli Buchbinder is a social work researcher with the Domestic Abuse Intervention and Research Unit, Women's League for Israel, in Haifa. He is also a doctoral student at the University of Haifa, where he works as a Research Associate with the Center for Youth Policy and the Violence Against Women Research Group.

Mary Ann Dutton is a clinical psychologist and forensic consultant specializing in domestic violence, with a focus on the psychological effects of violence. She is the author of *Empowering and Healing the Battered Woman* and is working on a new book titled *Understanding the Diversity of Battered Women's Responses to Violence.* In 1980, she founded one of the first graduate psychology training programs in domestic violence and directed the program for 12 years. Currently, she is a Research Professor, Department of Emergency Medicine, The George Washington University Medical Center in Washington, D.C. She is also affiliated with the George Washington University National Law Center.

Guy Enosh is a social work researcher at the Domestic Abuse Intervention and Research Unit, Women's League for Israel, in Haifa. He is a graduate student in the University of Haifa's School of Social Work and a research assistant with the Center for Youth Policy and the Violence Against Women Research Group.

Muhammad M. Haj-Yahia is a Lecturer at the Paul Baerwald School of Social Work, The Hebrew University of Jerusalem, Israel. He has conducted research on family violence in the Arab communities of Israel, and his current research includes studies on psychological and marital consequences of wife abuse, adolescents who witness abuse, attitudes of Arab women toward different coping behaviors used by abused women, and perceptions of child abuse among Arab professionals and lay people in Israel. He is also active in training Arab women to staff hot lines for battered women in the Arab communities of Israel.

Lori Heise is Co-Director of the Health and Development Policy Project (HDPP), in Washington, D.C., a not-for-profit organization dedicated to integrating concern for gender and social justice into international health policy and practice. A longtime advocate for women's health internationally, she has worked extensively in the area of gender-based violence, women and HIV issues, and sexuality education. She is author of *Violence Against Women: The Hidden Health Burden* and coauthor of *Sexual Coercion and Reproductive Health: A Focus on Research.*

Valli Kanuha is a longtime advocate for battered women. Since 1975, she has been involved in all aspects of domestic violence intervention, including direct services with battered women, organizational consultation with shelter boards and staff, and local, national and international training on mental health and domestic violence. She has worked extensively on the issue of lesbian violence and holds a particular interest in the relationship of race, ethnicity, sexual orientation, and other factors to an analysis of violence against women. She is currently studying toward a doctorate in social work at the University of Washington in Seattle.

Liz Kelly is a feminist researcher and activist. She has been active in campaigns and organizations on domestic violence, rape and sexual assault, sexual abuse of children, and pornography for more than 20 years. Since 1980, she has conducted research into violence against women and children and, since 1987, has worked at the Child and Woman Abuse Studies Unit of the University of North London. She has published widely, including a book titled *Surviving Sexual Vio-*

lence. She was recently appointed chair of a Council of Europe working group on the elimination of violence against women.

Einat Peled is a Lecturer in the Bob Shapell School of Social Work at Tel Aviv University. She has conducted research and published several articles and books on woman battering in Israel and the United States. She is particularly concerned with the effects of domestic violence on children and improving societal responses to them. Her books include (edited with Peter G. Jaffe and Jeffrey L. Edleson) *Ending the Cycle of Violence: Community Responses to Children of Battered Women* and (with Diane Davis) *Groupwork With Children of Battered Women: A Practitioners' Manual.* She received her PhD from the University of Minnesota.

Susan Schechter is a Clinical Professor at the University of Iowa School of Social Work and a research associate at the University's Injury Prevention and Research Center. She is the author of several books and monographs about domestic violence, including *Women and Male Violence: The Visions and Struggles of the Battered Women's Movement; When Love Goes Wrong* (coauthored with Ann Jones); and *Guidelines for Mental Health Practitioners in Domestic Violence Cases.* She has also founded and directed several clinical and advocacy programs, including AWAKE (Advocacy for Women and Kids in Emergencies) at Children's Hospital in Boston. She is currently a consultant to the National Resource Center on Domestic Violence, and the Family Violence Prevention Fund.

Michal Shamai is a Clinical Lecturer of Social Work and founding Co-Director of the Haifa Center for Intervention, Research and Education on Domestic Violence. She is a family therapist and social activist living on Kibbutz Mishmar Haemek and an author of several articles in leading family studies journals.

Richard M. Tolman is an Associate Professor at the University of Michigan School of Social Work. He has been involved in intervention with men who batter for the past 15 years, as both a practitioner and a researcher. He recently chaired the commission that developed a statewide guideline for batterer treatment in Illinois, one of the most populous states in the United States. He is involved in a similar effort in Michigan and consulted with Connecticut to develop alternative criminal justice sanctions for batterers. He has published numerous papers on violence against women and is coauthor, with Jeffrey L. Edleson, of *Intervention for Men Who Batter: An Ecological Approach*. He is associate editor of the *Journal of Interpersonal Violence* and a member of the editorial board of the *Journal of Emotional Abuse*.